MONOGRAPH 47
THE AMERICAN ETHNOLOGICAL SOCIETY
JUNE HELM, EDITOR

Double Descent in an African Society

The Afikpo Village-Group

By Simon Ottenberg

University of Washington Press   *Seattle/London*

To the people of Afikpo

PREFACE

THIS is written at a time when there are shifting concerns in the study of traditional Africa, and my own training and changes in orientation reflect these. The first period of field research at Afikpo, Nigeria, was carried out between December, 1951, and February, 1953, and resulted in my doctoral dissertation (S. Ottenberg, 1957), a study of leadership and government at Afikpo. At the time this was written my interest was moving from cultural anthropology, largely in a form which traces its history to Franz Boas of Columbia University, to a formalistic approach to social organization, represented particularly in the writings of A. R. Radcliffe-Brown, M. Fortes, and E. E. Evans-Pritchard. I was attracted by their structuralism and their apparently systematic approach to the study of social process. By the time I returned from my second period of field work, conducted at Afikpo between September, 1959, and June, 1960, with occasional visits until December of the latter year, I felt that I had a better grasp of some of the principles of social structure, and I was able to check and refine my data. Since then, I have had the opportunity to rework my material on double descent and to rethink my position, and I now find myself dissatisfied with any single approach to this topic. It is in this mood that the book has been written.

My former wife, Phoebe Ottenberg, also an anthropologist, carried out her own research on both field trips. On the first trip we lived at the edge of the Government Station, in a small wood-plank house not far from the central Afikpo villages, lent to us through the courtesy of the resident engineer, A. G. Farnfield. I employed an interpreter, Nnachi Enwo, later the Honourable Member from Afikpo South in the Federal House of Representatives. I never acquired sufficient fluency to do without his linguistic skills, and his knowledge of Afikpo culture and the Igbo dialect spoken there was of great help to me. We were constant companions during the entire trip. He quickly learned something of my orientation and needs and was an enthusiastic field worker, interested in meeting persons and in the history and the problems of his own people. He was not without his own opinions of course, and this had both advantages and disadvantages in the field work situation. I began my field researches in his village, Mgbom, and this is the Afikpo village with which I am most familiar, though on this first trip work was also carried out in other villages. Enwo was then a man approaching middle age who aspired to political office and was aligned with the "progressive" youths at Afikpo, then a much smaller group than it is now, who wished to bring modern and Western practices to the village-group.

I also carried out a great deal of work with Nnachi Iduma, also of Mgbom, a middle-aged man of great wisdom who held a traditional view of Afikpo, and who was rising in prestige within the framework of its customary government. Another good friend, J. C. Okoro, who had lived away from Mgbom for a few years in his youth, had a rich knowledge of traditional ritual, and was helpful in broadening my perspective on Afikpo culture. These three men formed the cornerstone of my work, though many others, including Chief I. Isu of Ngodo village, and Ndukwe Azu of Ukpa, were also very helpful. I was also fortunate to find a sympathetic District Officer at Afikpo, J. D. Livingston

Booth, who made available to me important government reports. His articulation of the government's view on social change and progress gave me a better perspective on my field research than would otherwise have been possible.

During the second field trip my wife and I lived in a tutor's house at MacGregor College, Afikpo, a teacher-training school of the Church of Scotland Mission (later the Presbyterian Church of Nigeria) under the directorship of Chima Oji. Our home was located several miles from the central Afikpo villages, near enough, as in the case of the first trip, to have visitors from Afikpo and yet far enough for privacy when they came. Much of my attention was focused on double unilineal descent, especially its matrilineal aspects, and on religious matters. I tried to roam further afield from Mgbom than on the first trip, to acquaint myself with villages I had scarcely known before, and to deal with problems of cultural and social variation in more detail. Again, the local government officials were of great assistance, especially E. M. Unaka, the Assistant District Officer at Afikpo, and A. Abbey, the District Officer.

The Honourable Nnachi Enwo and Nnachi Iduma again assisted me, to a limited extent; my interpreters and field guides were J. C. Okoro once again, and Thomas Ibe. The latter, about thirty-seven years old, had recently returned from a long period of work in the southern British Cameroons and was in the process of reintegrating himself into his own society, and here I shared his progress and problems with interest. Again, many others helped me, though on both trips I tried, not always successfully, not to rely too greatly on single informants but to keep broad contacts. Again, I never learned to speak the Igbo language adequately, though I obtained some grasp of its rudiments. This failure, I am afraid, has led to a lack of sensitivity in the data in some crucial areas.

Certain problems and facets of the field work in Afikpo should be mentioned. On the first trip, near the end of the colonial period, I was treated with great deference, and in some cases formality, much like a prominent visiting chief. This worried me considerably at first, but before long I became only too used to it. I suspect that I was never able to disidentify myself from the colonial regime. All the Europeans [1] in the area were employed by it or by the missions, and the idea that someone would travel such a long distance to study the Afikpo's customs without having any other purpose in mind was apparently not convincing to people who viewed the European as a man of action. Thus there was always some suspicion of my motives.

The second trip occurred when the government had been turned over to the Nigerians, in the atmosphere of coming independence for the country. I believe I was taken much more for granted, and much more as an American. At this time, also, Afikpo knew much more about the United States than before. Since nothing disastrous that could be attributed to my first field trip had occurred at Afikpo, there was less suspicion of me, less deferential behavior, and also less interest. The attitude toward Europeans had by this time changed considerably as a result of political developments in the country. I found that I was freer to move about and to make contacts, but also that the Afikpo were less interested in this strange person who wrote unreadable articles about them and who was probably harmless. As a result of the rewards following on the first trip, I was believed to be a wealthy person, and so I was by their standards.

On both occasions I found the Afikpo exceedingly courteous, carefully following custom as to social niceties. I was frequently involved in gift exchanges. I found that the Afikpo were quite willing to accept a stranger into their group once they knew him, and this turned out to be a characteristic feature of their social and governmental activities. I joined a village, a patrilineal lineage, a matriclan, and a village secret society on my first trip, and a village age set on my second. These incorporations immediately threw me into a host of activities in which I was expected to participate, and which led to some humorous commentary on my performance in these new-found roles. At the same time it was understood that I had my own work to do and could not always

---

[1] The term generally includes Americans, as well, in Nigeria.

take part; only rarely did the interrelationships which grew out of joining these organizations prove burdensome.

I found the Afikpo, like many other Igbo, a verbal and forceful people. They are not afraid to state their views frankly and to ask for help, and are sometimes uncomfortably direct. Others who have lived and worked with Igbo have confirmed my views (Le-Vine, 1966), as has my former wife. On the other hand, they occasionally can be evasive. I do not make these remarks disparagingly; this is simply how many Afikpo, but by no means all, struck me. In the field situation there was always a steady flow of conversation. The problem was to direct it and to sift out useful information. With a few exceptions, I was able to take field notes freely, there being little reluctance about this or about photographs.

I had the greatest difficulty in working with females. Afikpo is a society with striking sex polarity, and the women's world is thought quite inferior to and separate from the men's. Women talk little to men, even their husbands, except about routine or necessary affairs; they do not conceptualize, or at least are not able to articulate about social processes as freely as men. For much of my data on women I have relied on Phoebe Ottenberg's dissertation and publications (1958; 1959; 1965), and I referred to her field notes for the first draft of this book. Her counsel throughout both trips and subsequent to them was invaluable.

In discussing and writing up my field materials I am indebted to the late Melville J. Herskovits, who originally turned my attention to Africa and who showed me the exciting possibilities for research and scholarship that the continent offered. He and his wife, Frances, always held much interest in the Igbo. To William R. Bascom I owe more than I can repay for his encouragement and his evaluation of my materials. Professors M. Fortes and G. I. Jones, both of Cambridge University, have also discussed my field data with me at various times and have made helpful suggestions. And anyone who has worked on problems of double descent owes a great deal to Jack Goody and Daryll Forde for their own researches, as well as to the writings of George

Peter Murdock. Their work has established a high standard of analysis and set out many of the major problems discussed here. I wish to thank G. P. Murdock, Austin J. Shelton, June Helm, and Victor C. Uchendu for reading and commenting on the manuscript of this book.

During both field trips I received the help of many authorities. In particular, I wish to thank the West African Institute of Social and Economic Research, Ibadan, for the use of their facilities on the first trip, and the same institute, now the Nigerian Institute of Social and Economic Research, for similar assistance on the second trip. The University of Ibadan also kindly provided me with various forms of assistance each time. On both occasions Dr. Godfrey Hinds of the Medical Missionaries of Mary, Mater Misericordia Hospital, Afikpo, gave me medical aid, as did the nursing sisters and other persons working there. My first field trip was carried out with an Area Research Fellowship of the Social Science Research Council, with the help of a grant from the Program of African Studies, Northwestern University. The second was conducted under a research grant from the National Science Foundation, while on leave of absence from the University of Washington. The writing of this book was facilitated by a sabbatical leave from the University of Washington and a grant from the Joint Committee on African Studies of the American Council of Learned Societies and the Social Science Research Council. The Library of the University of Washington very kindly made available to me special funds to purchase useful material which has been of value to me, and many persons there have helped me in bibliographic research. From the University of Washington Graduate School Research Fund I received a grant to cover the costs of preparing the maps and charts. To all these organizations and individuals I wish to express my deep appreciation.

I have used the term Igbo, rather than the older form Ibo, throughout the book since Igbo is rapidly becoming the standard term, at least among scholars, and it is closer to the true pronunciation of the name than is Ibo.

This book is going to press in April, 1968, a time when there are serious political and military disturbances in the area where I carried out my research. Afikpo has become part of the new Republic of Biafra, which has broken away from Nigeria (since Afikpo was part of Nigeria during the time that I did my research and wrote this book, I have retained my references to this country). That these events are having profound effects on the matters that I discuss in this work goes without saying. It may seem hard for the reader to see any relevance in the quiet anthropological description given here to the hot issues of the day in Igbo country. I hope, however, that this social portrait, which I consider a sympathetic one, although expressing my affection for the Afikpo people in rather formal terms, may help some readers to better understand the cultural background to the present unhappy situation.

SIMON OTTENBERG

CONTENTS

ILLUSTRATIONS

MAPS AND CHARTS

DOUBLE DESCENT IN AN AFRICAN SOCIETY
THE AFIKPO VILLAGE-GROUP

I. INTRODUCTION

THE people of Afikpo Village-Group in Southeastern Nigeria are aware that their way of life is similar to that of some of their immediate neighbors, who share cultural and social features, and that it differs from that of other Nigerians and Africans. Their cognizance has grown broader as modern conditions have permitted and encouraged them to travel widely in Nigeria, occasionally to other parts of West Africa, to Europe, and America, and during the Second World War to the Middle East, India, and Burma. This takes the form of knowledge that they have important relationships with their mothers' relatives through ties going back a number of generations, as well as on their fathers' side, while in most other sections of Nigeria the predominant emphasis is on the paternal line.

They are correct in this observation. The form of relationship which they practice is unusual in Nigeria, where patrilineality is the rule. Called double unilineal descent, or double descent for the sake of brevity, or sometimes dual descent, it stresses ties through the mother as well as the father, in both cases in limited ways. In Nigeria it is found among a cluster of peoples in the southeastern region, on both sides of the Cross River, inland from the coast. It also occurs among a few groups in the north (Goody, 1961:12). This form of descent, in its pure form, is not common in human society, though the basic principles underlying it have been well known for some time.

This manner of tracing ties of individuals to other individuals through birth occurs when patrilineality and matrilineality are both found in a society, and normally when every individual traces descent in both ways and thereby has many aspects of his life organized for him. That is, individuals of both sexes reckon descent through males by way of their fathers, forming agnatic ties. They also trace descent through females via their mothers, resulting in uterine ties which are distinct from the agnatic ones. These two means of descent can usually be seen as a coherent whole in a society. There are differences of activities between the matrilineal and patrilineal spheres, and relationships between them also occur.

It was once thought that double unilineal descent was exceedingly rare in contrast to the number of societies which form unilineal descent, on one side only, either matrilineal or patrilineal. Recent thinking indicates that some societies which were formerly thought to be singular in unilineal descent have some form of relationships, with descent acknowledged, and sometimes activities carried out, on the other side, that are also of a unilineal nature (Goody, 1961; Schneider, 1962), so that the gradation from unilineal descent on one side to a condition of double unilineal descent is not a sharp one. Goody (1961) defines this form of descent narrowly, excluding the intermediate cases, as matrilineal and patrilineal groups which are named and corporate, the latter feature relating to property ownership. Others use a broader approach, in which corporate relations are not required to be present on both sides (Christensen, 1954; Murdock, 1940).

The data presented here do not throw much light on the question of definition, for no matter how double descent is delineated Afikpo has this form of organization, possessing it in its fullest form. There are named, organized, matrilineal groupings with well-established patterns of leadership and authority. This is also true of the agnatic ties. Both sides are property owning and controlling, and both play very important roles in the lives of individuals. Fully developed double descent systems with organized matrilineal and patrilineal groupings seem to occur mainly in Africa, where they are well dispersed.[1] Two of the best described are the LoWiili of Northern Ghana (Goody, 1956), and the Yakö of Southeastern Nigeria (Forde, 1964).

PROBLEMS

There is justification for preparing another account of an African system of double descent on the ground that the extent of variation of this type of structure is barely known. For example, the society to be explored here has both patrilineal and matrilineal land holdings, which the Yakö and the LoWiili lack. Again, the analysis of such an exceptional system throws light on the general principles of descent, a test case as it were. Beyond these points there are a series of interesting problems associated with double descent, which have been partially explored in four general articles (Murdock, 1940; Goody, 1961; Leach, 1962; R. Harris, 1962b). In the analysis offered here they will be touched upon, and further light will be thrown on them.

There is, first of all, the question of how this form of descent arose. Murdock's idea (1940:561) that "double descent would result when a people with strongly functional exogamous matrilineal kin-groups comes to adopt patrilocal residence and to organize politically on a local basis in consequence either of outside contacts or of internal adjustment" seems to be the most logical general statement of origin, and is supported to a degree by evidence published later (Murdock, 1949:50–56 and chap. viii). But the number of documented cases is small, and there are questions as to whether the reverse procedure could not also occur, or even whether this form of descent could not arise directly from bilaterality.

Questions of origin raise questions of stability. Full double

---

[1] Goody (1961:12) lists them.

descent is rare and complex, which, in addition to its probable manner of origin, suggests that it is a transitory form in the movement from matrilineality to patrilineality. Possibly it is an inherently unstable social form, extremely sensitive to changes in productive controls and other economic factors, and to alterations in marriage rules and residence patterns.

There is also the matter of to what extent there is a balance of functions and activities on the uterine and agnatic sides. To what degree is there complementariness or conflict and competition over activities and functions? In the case of both the Yakö and the LoWiili there is a high level of distinctiveness of activities for each type of descent. But if double descent societies are in some ways in a transitional stage from descent on one side to descent on the other, as Murdock implies, we might expect there to be points in the reorganization where there must be competition over control of like activities; it is hard to see how these could be avoided.

Then there is the problem of the degree to which in such a society there is uniformity in the internal organization, and in the system of authority and leadership, in both types of descent structure. There is a logic which says that they should be quite different. If each side carries out different activities we would expect them to show differences in structure which relate to these. And while authority in both is in male hands, in patrilineality the descent lines run through men and in matrilineality through women; this should make for organizational differences. On the other hand a society tends to have uniformities of leadership and organizational principles which operate in many sectors and which are related to early child-training practices. So we would expect to find some tendencies which push toward distinctiveness, and others which pull toward common practices. Perhaps, if we may reify our subject for a moment, we may look for a sort of warring of these two principles with one another.

There is the related question of the influence of the structure of each type of descent upon the other. We are accustomed to think that matrilineal descent shows certain characteristics and patrilineal descent others. For example, Richards (1934; 1950) and Schneider (1961) have discussed the important features of matrilineality, and the latter has contrasted them with patrilineality. What occurs when both types of descent are found in the same society? Are modifications necessary as a result of conflicting principles, and if so in what direction? For example, in the case of both patrilineal and of matrilineal societies there is often a regular procedure for the selection of leaders of the descent group based on the unilineal principle, and this pattern is usually related to the form of government found in the larger society. But to some extent patrilineality and matrilineality are contradictory principles, for one emphasizes father-son succession and the other ties of mother's brother to sister's son. How are these resolved when double descent exists? Again, in a patrilineal society the ties of a man with his father are often legal and involve authority, and with his mother's brother they have an affective element. The reverse is more or less true in matrilineal societies. How is this resolved in double descent?

Another question is the extent to which this form of descent dominates and permeates the society in which it is found. The query takes two forms. First, in a condition where descent plays such an important role through both the matrilineal and the patrilineal sides, to what extent are the domestic groupings and bilateral ties able to exist with autonomy or even with visibility? Schneider (1962), for example, has argued that certain kin ties that outwardly may look unilineal in a double descent society are in fact not so at all. This is an important point to be explored. Again, to what degree do other nondescent structures, such as association groupings, exist in this form of society, and how do they interrelate or remain distinct from the groups of descent?

Then there is the matter, which Leach (1962) has raised, of alternatives and choices. If, in these societies, many of an individual's activities are dominated by matrilineality and many others by patrilineality, to what degree is there freedom of action and choice for the person? Logic might suggest that there will be very little, but Leach (1962:133) feels strongly that in every society there are alternatives for the individual, and that writers on dual descent have not dealt with this question adequately in that through their manner of handling data on double descent they imply that there is little choice for the individual. This is not completely fair. For example, Forde in his monograph on Yakö marriage (1941; see also Forde, 1965) discusses this question, though in other contexts, and Goody (1957; 1959) has dealt with it as well; but the matter has yet to be fully explored.

These form some of the major problem areas in the study of this type of descent system, and they will serve as an orientation for the reader.

In thinking about the analysis of double descent it seems useful to distinguish two broad approaches. First, there is the structure of the descent groups. These can be studied in terms of the internal organization of each type of group, its external relations with like and different groups, and its functions and activities. It is then possible to compare the organization and functions of each type with its lineal opposite and to relate them both to the larger society. This is the kind of analysis which Forde has used in his essays on the Yakö (1964), and Goody in his review of double descent societies (1961).

The second approach is to examine double descent from the point of view of interpersonal relations in the society, from the orientation of the individual in a network of relationships dominated by descent. Here, for example, we are very much concerned with the relation of a male adult to his father, his mother's brothers, his wives and their male uterine relatives, within the framework of descent. It is largely in terms of this second view that the question of choice and alternatives for the individual is best explored.

Both views are important to the study of double descent as a totality. They are analytically separable but they concern the same persons; they are essentially different ways of looking at the same data. They are two views, one of the larger structure, the other of the individual in his role relationships. The first has logical priority and is mainly concerned with the question of what activities groups of persons carry out and how these are done. The other view involves the analysis of the interconnections of descent ties through single individuals and the relationship of persons to one another. It asks the question that given the fact that individuals belong to certain descent groups by birth and others through marriage and other ways of affiliation, how do they act toward other individuals who also have such associations? Both the larger and the more personal view are complementary aspects of the total analysis. Chapters II and III discuss the broader aspect, Chapter IV takes a look at the interpersonal and individual aspects, and the last chapter summarizes both approaches.

SETTING

Afikpo Village-Group is one of more than two hundred relatively autonomous groups of Igbo-speaking peoples in southeastern Nigeria (Uchendu, 1965). These are stateless societies characterized by the presence of unilineal descent and associations based on residence, both of which play important roles in government. They live mainly between the Cross River on the east and the Niger River on the west (see Map 1) but some Igbo groups also reside west of the Niger. They extend southward to the Guinea Coast on the Atlantic Ocean, but are separated from it by a number of smaller groups of people who speak different languages, especially the Efik (including the Ibibio), Ijaw, Ogoni, and Okrika. To the north are found Igala, Idoma, and Tiv, to the east are numerous small Cross River societies, such as the Yakö, while to the west live the Edo-speaking Bini, Ishan, Urhubo, and Isoko. All of these peoples surrounding the Igbo, except the Bini, and two groups which have had contact with them, the Ishan and the Igala, have stateless traditional governments, though the forms that they take vary greatly.

Much of Igbo country is within the West African tropical rain forest belt with heavy forest growth and annual rainfall generally between 60 and 140 inches (Nigeria, 1954:5–9). The country is low-lying, with numerous rivers and creeks, particularly in the

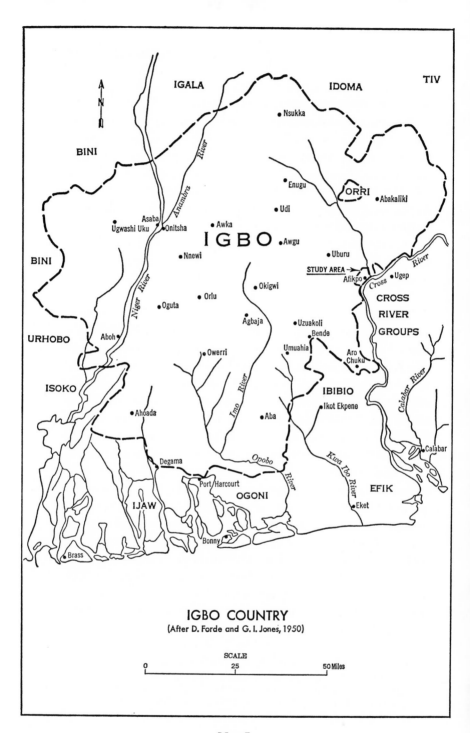

IGBO COUNTRY
(After D. Forde and G. I. Jones, 1950)

SCALE

0   25   50 Miles

Map I

southern sections where the rainfall is heaviest. In the north, the land is largely savannah interspersed with orchard bush. The total population of Igbo is more than five million, probably as high as seven million. Over a million Igbo have migrated to other parts of Nigeria in the past eighty years, but many have now returned as a result of recent political troubles in the country. The Igbo have one of the highest population densities in Africa, ranging up to over one thousand persons per square mile in rural Owerri Province in the central Igbo region (Forde and Scott, 1946:42). The reasons for this are not fully known, but it has had marked effects on the forms of social groupings and reactions to European contact (Gourou, 1947; Trewartha and Zelinski, 1954:153; Stevenson, 1968).

There is no single Igbo "tribe" in the sense of a unified governmental organization. Rather, the characteristic structure is that of numerous autonomous village-groups, which range in population from several thousand to more than seventy-five thousand,[2] each with its own territory and distinctive name. These village-groups, which have been referred to in several different ways,[3] were in precolonial times interrelated through trade, intermarriage, common descent, and occasionally by joint ritual activities. On the whole, however, each village-group was self-sufficient, and warfare and head-hunting between some of them were common. Any centralizing tendencies in Igbo country, where a marked spirit of individualism did and still does exist, occurred through the agency of certain oracles. These included, most notably, *Ibini ɔkpabe*, the "Long Juju" of Aro Chuku; Agbala of Awka; and Igwe-ke-Ala from the Owerri area, apparently from near Okigwi (S. Ottenberg, 1958). Agents of these oracles, usually residents of the place where the oracle was located or their descendants, traveled and settled in many sections of Igbo

[2] Forde and Jones (1950) provide a useful listing and discussion of these groupings.

[3] Talbot (1926) uses the terms subtribe and clan. Forde and Jones (1950) use tribe, subtribe, group, and village-group. Persons in the eastern area of Nigeria often use the term clan for all or some of these groups, and it is sometimes used by government as well.

country. The oracles were consulted for a variety of problems: the resolution of land disputes; charges of murder, theft, sorcery; and personal misfortunes. Many agents, especially those from Aro Chuku, were also actively engaged in the slave trade, shipping slaves south to the coast in the days of the European trade (Dike, 1956:37–41) and around and out of Igbo country until the beginning of this century. These agents also traded in European goods.

Internal organization of Igbo village-groups shows considerable variation. There are common denominators, however. Each village-group usually consists of a series of "villages" as they are called in the literature, and each village is composed of a number of residential corporate agnatic groups (often both lineages and clans are involved) which may or may not be related, which are the land-owning groups, and through which most of the valuable movable property is inherited. In the eastern Igbo area, where Afikpo is located, villages are often compact in form, but elsewhere they are more dispersed about the countryside, usually in a pattern of contiguous homesteads. Each village has a common meeting place where social and ritual activities occur, and has shrines and rest houses for the public use of its members. The government of the village consists of the elders who lead the agnatic groupings, priests and other ritual leaders, and sometimes members of titled groups and secret societies.

The villages are themselves joined together in the village-group by a common meeting place, one or more public markets, and by common ritual activities. Here again, there is a clearly delineated government which consists of the same type of leaders as those who direct the agnatic groupings and the villages, often the same individuals. An age-grade system frequently occurs within both villages and the village-group and forms a framework for status distinctions which are important in government and in general social life. The typical Igbo governmental structure is strongly dominated by males. Thus there is an underlying basis of Igbo life in patrilineal descent groups, joined together on a residential basis for common activities. Also, in all Igbo village-groups, so far as is known, personal achievement in government and every-day life is stressed, and some authority roles are open to enter-prising and energetic individuals.

There has been little detailed analysis of patrilineality in Igbo country. Meek's work (1937; Nigeria, 1933), mainly in Owerri Division, is helpful but unsophisticated. Ardener has published two papers (1954; 1959) on this topic for the Mba-Ise, also in Owerri, which are detailed and very useful, but we lack much of an idea of how these agnatic groupings relate to the rest of the society. Henderson (1963) has recently written an interesting study of traditional Onitsha which integrates the material on descent with the larger society,[4] but Onitsha is not a typical Igbo society. The study of Afikpo must be understood in terms of this lack of substantial data from other Igbo areas.

There have been no detailed studies of Igbo societies practic-ing double descent. It is found among the eastern Igbo, though it seems to be absent elsewhere. This includes the so-called Ada village-groups of Afikpo, Okpoha, Edda, Amaseri, Unwana, Aka-eze, and Nkporo, those found in Ohaffia to the south, and proba-bly also Aro Chuku, still further south (Forde and Jones, 1950:51–56). The presence of uterine groups in this area sets these Igbo off from others in many ways.

The twenty-two villages which are collectively known as Afikpo Village-Group, or in colonial government usage Afikpo Clan, lie in the easternmost portion of Igbo territory, on the west bank of the Cross River.[5] Afikpo forms one of sixteen village-groups, all but two of which are Igbo, which make up Afikpo Division, an administrative unit in Abakaliki Province. The District Office for the entire division is located near the central villages of Afikpo Village-Group. It is the most acculturated village-group in the division, having had considerable contact with Europeans for the past six decades, and now with Nigerian administrators. The area also has the largest concentration of schools in the division.

The population of Afikpo in 1953 was given at 26,305 out of a

[4] See also Henderson's recent paper on kinship terms (1967).
[5] See P. Ottenberg (1965) for a general characterization of Afikpo.

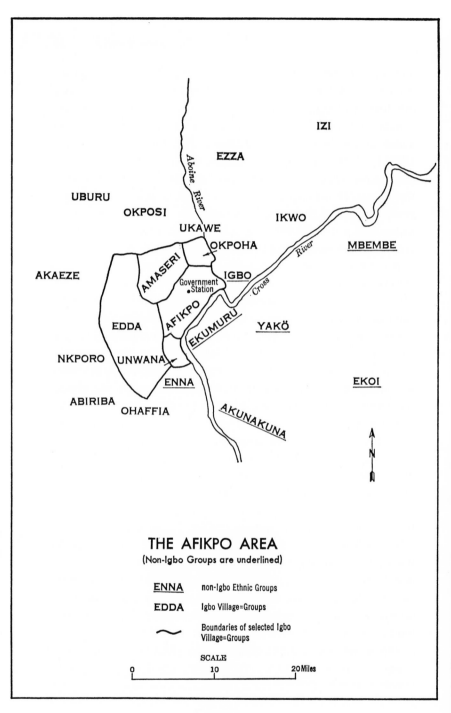

IZI

EZZA

UBURU

OKPOSI

UKAWE

OKPOHA

IKWO

MBEMBE

AMASERI

Government
Station

IGBO

Cross River

Aboine River

AKAEZE

AFIKPO

EDDA

EKUMURU

YAKÖ

NKPORO

UNWANA

ENNA

EKOI

ABIRIBA

OHAFFIA

AKUNAKUNA

N

THE AFIKPO AREA
(Non-Igbo Groups are underlined)

ENNA   non-Igbo Ethnic Groups

EDDA   Igbo Village=Groups

     Boundaries of selected Igbo
     Village=Groups

SCALE

0   10   20 Miles

Map II

total of 246,796 in Afikpo Division (Nigeria, Census Superintendent, 1953–54, Pt. IV, p. 25), but the figure for Afikpo from this first systematic census of all Nigeria seems to be low; the population is probably at least as large as 35,000. The area of the village-group is roughly sixty-four square miles (Chubb, 1948:105), giving a probable density of close to five hundred persons per square mile. This is not high compared to the central Igbo areas, though it is so relative to some other eastern Igbo groups. Many of the compact villages that make up Afikpo are within half a mile of others, separated only by a narrow area of groves, farmland, and bush.

It is a hilly region, with sandstone ridges which run in various directions. The altitude is not high, being about five hundred feet above sea level. It is a transitional area between open grassland and tropical rain forest, the rainfall of about seventy-seven inches a year (Wallace, 1941:89) coming mainly between June and November.

The long broad valleys tend to become swamp during the rainy season, but the best farmlands are there. The practice of planting crops in large mounds of earth, some as tall as a man, prevents their rotting during the wetter periods. The villages are generally located near the tops of ridges, but rarely on their highest points. The area is well watered and the major streams run throughout the dry season. The villages nearest the Cross River are not so much on it as above it on high cliffs overlooking the water. The descent to the slow-moving river is not difficult, and many beaches are found along its western bank on the Afikpo side.

The Afikpo are mainly agriculturalists, though men of some of the villages near the river are actively engaged in fishing. The basic subsistence crops are yam, coco yam, and cassava, which are also the main cash crops. In 1960 rice was beginning to be grown in quantity in some of the swampy areas. Yams, the only food grown by the men, are a prestige crop, and play a major role in ceremonials; no respectable feast could be held without them. Cassava, in particular, is a major cash crop for women, and many females prepare *gari* (cassava meal) for sale. Cassava may be harvested through the year, but yams are planted during the dry season (February to April), and harvested during the wetter period (September to December). The time from June until the yam harvest was formerly one of hunger, when the new crop was not ripe and the previous one had been consumed or had rotted. Cassava and maize, relatively new crops at Afikpo, are now present in sufficient amounts to prevent undue hardship during this season. Between the beginning of the yam harvest in September and the planting of new yams in February is the season when many important ceremonies and rituals are performed, when the village secret society is active, and when land disputes and other cases are tried and settled.

People of the villages near the Cross River, particularly the Ozizza villages in the north, and Anohia and Kpogrikpo in the south, not only farm but fish as well. Many of the young men are away from home during all or part of the time from December to July or August, when the water is low and the fishing is best, and when it is possible to live on sandbanks on the river. Fishermen travel as far south as the port of Calabar and north to the Cameroun border. Older men from these villages concentrate more on farming, which is less demanding physically. This study, however, deals mainly with the central Afikpo villages, which are agricultural.

Afikpo is outside the major Igbo palm-forest area. While palm products are available and are consumed and traded locally, and some even enter the export trade, Afikpo is not a region of high productivity compared with the Owerri area and other regions to the south and southwest. Dwarf cattle (*muturu*) were formerly kept in small numbers in some of the villages but have now been barred in all as being too destructive to the crops. They were used mainly for ceremonial feasts.

Market trade on a part-time basis is a common activity for many Afikpo; for a few it is a full-time career (S. and P. Ottenberg, 1962). Afikpo traders are active on the Cross River, shipping yams and other foodstuffs and pottery (made by women at Afikpo) south and Europeans goods and dried fish north by canoe. The major Afikpo trading center is ɛkɛ market, named for the day on which it meets. It is one of a connected series of markets found in adjoining village-groups to the west and north, which generally meet on different days of the four-day Igbo week. Men and women from Afikpo trade regularly in almost all of these markets. While they contain similar goods, they differ in price and the available quantities of certain products. The central Afikpo market is a place for the sale of dried fish, while Afikpo traders go to other centers for yams and cassava, which the Afikpo apparently do not grow in sufficient quantity. The dried fish and many European goods are brought by canoe from Calabar to the Afikpo markets and small stores in the strangers' settlement, called Afikpo Number Two, and Afikpo is a transshipment point for products going to Igbo areas to the north and northwest. Goods come also by truck from the cities of Onitsha, Umuahia, Aba, Port Harcourt, and Abakaliki.

Within Afikpo there are small local markets that supplement the main one. While the day following ɛkɛ has no market, on the next day (ahɔ) petty trading is carried out in the village of Amachara in the western Afikpo area and near Ugwuego Elu, in the central area. On the following day (Nkwɔ) there is a market at Ozizza, in the north. Since 1920, currency has largely replaced barter and the use of a traditional form of money, brass rods, as a medium of exchange; it is increasingly employed as a substitute for foods and goods in ceremonial exchanges.

Everywhere one looks there are shrines. Often the sacred object is composed of rocks, grouped under a tree, with pots among them, or pots found inside a compound gate, behind a home, or in a special house. Shrines symbolize the diversity of beliefs and rituals at Afikpo. Religion is based on a belief in a variety of spirits which can be sacrificed to at these shrines, often through the agency of priests. There are a very large number of spirits, and the Afikpo have considerable choice, often working through diviners, of which shrine to approach. Many shrines are associated with and controlled by the residential and descent groupings. Ancestral spirits are also important. In addition there is a general high spirit or God, called by various names, such as *cukwu na ɛlu* (God-in-sky), who takes no particular form, and a number of other spirits, also having no shape, associated to a greater or lesser degree with the ground. Others are connected with curing certain types of diseases and still others are for fertility and general welfare. Belief in many of these spirits is associated with important rituals, as we might expect. While the religious system is not codified and systematized in the minds of the Afikpo, it plays a pervasive role in everyday affairs.

The villages are closely packed one upon another, often with less than a mile separating them. In the valleys going out from the center of Afikpo many of these have their sections of farmland, the outmost limits sometimes being seven miles or so from the village. The village usually has a central common where its elders meet to discuss important issues. Facing the common are the entrances to many of its compounds, each one usually housing a patrilineal grouping. To the casual visitor walking into the square the settlement seems dead. He cannot see into the compounds, and unless there is something of importance, some ritual, dance, or meeting going on in the common, there are liable to be only a few senior men sitting in the men's rest house there, roasting a yam or two and gossiping and sleeping. They are likely to be talking about some event in the past, or thinking of some current matter in terms of the past events which it brings to mind, for the Afikpo rely much on tradition, on an orientation to past events as precedent.

The history of Afikpo is complex. It has involved the gradual movement into the area over the past several centuries of various peoples, mainly Igbo-speaking, with very little emigration. This has resulted in a rather complicated organizational structure in the village-group, including double descent, and considerable variation in rituals among different sections. There has been strong influence from the Igbo village-group of Aro Chuku, since agents of its famous oracle, *Ibini ɔkpabi,* have been active at Afikpo for many years, and persons from Aro have settled in the village-group. The dialect of Igbo spoken by the Afikpo is that of Aro Chuku (Adams, 1928).

There have been three basic periods to the history of Afikpo social-political organization. First there was an early pre–slave-trade governmental structure that was simply organized and based on uterine descent. This was followed by the growth of double descent associated with the slave trade, in which class factors in government were very important. Then we find the colonial and present period when double descent has taken on a more egalitarian aspect and class factors are negligible. These three stages in Afikpo history need to be discussed here briefly by way of background.

An early non-Igbo population formerly lived at Afikpo, as it did in other areas where other eastern and northeastern Igbo are now found. Non-Igbo today still live east and north of the Afikpo, and in the Northeastern Igbo area where they are surrounded by Igbo. There is a traditional name for the main indigenous group at Afikpo, the Ego, and Nkalo for another early people. But of non-Igbo at Afikpo little is known by the Afikpo today. A few shrines are said to be of Ego origin, and they are believed to have descendants living in the central villages of Ugwuego Elu and Amaizu. The Ego may have been Enna (Erei) or Akunakuna, non-Igbo who today live south of Afikpo.

It is likely that these people were primarily agriculturalists, growing only a few basic crops, and carrying out little fishing as warfare restricted movement on the Cross River, and fishing techniques known further south toward the coast had not then reached Afikpo. They also hunted considerable game. Population density was undoubtedly very much lower than today, and the people lived in small settlements, probably compounds or tiny villages, dispersed about the countryside. Possibly they already possessed double descent, as do many other non-Igbo groups in the area today, but more likely only matrilineal descent was present. In any event, it seems clear that land and most property were matrilineally controlled, and that the uterine groups also owned a small number of important shrines. It is likely that this was a relatively classless society, at best having a small number of slaves. Government apparently centered around the few shrines and the matrilineal groupings, and was simple in organization.

Beginning sometime during the major period of the slave trade in southeastern Nigeria, between about 1700 and 1830 (S. Ottenberg, 1958), and continuing up to the end of the nineteenth century, there was in conjunction with this trade a gradual movement of Igbo from the Aro Chuku and Ohaffia areas to the south into the region. In addition, there were movements of Igbo from the west, for example from the Okposi and Okigwi areas, probably because of population pressure. The exact details of these migrations are unknown, but there is no doubt that they occurred and were paralleled by other migrations of Igbo into the Northeastern Igbo area (Jones, 1961; R. Harris, 1962a; Allen, 1935). The cultural and social associations of Afikpo with Aro and other Igbo areas, and the tales of the founding of Afikpo compounds and villages, make this clear. It seems evident that the Igbo who moved into Afikpo were basically patrilineal in descent, the persons from Aro mainly so, and those from some other Igbo areas probably more completely so. The tales of their movements into Afikpo are the stories of the founding of patrilineal groupings, not of matrilineal ones.

The Igbo seemed to have come in stages in small groupings of families, sometimes led by two or more brothers, bringing patrilineally controlled shrines with them. But they pressed in in considerable numbers, gradually conquering the smaller matrilineal groupings, who probably lacked firearms or other weapons the invaders had acquired through their trading activities. Even without firearms it is doubtful whether they could have been stopped, coming as they did, in numerical strength over a period of time.

Igbo did not kill all the indigenous population, though some apparently fled east of the Cross River, nor, we hypothesize, did they destroy the matrilineal system of land tenure. Igbo married indigenous women and acquired matrilineal land rights by doing so, involving themselves in the uterine descent system. In addition, they retained their patrilineal organization, which was the basis of their pattern of residence, and cleared virgin land which they passed agnatically. Thus arose the seemingly strange custom, as stated by Afikpo, that if land has been acquired by clearing it can pass either patrilineally or matrilineally, according to whoever aids the original clearer, or to whom he gives the land. This custom is nonexistent today as virgin land has disappeared, though it still figures prominently in court cases involving the origin of farmland. What is meant is not that the person clearing the land freely chose whether to pass it patrilineally or matrilineally, but that he followed whichever custom was his by experience, either patrilineal or matrilineal. The later virgin land to be cleared seems to have been primarily patrilineal (Cf. Chubb, 1948:22). The pattern of marrying and incorporating strangers into their group, as followed by the invading Igbo with regard to the original inhabitants, is mirrored in the willingness today of Afikpo patrilineages to absorb strangers. The newcomers, as they came to dominate the matrilineal landholdings, apparently did not change them to patrilineal controls, but placed shrines on them, mainly to the Aro oracle, *Ibini ɔkpabe,* to protect the lands. They also brought many patrilineal shrines from their original homes which today dominate the Afikpo supernatural system.

The newcomers, coming in large numbers and involved in the slave trade and in warfare under the aegis of Aro agents, developed a highly compact, easily defensible village structure built on high ground, replacing the earlier, more dispersed settlements. The residential organizations, associated with patrilineality, became the basis of warfare and headhunting and associated rituals, and also of the governmental confederation today known as Afikpo. A number of patrilineal groups, the *amadi,* with their special shrine, *ɔtɔsi,* who were either from Aro Chuku or became associated with the Aro, came to dominate important aspects of village and village-group government, partly in terms of their interest in trade. They formed the basis of a class system in government, since they had special controls in judicial matters, and were feared by other Afikpo. Physical strength played an important role as a basis of authority. There was an emphasis on the rapid settlement of litigation, with the frequent use of force and seizure of persons and property. However, a fundamental system of group authority based on the consensus of elders, which seems typically Igbo, and may also have existed among the indigenes, played an underlying role as the larger population group faced the problem of coordinating rituals and other activities, and of unifying custom for the increasing population. The Aro oracle agents came in small numbers during and after the slave trade, moving into various compounds, and carrying out their special work. They came not as settlers but as representatives of their oracle, and did not, until recently, marry local persons, or adopt local customs. These agents were closely associated with the *amadi,* who were, in contrast, permanent settlers who married local persons as well as persons who came with them.

European contact brought further change to Afikpo. Although in the last century the Afikpo were involved in trading slaves and European goods and possessed European guns, cloth, and metals many years before they ever saw a European, the period of direct Western contact has been relatively brief. It also began later than in some other parts of Igbo country. Members of Captain Beecroft's party were probably the first Europeans to pass by Afikpo on their trip up the Cross River in 1841 (Beecroft and King, 1844),[6] but it was more than forty years until further contact was made. In 1883 a party of Scottish missionaries visited the cliffs overlooking the river on the Afikpo side and met a delegation from its village-group at Ebom, across the river (Goldie, 1901:333–34). In 1884 another missionary group visited Afikpo (Goldie, 1885), and in 1888 a missionary of the United Presbyterian Church, later the Church of Scotland Mission, opened a station just south of Afikpo at Unwana Village-Group (McFarlan,

[6] Beecroft's name is erroneously spelled "Becroft" in this article.

1946), though for the first years it was not fully maintained and there was little direct contact with Afikpo.

In 1902, during the Aro Chuku military expedition to pacify the areas west of the lower and middle Cross River, British-directed African troops based at Unwana fought their way into Afikpo, shelling and burning some of the major villages (Heneker, 1907:35–37, 158–62). There they established an administrative center which eventually became the District Office, and which served for some fifteen years as a base for patrols moving out to the north and northwest.

The British administrative post in Afikpo Division was small, consisting usually of two or three Europeans for the more than quarter of a million persons, but it was backed by force and was generally respected. The colonial officers soon established a system of Warrant Chiefs to act as judges in certain minor cases, and as advisors and points of contact with the administration. In the 1930's the system was changed so that Afikpo Village-Group had a representative Native Authority Council with limited powers and a Native Authority Court to try minor matters. In 1955 the Afikpo District Council was created, representing all village-groups in the Division except Edda. The colonial administration is now gone, of course, and government is in Nigerian hands, but its senior administrators are rarely from the village-group or the division.

With the coming of peace in the past sixty years trade has expanded and safe movement of persons is now possible at all times for fishing as well. Women, in particular, travel much further from home than formerly. Many primary and secondary schools, sponsored by both the government and various missions, have been established and roads have been built. Much of the old isolation of the village-group is gone, but its separate identity has remained. In fact, British recognition of the village-group in the establishment of the local native authorities has helped to reinforce its sense of unity.

The influence of the British removed the special powers of the *amadi,* which they took for themselves, and this led to a situation where the ranking of persons has largely disappeared and the role of groups of elders in decision-making has increased. Double descent remains strong though modern conditions have modified it.

The Afikpo still recognize ties with Aro Chuku, and with certain of the neighboring Igbo village-groups in the Ada subgroup of Igbo: Unwana, Edda, Amaseri, and Okpoha (Forde and Jones, 1950:53–54).[7] Although all are autonomous in relation to one another, there is a sense of common identity among these historically related groups. While Afikpo recognize no special ties with the non–Igbo-speaking peoples east of the Cross River, Afikpo are aware that they have accepted many Efik and Ekoi cultural influences, particularly in language and ritual, from the coastal region and from the area to the southeast.

Nevertheless, in terms of some aspects of Afikpo social organization and culture, the village-group should be classified not so much as Igbo but as similar to a cluster of non-Igbo groups on the Cross River which include the Erei (Enna), Akunakuna, Ekumeru, Yakö, Mbembe, and probably the Ekoi. Intensive research has only been carried out on the Yakö, by Daryll Forde, and on groups to the north, by Rosemary Harris, but the publications of both anthropologists have been extremely helpful in preparing this analysis.[8] Not only the Afikpo but probably many other Eastern Igbo would also be included. Features which seem characteristic of all these peoples are double unilineal descent, relatively compact villages with an age-group structure, and secret organizations of various kinds. There are other commonalities, such as certain types of mud and stone shrines and some kinds of dances and plays prevalent in the region. While the Afikpo also have features in common with other Igbo it must be made very clear that it would be very much in error to think of them as typically Igbo, or their social organization as a model of traditional Igbo society.

[7] However, the other two groups in this category, Akaeze and Nkporo, are not recognized by Afikpo as being closely tied to them.

[8] See the references in the bibliography, and also Charles and Forde (1938).

II. THE PATRILINEAL GROUPINGS

ALTHOUGH historically the matrilineal groupings were the first to form we will begin our review with the patrilineal ones, in much the same manner as this research worker first became aware of the agnatic life at Afikpo, then the uterine ties. These patrilineal groupings are socially visible, being residentially based and forming distinct units in the villages. The most important agnatic form, the major patrilineage, usually is located in its own compound, a clearly demarcated residential unit. The compound is called *ezi* followed by the name of its founder, who is also usually the original ancestor of the patrilineage. As we approach the compound from the village common, on which it usually faces, we see a narrow roofed entrance from which hangs a protective shrine, *egbo* (S. Ottenberg, 1968b). The compound is normally separated from the village common (see Map 3) by mud walls, with wood and bamboo fences at its sides, bordering other compounds or unused residential land. From the common it is difficult to see anything within the compound other than the raffia and galvanized iron roofs of its homes; there is normally no place from which one can obtain a full view of it.

A short distance inside the compound entrance is the ancestral

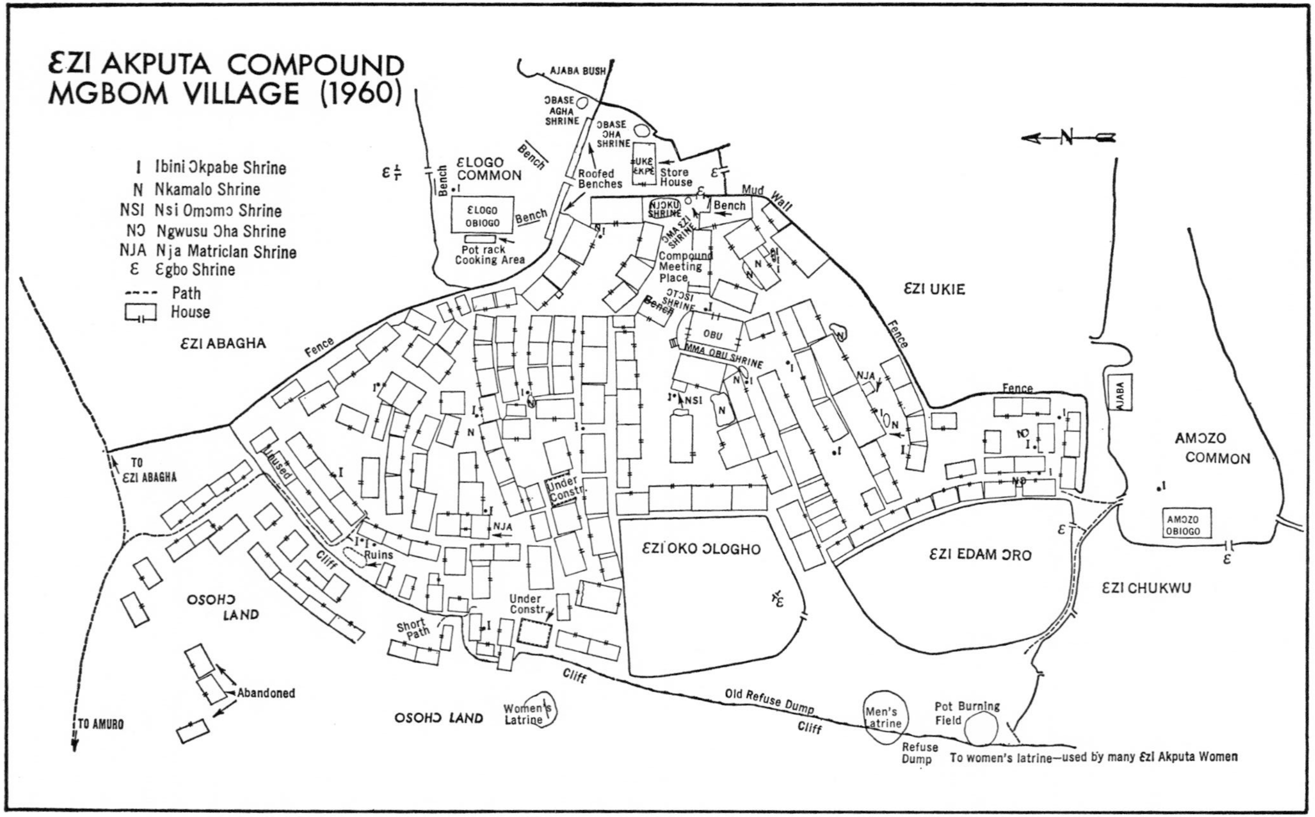

Map III

ƐZI AKPUTA COMPOUND
MGBOM VILLAGE (1960)

I   Ibini Ɔkpabe Shrine
N   Nkamalo Shrine
NSI Nsi Omɔmɔ Shrine
NƆ Ngwusu Ɔha Shrine
NJA Nja Matriclan Shrine
Ɛ   Ɛgbo Shrine

--- Path
☐   House

ƐZI ABAGHA

ƐLOGO COMMON
ƐLOGO OBIOGO
Bench
Bench
Pot rack
Cooking Area

Fence

AJABA BUSH
OBASE AGHA SHRINE
OBASE ƆHA SHRINE
Roofed Benches
UKE SHRINE
Store House
NƆRƆ SHRINE
DINING
Compound Meeting Place
NSI SHRINE
Bench
Mud Wall
Bench
OBU
IMMA OBU SHRINE
NSI

ƐZI UKIE
Fence

ƐZI OKO CLOGHO

Under Constr.
NJA
Women's Latrine
Short Path
Cliff
Ruins
Abused
OSOHO LAND
Under Constr.

ƆSOSO LAND
Abandoned

To ƐZI ABAGHA
TO AMURO

ƐZI EDAM ƆRƆ

AMƆZƆ COMMON
AMƆZƆ OBIOGO
AJABA

ƐZI CHUKWU

Fence

Old Refuse Dump
Cliff
Men's Latrine
Pot Burning Field
Refuse Dump
To women's latrine—used by many Ɛzi Akputa Women

N

shrine of the lineage founder, *Mma obu* (ancestor–rest house),
which also serves as a rest house and meeting place for the
lineage elders, and near which is a small cleared area used for
public meetings and feasts. The houses in many compounds,
particularly those increasing in population, are built wall to wall
and back to back, separated by narrow alleyways and streets
winding tortuously here and there. The dwellings are small, perhaps fifteen by twenty-five feet, with mud walls, a small door, and
a thatch or galvanized iron roof. There is usually a separate
house for each man and for each woman and her young sons and
unmarried daughters. There are numerous shrines in the compound area, arranged in distinctive patterns, located in tiny huts,
shielded from view by raffia hangings covering their entrances.

The rear of the compound is not clearly demarcated and opens
onto bush or groveland, called *osohɔ*, the area into which the
major patrilineage expands as it grows. Here are small gardens,
a garbage dump, and perhaps one or more latrines and a field
for firing pots. From the *osohɔ* paths go out to the farms and to
nearby streams.

The residents of a compound are members of two broad social
categories: the agnatic groupings, consisting of a major patrilineage with its component minor lineages, and the domestic groupings. We will describe briefly these two forms of organization and
then analyze the agnatic groups in detail. They are sometimes
hard to distinguish from one another for they interpenetrate in a
seemingly infinite variety of ways.

While a single major patrilineage normally occupies a compound by itself, there are occasionally some variations on this
pattern. Two unrelated patrilineages may share one compound
area, or a single major patrilineage may be associated with two
compounds. Such variations are not really exceptions to the rule,
but are normal in terms of the principles of Afikpo social organization, and are important in the analysis of patrilineality. But we
will delay their discussion until the general features of the patrilineal system have been examined.

The major lineage is a named, corporate group, lacking a rule of exogamy and claiming descent from a single male ancestor, its founder. The genealogies show a generational depth of approximately five to seven generations. This descent group can usually be referred to by the word *εzi* followed by the name of the founder, the same terms used for the compound itself, and also by *Ndε* (people), followed by the founder's name. The former is employed when referring to the residential unit, the latter in reference to the descent line, but Afikpo sometimes interchange the two. The general term for any patrilineal grouping, here applied to both the major and minor patrilineages, is *umudi* (children-husband). The more common Igbo term *umuNna* (children-father) is understood, though rarely employed. When used, it is usually with reference to the children of a particular man (Cf. Ardener, 1954; Meek, 1937:88; Green, 1947:17; Forde and Jones, 1950:15). Afikpo usage would seem to imply that the speaker is external to the group, specifically that it is a wife referring to her husband's patrilineal relations. In fact, it is a term persons use for their own patrilineal groupings; men, for example, employ *umudi* when talking about their own major patrilineage. The reason for this deviation cannot be discussed here, but seems related to the presence of double descent.

The major patrilineage usually is formed of from two to four minor lineages. These trace descent to the first son of each wife of the founder, the lineage of the first-born son being the most senior. However, conscious ranking among the minor lineages of a major patrilineage by order of birth or any other device is virtually nonexistent, and is unimportant in everyday affairs. The lines of other sons of a wife of the founder are usually amalgamated with that wife's first son's line, forming part of the minor lineage, and again these lines are not inferior in rank. If the founder had only one wife who bore male children the subdivisions of the major patrilineage are by the sons of that wife, with the line of the eldest forming the senior minor patrilineage. If the wife had many sons, the lines of the younger ones are generally amalgamated with the minor lineage of an older one to form a separate minor lineage. There is distortion and fictionalization in these genealogies, as is common in Africa. Minor lineages use the term *Ndε* (but not *εzi*), followed by the name of the founder of the minor descent line, though sometimes this name is changed over a period of time to that of some other prominent member of the minor lineage or to the progenitor of one of the descent lines within it which has grown most numerous in numbers (see Chart 1).

Each minor lineage tends to reside in a particular part of the compound, but since persons can build on any fresh site considerable intermixture occurs, particularly toward the rear, where new homes are most commonly built. Thus this area is usually dominated by the fastest growing minor lineage. It is in the sector nearest the compound gate, where the older houses and the important shrines are found, that the clearest division of residence according to minor patrilineage occurs.

The largest domestic grouping in the compound is the extended family, generally comprising a group of agnatic full and half brothers who live near one another and their wives and children and headed by their father or eldest brother. It is also called *umudi*, and again the term *Ndε* is used in referring to it, reflecting its dominant patrilineal relationships, though the matri-

Chart I. The Minor Patrilineages of Ndε Akputa Major Patrilineage, Mgbom Village

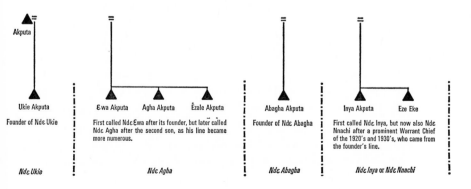

| Akputa | | | | | | |

Ukie Akputa	Εwa Akputa	Agha Akputa	Ēzale Akputa	Abagha Akputa	Inya Akputa	Eze Eke
Founder of Ndε Ukie	First called Ndε Εwa after its founder, but later called Ndε Agha after the second son, as his line became more numerous.			Founder of Ndε Abagha	First called Ndε Inya, but now also Ndε Nnachi after a prominent Warrant Chief of the 1920's and 1930's, who came from the founder's line.	
Ndε Ukie	*Ndε Agha*			*Ndε Abagha*	*Ndε Inya or Ndε Nnachi*	

lineal and affinal ties of its members are also of significance in family life.

The extended family thus includes the polygynous and monogamous families of its married male members. The terms *umudi* and *Ndɛ* can also be used in referring to the polygynous family, but there seems to be no term for the monogamous one. Except for newly married men, each husband generally has a house of his own and supplies one for each of his wives within the compound, but there are variations on this theme. Wives frequently do not live close by their husbands, and the cowives of a man seldom live near one another. In this regard the Afikpo differ from the Igbo to the west, where a husband and his wives form a distinct grouping in one enclosed area (Green, 1947:18–19; Meek, 1937:124–44). This arrangement in Afikpo is reflected in a lack of a well-defined cooperative spirit among the cowives of a man and the marked emphasis on the separate relationship of each wife to her husband (P. Ottenberg, 1958).

FORM OF THE MAJOR PATRILINEAGE

There are over 200 major patrilineages in the 195 compounds that make up the 22 villages of Afikpo. These descent groupings vary in size from fewer than fifty persons to more than five hundred. There is even a compound with only one surviving lineage member, who lives alone and cares for its shrines. It would be difficult, however, to call this man a descent group, and if there are less than ten or fifteen adult members in a major lineage it is virtually impossible to carry out full lineage activities, though its members may still tend to its important shrines and care for lineage properties. On the basis of an Afikpo population of about 35,000, the average size of a major patrilineage is over 150 persons. However, since its adult females usually live away from its compound and have only limited contact with the group, and since there are other persons living in the compound who are not members of the agnatic group, the average functioning size is probably less than one hundred persons.

The genealogies usually trace all living members, except adopted ones, to the founder, and for this reason these descent groupings are patrilineal lineages and not patrilineal clans. There is usually some legend of the founder's moving by stages to Afikpo from outside, though a fair number of lineages have grown out of resettlement within the village-group. The range and direction of movement is wide and includes both Igbo and non-Igbo. At times the founder of a major patrilineage came to Afikpo with one or more brothers who settled separately and founded their own major patrilineages, sometimes in the same village, sometimes in others. Occasionally a younger brother settled with a founder, and his line became a separate minor lineage within the larger one. No totemic system is connected with patrilineal groupings, although some major patrilineages control shrines with which a taboo is associated. For example, a number of special lineage shrines forbid persons wearing anything black in the compound. One forbids using glass or mirrors, another has a taboo against the lineage members eating and killing snakes, still another against crocodiles. These taboos are not common, and no elaborate rituals or mythologies are usually associated with them. Rather they are restrictions which the founder of the shrine learned of when he first obtained it, and which should be practiced.

Genealogies usually provide explicit information on the sons of the founder of the major lineage, as we might expect, since it is with them that the internal segmentation into minor lineages begins. However, there is little evidence of internal differentiation as a result of some dispute or friction within the lineage. In fact, Afikpo say that it is "natural" to claim a line of descent from a first son of the founder by a certain wife, and that this occurs among the developing lines without friction.

Although persons of the founder's generation and his male children are definitely known, and so are the living and one or two antecedent generations, there is considerable vagueness, telescoping of generations, and lack of recollection of certain persons between the two ends of the descent line. Of course, persons who fail to produce children are likely to be forgotten. Many major lineages are generations older than the genealogical record indicates. New major patrilineages rarely form today, and the depth of roughly five to seven generations probably dropped to as low as three in former times, when new major lineages formed.

If we return to the question of residence for a moment, clearly the major patrilineage has a specific residential base for virtually all of its males, whether adult or not, plus most of its unmarried females, and a few of its married women. However not all lineage members live at home. Its major external population consists of the majority of its married females, who, though they live elsewhere in Afikpo, retain some ties with the descent group. In addition, there are some children living away, offspring of women who have left their husbands, and there are also children without their mothers who are living and working elsewhere. In general, no person who lives outside of the lineage area, though still considered a member, has much say in its activities or decisions, which are dominated by its adult males at home.

There are others living in the compound who are associated with the major lineage to varying degrees, for it is possible for persons from outside Afikpo to be adopted into a lineage and for individuals within the village-group to change their patrilineal affiliations. Although Afikpo do not distinguish these different types of affiliations by name, there are three in terms of the persons involved: those who are free to play a full role in the administration of the major lineage, those who play a partial role, and those who have virtually no position at all.

The first type includes strangers who have been completely assimilated into the major lineage. Among these are individuals and their patrilineal descendants from other parts of Afikpo or elsewhere who have settled in the compound permanently and joined its major lineage, and sometimes, after several generations, formed a minor lineage of their own. They may have been remnants of a dying lineage, or have been attracted to the major patrilineage because it could protect them in the days of warfare or because it seemed a wealthy or influential group. Lineages, unlike matrilineal clans, are anxious to increase their size by adoption, as we shall see.

Another form of total adoption comes about when a previously wedded woman marries into a compound, bringing children with her. On reaching adulthood these children are allowed to choose whether they will affiliate with the major patrilineage of their mother's first or second husband. Since daughters generally marry into another compound this choice is rarely meaningful for them. For a son it is a different question, as each lineage wants to keep him. If he remains with his adopted father, as he often will, he becomes a full member of this man's patrilineal descent line, as his son; otherwise he returns to his own father's lineage, taking up residence in its compound. Occasionally a widow or a woman separated from her husband does not remarry, but returns with her children to her compound of birth, or sometimes moves to one where a married sister is living. Again, the sons have a similar option. A like situation arises when a man rears a child of a friend or matrilineal relative, sometimes an orphan boy, who works for him as a houseboy or servant. Whether a son remains or returns to his father's compound depends to a great extent on whether he has developed strong emotional and personal ties in his place of residence. Attempts to lure sons back to their original home with offers of housing, farmland, arranged marriages, and through sacrifices to the patrilineal ancestors and other spirits are common.

In addition, there was formerly a class of slaves, *ohu*, which has now disappeared, who were persons captured in warfare or obtained in trade. An *ohu* was adopted into the major and minor lineage of his male owner, usually as a "son" (and into one of the owner's wives' matrilineal groupings as well). A man's slaves worked for him at the farms and as servants, and were usually given Afikpo names. They could marry freeborn persons or other *ohu;* they and their descendants gradually became full adult members of the major and minor lineage. However, an *ohu* was never considered to be an eldest son, a head of an extended family, or a lineage leader or priest, though these restrictions do not seem to have applied to his descendants. Today, it is virtually impossible to locate persons who are *ohu* as this form of slavery is no longer found. Distinctions between *ohu* and other lineage members are not stated publicly, as is true also for strangers adopted into the lineage, for it is said that this would drive them away and the lineage is anxious to keep as many persons as it can.

The extent of full incorporation of persons into the major patrilineage is high, as in the case of the neighboring Yakö (Forde, 1964:71–82; 1965), mainly a result of the adoption of non-Afikpo. The resettlement and adoption of adult males born in Afikpo into a new major patrilineage is not very common.

The second type of affiliation, partial association with the agnatic descent group, includes lineage members' wives born in other patrilineages, for marriage residence is patrilocal, and most women marry outside their own descent group. A married woman's ties with her husband's lineage will be discussed elsewhere, but it should be noted that there is no pretense of fully adopting her into it. There is also a second class of slaves, *osu,* who trace their inferior status matrilineally, and who are found in some Afikpo compounds. These people belong to patrilineal groupings as well, as minority members. There are ritual restrictions on them, and they are allowed to play only a very minimal role in the government of their major patrilineages (see "The Slave Matriclan" in chap. iii). Some major patrilineages forbid them to live in or to marry into the compound.

In addition, there are persons of Aro Chuku descent who settled in many Afikpo compounds or whose patrilineal ancestors did so, who act as agents of their famous oracle. In former times they also traded in slaves and certain specialized goods (S. Ottenberg, 1958). These Igbo maintain ties with home and follow their own customs. Until recently they married other Aro, and rarely Afikpo, but this is now breaking down. They act as advisors to the elders of the major lineage, who, like others, fear them. They are involved in land litigation and in other matters which potentially can be resolved by their oracle. While they are

not really lineage members and remain outside of its formal
authority structure, they are interested in some of its activities.
The third type of affiliation includes persons who at any given
time may have little direct connection with the major lineage, or
a role in its government, though they live in the compound. These
include persons who may eventually affiliate with it if they remain and others who are not likely to do so. In the former
category are children of women living in the compound whose
fathers belong to other major patrilineages, as discussed above,
as well as houseboys and trading boys, those who are unlikely
ever to settle permanently. The latter category includes prostitutes, traders, Ezza Igbo blacksmiths and farm laborers who
come south for the farming season, and palm-wine tappers,
mainly from Okposi, northwest of Afikpo. All these persons rent
houses in compounds, but except for prostitutes live there only on
a part-time basis. Prostitution, said to have been rare in Afikpo in
the past except for that involving *osu* slave women (see "The
Slave Matriclan" in chap. iii), is now common. Today most of
the prostitutes, who come mainly from the non-Igbo areas east of
the Cross River, live and work outside of the villages, near the
market or at roadside hotels. Lineages do not particularly care to
have them in their midst, since they are associated with drunken-
ness and fighting.

Thus there is a considerable number of individuals not born
into a lineage who are associated with it and live in its compound
area, and who take part in its activities to varying degrees. There
is an atmosphere of acceptance toward most of them, reflecting
the members' feelings that increasing size is associated with
lineage health and influence. Conversely, a lineage that is unable
to attract outsiders may fail to do so because it is considered
weak or in a state of decline. Persons in all three types of
affiliations are bound by the rules of conduct of the major lineage, but only those of the first type play a full ritual role; those of
the second have varying roles, while those of the third virtually
none at all. The importance of a person's patrilineal affiliation at
Afikpo cannot be overestimated, relating to his role not only in

the major lineage, but also in the village and village-group. Membership in a major patrilineage is, in a sense, necessary for full citizenship. It provides a person with a residential identity and a place in the total social setting.

THE LINEAGE ELDERS

The leaders of the major patrilineage are its elders, *Ndɛ iciɛ* (people-old). They hold ultimate authority and control conflicting forces within the descent group. The elders in Afikpo include all adult males above approximately the age of fifty-five years, as determined by membership in certain age sets and grades formed on the village and village-group basis, in which they generally also have leadership roles (see chap. iv).

Within the elders' group, age is a secondary consideration in leadership and decision-making. The primary factors are (1) ability as a speaker, (2) knowledge of historical and recent events in the compound, village, village-group, and even in matrilineal matters, and (3) interest in patrilineal affairs. Secondary factors include not only seniority in age among elders, but also wealth, the number of ceremonial titles a man has taken, his leadership position in the village and village-group, and whether or not he heads his minor lineage. Among the elders descent position within the major patrilineage is unimportant, for they are not ranked according to their minor lineage affiliation: whether it is the senior minor lineage that they belong to or not, or whether they are closest genealogically to the founder. Nor is the nature of matrilineal ties important, except in the previously mentioned case of *osu* slaves.

A good speaker states his ideas clearly, debates without making enemies, and is skillful in the use of proverbs (this is highly regarded in Afikpo). These features, coupled with a general interest in local affairs and a good sense of history and tradition, are almost certain to make an elder prominent in his major patrilineage. Nevertheless, there are some elders who have excellent historical knowledge but do not speak well. These men say little at lineage meetings until consulted, when their opinions carry weight. Such a person may be given the spleen of a goat or other animal being divided in the compound as a mark of respect; this organ is considered a "hidden thing." Similarly, a good speaker is sometimes given the tongue. There is also often a senior male who summarizes publicly the results of the elders' deliberations. This lineage spokesman is not usually chosen formally but gradually grows into the role. Such a man must be careful to give an exact view of the matter and not arouse conflicts that have been quieted in the settlement.

Age within the elders' group is not always a significant factor in leadership. While the two or three oldest men in a major patrilineage may be priests of its shrines, younger elders often hold these positions. The most senior men may lack the primary qualities of leadership, or may be ill or senile. In keeping with respect for age, their opinions will be considered, especially in ritual matters, but their advice is by no means always followed. Ranking by age, however, is clearly followed at feasts and rituals. Food is served in order of age, the most senior men, as determined by membership in the village age sets, will be given the largest shares. Younger men sometimes feel that little food is left for them but concede that good eating is one of the rewards of seniority. In contrast, this careful delineation of age differences is not followed in the elders' group in discussions or in the decision-making process, where there is great freedom for any elder to speak at will.

Middle-aged men are not usually major patrilineage leaders. However, such a person, or even a younger man, may achieve a position of some leadership if he is an exceptionally good speaker, has knowledge of history, and shows a strong interest in lineage matters. His position is strengthened if he is wealthy and if he has taken many ceremonial titles. And when there are few or no elders living in a major patrilineage, as occurs in smaller ones, the middle-aged men hold a strong position. In any case they exercise more authority in the major lineages than they do in the village or village-group, where the predominance of elders affords them little leadership opportunity.

The fact that wealth is not a primary feature of leadership is curious. Although riches and titles are not inseparable, a wealthy man probably will have taken many of the important titles. However, his resources are also likely to depend on the quantity and quality of farmland he controls, and on money obtained through trade or farming. But one does not use wealth to buy power in the patrilineage, perhaps because the descent group does not own much farmland and contributions to lineage funds for various purposes, mainly ritual, are believed best given on an egalitarian basis. An example which illustrates the secondary nature of wealth in patrilineage leadership is the case where the wealthiest man of a lineage was an inadequate speaker and easily became irritated in discussion. As a result he was not considered a leader. Another lineage member who was poor but who spoke well and was interested in the personal problems of others, was more influential in lineage affairs. But an elder who is poor and who has taken few titles will lack influence unless he is gifted in such a primary quality as those discussed above. He may be afraid to speak publicly for fear others may mention his poverty obliquely and make him feel ashamed.

Wealth differentials were not so great in former times as today, but physical strength, as exhibited in warfare and wrestling, or having taken a head in warfare (formerly an important title), was a major qualification for leadership. This was particularly important if lineage members were engaged in a matter or case involving outsiders, for if fighting broke out, the leaders were expected to defend their group. Today such altercations are rare, and physical strength is unimportant.

A man whose father was a well-known leader has an advantage in competition for leadership recognition, but if he does not exhibit the desired qualities he will lose this lead. A well-to-do man may take titles on behalf of a son and pass wealth on to him. This will work to the son's advantage, even if he lacks other qualifications, but the son must also show his capabilities by his own behavior. The continuation of a patrilineal line of leaders within a major lineage over several generations is rare.

Sometimes a younger brother is a better speaker, and is more aggressive and more knowledgeable in lineage matters, than his older full brother or a more senior agnatic half-brother. This creates a difficult situation, especially if the younger sides against his elder, as this is an insult to the latter. Such a situation requires considerable tact on the part of the younger person. The same is true of a father and son, though here the age difference is likely to be so great that the son will not offer the father serious competition in lineage leadership. It is felt that a son should wait until his father dies before becoming very active in lineage affairs.

An elder who is active in the village and village-group invariably will be influential in his major patrilineage. He will often speak for his lineage in village gatherings, where other elders will ask him for the lineage's views, and he will report to the lineage on matters in the village and village-group. In a few cases a very prominent elder in the village dominates the decisions of his lineage, and some compounds are known for having such an outstanding leader. He is always a man who has the primary leadership qualities already mentioned. Such a person is sometimes addressed or referred to as "chief" (ɛzɛ), particularly in matters relating to the Nigerian administration at Afikpo, but he does not have the qualities of chiefs in other areas of Nigeria.

The converse—that a lineage leader takes an active part in village or village-group affairs—is not necessarily the case, since some leaders restrict their interests to the patrilineal groupings. While leaders in agnatic groupings are sometimes also leaders in matrilineal ones, there is no direct association between the two; leadership in one does not automatically confer leadership in the other.

Agents of the Aro Chuku oracle live in most of the important compounds in the Afikpo villages, but they are often away on business connected with the oracle. Even when at Afikpo, they do not usually participate in routine matters of the major patrilineage. However, the Afikpo say that they "seek out trouble," and if the lineage is engaged in a dispute, if it has few children, its members have poor crops, its male members are leaving to settle elsewhere, or some other problem occurs, the agent may suggest that a consultation with his oracle is in order. Or the elders may go to the agent after a diviner has advised them to visit the oracle. For this trip the agent is in complete charge. He thus has a special role in patrilineage affairs regardless of his age and personal qualities.

Educated and acculturated Afikpo rarely live in the compound. Sometimes they live nearby but most often, while they retain a home in or near the compound where some members of their family live, they reside and work away from Afikpo. They may occasionally take part in some lineage matter if at home, and if so they are likely to have influence, regardless of age and personal qualities, but generally they leave alone the traditional system of decision-making.

In summary, the role of leader in the major patrilineages is potentially open to all lineage adult males, except *osu*, and there are no formal limits to the number who may hold it. Virtually all men who reach old age take at least some lead in lineage affairs: to refuse to do so is considered antisocial. Thus the leadership role in the lineage is almost universal for all adult males who attain the proper age. It is an ascribed one within which achievement based on personal qualities is extremely significant in determining the most outstanding leaders.

There is no specific meeting time for the leaders of the major patrilineage, but they usually gather in the morning or late afternoon of a market day, either at the ancestral rest house or in the open meeting area nearby. Decisions are reached only after thorough discussion, and perhaps calling in persons with special information or witnesses to some event. Elders of a minor patrilineage, but especially the most senior member, who is its head, speak for the subgrouping. The elders attempt to reach agreement even though this may mean some compromise. Persons in a clear minority are expected to give way, but only after freely expressing their views. It is the consensus of elders' views which regulates the lineage, not the authority of a single individual.

This pattern of decision-making is characteristic of many Afikpo organizations—the ward, the village, the village-group, and the matrilineal clan—though the basis for selection of leaders varies from group to group. There is no special dress or insignia for major patrilineage leaders.

The elders are mostly involved with the orderly administration of the lineage, that is, with routine matters of authority. Political competition, factionalism, and internal disputes do occur, and the elders must deal with them, but they seem less significant within the major patrilineage than in some other Afikpo groupings, and internal solidarity in this form of descent group is high.

They are concerned with the health and welfare of the lineage, and they may consult a diviner when they feel that it is not prospering. They have over-all responsibility for upkeep of the lineage shrines, and they assist in the selection of the shrine priests. They are also involved in the care of lineage properties, and they represent and defend the lineage in village matters and in disputes involving it. These activities are examined below, but they cannot be understood without first describing the roles in the major patrilineage of the ancestral priest and of the young men's grade.

THE ANCESTRAL SHRINE PRIEST

The ancestral shrine of a major patrilineage is hidden from view behind raffia strands in the rear of the *Mma obu* shrine house. It consists of a large number of pots, many old and broken, put there during the lifetime of male lineage members and again after they die. There is usually one that is identifiable as that of the lineage founder, placed there following his death, and sometimes one for the founder of each minor lineage. Other pots are not specifically identified, though they may be grouped by minor lineage affiliation. The founder's house is believed to have been located where the shrine stands and his body to be buried beneath it, and the spirits of the male ancestors of the major patrilineage, *Ndɛ Mma* (people-ancestors or spirits), are said to reside in the shrine. Contact with them is made through it, so that they can be appeased or notified of festivals or events, and their assistance sought.[1]

Not only do lineage elders meet in the shrine house or in the area outside it to discuss lineage affairs, but it is here that most of the lineage feasting occurs. Here also adult men relax, and boys rest and play as they will. Women often fear this shrine, entering the house only for rituals, and they do not tarry in its vicinity.

The priest of *Mma obu*, a lineage member, holds the position for life. When he dies his successor is soon chosen, and no person acts as interim priest, unlike the case of the matrilineal clan shrine. He is selected by the lineage elders, generally with the aid of a diviner. If there is such a ritual specialist within the lineage he will often be consulted, but diviners are not found in most lineages so that an outsider is often chosen. Although the diviner often suggests a man whom the elders desire themselves, it is considered helpful to obtain supernatural assistance in the selection, for it is believed that the diviner names the person that the shrine spirits are "calling" to take charge. The person chosen may not wish to accept the priesthood; considerable work is involved, and he often automatically becomes priest of other lineage shrines as well. Sometimes a man may fear the work, for a priest observes ritual restrictions, and if a lineage member offends the ancestors it is believed that this may kill or harm him. If a man chosen is in doubt about accepting he may consult another diviner. Sometimes the elders may not like the person selected, or they may feel that he is a troublemaker, and may ask the diviner to choose another.

Before taking office the designate performs a series of rituals under the direction of the diviner who has chosen him. He also feasts the elders, giving them a small sum, perhaps one shilling, "to buy the shrine," and to be blessed by them. He performs sacrifices at the ancestral shrine, and at any shrines of which he

---

[1] It is also possible for a person to offer sacrifices to them at a crossing of paths, particularly if he is away from home, but it is usually preferred, especially for important sacrifices, to do this at the shrine.

becomes priest at this time to announce to them that he is taking over. There is no special priest's costume or insignia of office.

The priest is usually an elder, and he may be from any minor patrilineage within the descent group. In fact, personal character is an important basis for selection. He must not be an adulterer or a philanderer. He is expected to be a quiet person, who does not engage in secular political activities or join in settling disputes to any great extent. The restriction on political participation is not a taboo; it relates to a general feeling in Afikpo, often expressed in song, that public politics, disputes, or "palaver," cause the death of elders and that the priest should refrain from these to protect himself. There are, however, some shrine priests who do take part in politics.

Other restrictions are more clearly stated. The priest should have at least one wife, since at certain feasts the food he eats must be cooked by a spouse and a portion of it first given to the ancestral shrine as a sacrifice. He is expected not to have sexual relations with anyone but his wives, most especially not with other married women living in the compound or women who have once married there; it is believed that this would anger the ancestors. While these restrictions apply to all lineage males, sexual purity is particularly important in his case. Wherever he goes, a priest is careful to avoid contacts or the suggestion of such contacts with married women, or to eat food prepared by women other than a wife. Another woman may be "impure," for example, may have borne twins. If he has only one wife and she dies, he is expected to marry another.

If the priest violates the shrine's sexual taboos, Afikpo say he must perform a sacrifice of expiation to appease the ancestors and that the lineage elders may remove him from office. However, no case of such a violation was recorded. The elders may remove him for other causes, though this is rare. The only instance noted was of a priest who, lacking sons of his own, refused to put a surrogate eldest son through the village secret society initiation (that is, to sponsor the son of another lineage member), as he should have done, and who was fined by the lineage elders. He refused to pay and the elders, feeling that he could not be their priest while being so at odds with them, removed him from office. The new priest named by a diviner was soon found to be a leper; he had not yet performed the rituals to take office when the elders and the diviner chose yet another man. In another case the lineage elders threatened to remove a priest because he was lazy in performing the proper rituals, but after they warned him his behavior improved and he was retained. These exceptional cases indicate that the ultimate control of the ancestral shrine priesthood rests in the elders' hands.

The priest meets with the elders in lineage matters and advises them on ritual actions. He is an equal among them, outside of his specialized experience, and holds no position of authority over them. If anything except a routine ritual matter is involved, he and the elders consult a diviner to determine what steps should be taken, rather than depending upon their own judgment.

The priest's role as ritual leader is limited. He may determine, often through discussion with lineage elders, and sometimes a diviner, when to perform sacrifices for the lineage as a whole, but he does not usually diagnose individual "troubles" nor attempt to control who shall sacrifice at his shrine. He is more a ritual intermediary rather than a strong authoritarian figure.

His position illustrates another aspect of Afikpo leadership. This is that while secular roles, such as those of the lineage elders, are multiple, sacred roles are single, filled through supernatural guidance and elders' assistance.

THE YOUNG MEN'S AGE GRADE

This is an organization of young lineage men formed into an age grade composed of two or three age sets.[2] Called *ukɛ ɛkpɛ* (grade-society), or sometimes by other terms, such as *ɛkpɛ ukɛ*

---

[2] In Afikpo an age set is a grouping of persons whose ages are within about three years of one another; an age grade consists of two or more sets grouped together for certain purposes.

ɛzi (society-grade-compound), it forms part of a larger village and ward system of age sets and grades to which all males above the age of about twenty-eight years belong. The *ukɛ ɛkpɛ* in the compound is generally a section of the larger ward or village *ukɛ ɛkpɛ* and is composed of its major patrilineage members, plus other males of the proper age who regularly live in the compound and belong to the proper sets. It remains active for roughly five to fifteen years, the members being about thirty to forty-five years old. Membership in the *ukɛ ɛkpɛ* grade in a compound usually changes when it does so in the ward or village, where the shift originates. The relationship of this lineage grade in the compound to that of the ward and village age groupings is discussed later (see "Patrilineal Groupings in the Village" in chap. iv). Here we show how it is organized within a single major patrilineage.

The age grade meets in the house of its leader, generally an active and interested person of the senior set chosen by the members when they take office. The leader need not come from a particular minor lineage within the major patrilineage; he is informally selected because he is interested in organizing the grade, and is amiable. Seniority of age within the grade, as determined by set membership, is important in the selection, however. Several of the leader's age-grade friends who are interested assist him. The grade sometimes also has a member, who may be from any set within it, who likes to direct work parties and communal labor, and comes automatically to fill this post. The *ukɛ ɛkpɛ* also usually has a secretary, an educated grade member, or a schoolboy, who keeps records of the group's finances, and often of the lineage finances as a whole, as well as records of title societies within the compound. All males of the proper sets in the compound belong to the grade; the *ukɛ ɛkpɛ* role is multiple and universal for males, as is being a lineage elder. Yet, while grade activities frequently appear to be based on consensus of all members, those of the most senior set usually wield the greatest authority.

THE ANCESTRAL ASPECT

The elders, the ancestral shrine priest, and the young men's grade are the three focal points for the activities of the agnatic descent group. Guidance and control of lineage activities are carried on through both secular and sacred means, most often a combination of both. The link between priest and elders is an important one, and, of course, is heavily sacred. Also of great significance is that between elders and the young men's grade, more secular in nature. But there is little direct tie between the young men's group and the priest. Let us first examine the more sacred aspects.

The priest is the direct link and the intermediary between the living lineage members and the agnatic ancestors: a facilitator of contact rather than a highly authoritarian person. The key tie is that between lineage males and the ancestral spirits; the key ritual is the process of associating the spirit of the newly dead with the shrine.

A pot representing a man's spirit is placed in the ancestral shrine shortly after his death, but only if he has had children, particularly sons. This forms part of an important second funeral ceremony, *olili madθ* (bury-person), the so-called "goat" funeral. The eldest son who directs the ritual, obtains from an elderly women a specially designed pot, *Mma* (the word for ancestral spirit), one of several types of shrine pots made only by senior women. He then gives it to an old woman of the compound, who has passed the menopause and is therefore considered free from possible sexual contamination. She washes it and decorates it with chalk and camwood dye, for which the son gives her a few pennies. After this he takes it to the lineage shrine house, where the priest places a variety of objects in it.[3] Both the priest and son

[3] For example, in some lineages he uses an iron gong (*εgεlε*), four palm nuts, four palm kernels, bits of chalk, kola, dried fish, the feathers and blood of a cock, the blood of a dog, and, if the son is wealthy, the blood of a goat as well. The priest kills the animals. The explanation of why certain foods or materials are used in sacrifice is invariably that this is what the spirit or spirits of the shrine "like." The gong is em-

1. New housing, built outside the compounds, along the road between Mgbom and Ukpa villages

2. Looking in at the compound meeting-place (*ihu εzi*, face-compound) from the entrance to Ezi Akputa, Mgbom Village (see Map III)

3. Ancestral shrine house (*Mma obu*), with *Ibini ɔkpabe* shrine outside

4. Matrilineal clan shrine, *Nja*, of *Ibɛ ɔkwu* clan

put in a little yam fufu and soup. Sacrificial materials are supplied by the eldest son, sometimes with the aid of his younger brothers; he performs the rite not only on his own behalf but for all his agnatic brothers.

He then feasts a member of his father's matrilineage [4] and separately in the compound the men of the major patrilineage who have performed this ceremony for their dead fathers. The feast is a sort of lineage title but without money payment. The spirit of the dead, *Mma,* is now believed to be in the rest house and the burial finished, though a series of further funeral ceremonies may be performed (S. Ottenberg, 1965). It is said that if this ritual were not done the deceased's spirit would become angry, causing illness and trouble in the patrilineage, perhaps harming his matrilineal relatives as well—a reason why the latter send a representative to see that the ceremony is properly performed.[5]

Any male who belongs to the village secret society, and this normally means all men and some boys, is entitled to a pot in the ancestral shrine, but one is not usually placed there for a childless man unless a diviner indicates that his spirit is causing illness or some other trouble. Then the ceremony is directed by a closely related elder of the deceased's matrilineage, sometimes a person who is also a patrilineal relative of the deceased, living in the same compound. If a father is alive when his son dies, the father

ployed to clear the way in ceremonies of the village men's secret society and other organizations, and it is used here to "clear the way" for the dead man as he goes along in the next world.

[4] Usually an elder who is a close matrilineal male relative of the deceased, and who represents the dead man's matrilineal groupings in seeing that the ceremony is performed properly.

[5] If a man commits suicide, is murdered, is killed in warfare or fighting, or dies away from home, the normal ritual of placing the pot is followed. However, if he dies from a loathsome disease, that is, smallpox or one in which the body swells up, the ceremony is delayed a number of weeks, and before it is performed his compound must be ritually cleansed. For death due to leprosy, it is delayed for seven years. See S. Ottenberg (1965). In all these cases, once it is performed the ancestral spirit can reincarnate and is not necessarily an evil spirit.

is said to be angry that his offspring has died before him, and will refuse to place the pot in the shrine. This would be a reversal of generational roles. If the son's spirit causes trouble, a close matrilineal male relative performs the ceremony, but this person must be from a different major patrilineage and must perform the rite at the ancestral shrine in his own compound. It is believed that if the pot were put in the father's ancestral shrine it would cause the father's early death.[6]

A similar ceremony is performed for a living male child, which is said to place his personal spirit (*owa*), in the ancestral shrine. This is usually done by the time the boy is able to walk. Until then the child is forbidden to eat anything in the shrine rest house or any of the food cooked there for lineage feasts, and there is fear that he may accidentally do so by the time he toddles. The ceremony is similar to that for a dead male except that fewer sacrificial goods are given. *Owa* represents the personal spirit of the male child, not the spirits reincarnated in him, and throughout his life it may be sacrificed to at the shrine upon the advice of a diviner if he is ill or has other troubles. No matrilineal relative of the boy need attend this function, which is directed by the child's father, or if he is dead, by a close patrilineal male relative. It is considered a patrilineal affair, as the *owa* of a person has no effect on matrilineal relatives, or on anyone but the person himself (S. Ottenberg, 1969). No pot for females is placed in the shrine during life or at death, but they have an equivalent, though individual shrine, *adudɔ* (see "Other Lineage Activities" in chap. iii), which is matrilineal in nature.

Thus *Mma* and *owa*, spirits of the dead and the living, are symbolically linked through the ancestral shrine. When the priest performs shrine rituals for the major lineage he is sacrificing to

[6] The deceased is then considered a fictive ancestral member of the lineage and compound where his pot has been placed. Sacrifices to this ancestor will be made where his pot is by his true patrilineal relatives with the aid of the priest of the shrine where the pot is located. If the deceased had wives no one in that compound can marry them. This restriction is an extension of the normal lineage rule against a woman's remarrying in her husband's compound.

both types of spirits, though he mainly calls upon the ancestors, particularly the founders of the major and minor lines, other prominent members, and former priests. A person's *owa* becomes an *Mma* upon his death; placing the pot in the shrine house at the funeral completes this transformation and enables the ancestor to reincarnate. Every Afikpo is believed to be the reincarnation of two ancestors. Normally at least one of these is in his agnatic line. Reincarnation is complex and cannot be discussed here, but it links into the concepts of *Mma* and *owa*.

The *owa* is a vague spirit, neither benevolent or malevolent, less often considered to be the cause of personal troubles than the ancestors, especially ritually neglected ancestors. Many cases of personal troubles, illness, poor crops, and so on, are said by diviners to be caused by ritual neglect, the ancestor concerned demanding sacrifices beyond what has been given to him. Some ancestors, however, seem to be inherently angry or harmful and repeatedly cause difficulties for the living, though the character of an ancestor is not believed necessarily to be similar to that of the deceased during his lifetime. Persons generally are affected by individual ancestors, whether the persons from whom they are reincarnated or not, and the lineage as a whole by collective ancestors. However, Afikpo believe that misconduct by individuals, particularly violations of sexual regulations, may anger the spirits of the dead who may then harm the priest and other lineage members unless the violator is punished and a sacrifice to the ancestor carried out.

Ancestors are thought to cause a wide variety of illnesses and other "troubles," though other types of spirits also create unpleasantness. Difficulties concerning ancestors usually are discovered through consultations with diviners, not with the priest of the ancestral shrine; diviners play a key role in the ancestral belief system. Persons can be affected by ancestral spirits related to them matrilineally or bilaterally, as well as patrilineally, so the focus of the belief system lies within the major patrilineage but also cuts across it. Finally, the priest of the ancestral shrine does not refuse to offer sacrifices on behalf of anyone who approaches him, except "contaminated persons," such as a menstruating woman or the mother of twins.[7]

Should a man who is ill or has other troubles be advised by a diviner that an ancestor is angry because he has been neglected, as frequently occurs, the person offers a sacrifice, the food being eaten by the petitioner, the priest, and the major patrilineage elders.[8] A female will have a close patrilineal relative offer the sacrifice on her behalf through the priest in her compound of birth, if her male ancestors are "calling" her. Her husband will offer it if his ancestors are involved, as may sometimes happen. A man may have this sacrifice performed without consulting a diviner to insure his welfare before clearing land for farming or during village feasts.

The priest offers sacrifices on behalf of the lineage at most of the general village feasts, during the New Yam Festival, and at the beginning of the yam-farming season, to insure prosperity. If there is sickness or death in the lineage, if there is a dispute with another group, if its birth rate is declining, its members' crops are poor, or if its sons who moved away with their mothers when they remarried out of the compound fail to return upon reaching adulthood, the elders may call for a sacrifice.

The ancestral shrine is the symbolic focus of the lineage. The lineage members' belief in a common set of agnatic ancestors gives the descent group a common identity which strengthens its organization and defines it in relation to other units. The belief in ancestors is tied to social control within the lineage. Since certain forms of misbehavior are said to harm the miscreants and other lineage members through the actions of ancestors, ancestral beliefs help check misbehavior. Thus, in addition to the elders' authority and the leadership of the ancestral priest, automatic supernatural sanctions play a role in regulating behavior. These

---

[7] In these cases the sacrifice can still be done through her spouse or another male relative.

[8] This generally consists of the flesh of a chicken, roasted by the shrine priest, the blood and feathers and other sacrificial materials being given to the shrine.

aspects of the lineage administration are crucial in maintaining internal harmony and controlling potential tensions in the lineage.

One of the most important functions of the ancestral shrine is to bind the wives of lineage men, thereby restricting their sexual activities to their husbands. Soon after a woman comes to live with her husband, whether it is a first or a later marriage for either of them, whether she comes from an agnatic lineage outside the compound, or, more rarely, from her husband's major patrilineage, she performs *imo ɛkwu* (putting-cooking stand). This binds her to the sexual rules of the ancestral shrine. Her husband brings her a cooking pot, elderly women of the lineage carry in stones to place it on, and she cooks and feeds yam fufu to the compound women. The women fix her hair in a special style and explain to her certain lineage rules which are extended to anyone living in the compound. She must not have sexual contacts with men other than her husband. If somebody makes advances at her she must report it to her husband or his patrilineage, if a man tries to give her a present she must do the same, and she allows no one except her husband to touch her vaginal area. This ceremony can be done whether the bride price has been paid or not. The ritual expresses the fact that sexual rights over her are exclusively her husband's unless she leaves him or he dies, after which she cannot remarry or have sexual relations with any persons of his lineage or compound. These rights are not transferrable to another lineage male. She is the sexual property not of the lineage but of her husband, though the descent group is concerned with any violation of this claim. The bride price paid by the bridegroom to her parents, on the other hand, concerns her legal status as wife as well as that of her future children, who will be members of his patrilineage.

On the *ɛkɛ* day of the annual Afikpo feast, *iko okoci* (feast-dry season: usually held in December), wives prepare yam fufu and soup, some of which is offered to the ancestral shrine by its priest. Each wife in the compound then eats a little herself, in the ceremony *itθ Nri Mma* (throw-food-ancestors), a renewal of the sexual restriction of a woman to her husband. It is said that a wife who has secretly violated the ruling will be afraid to eat for fear the ancestors will harm her, particularly by making her ill. She may try to avoid the ceremony which, of course, makes others suspicious of her, or she may confess. Although the manner in which this ritual is performed varies in different lineages, women who have not done the cooking-pot ceremony do not do this one. Adult lineage males, whether married or not, are also supposed to do so to bind themselves to the rules, and men who have violated them are said to fear to eat the yam. In neither ceremony do matrilineal relatives of the persons involved appear as witnesses.

It is believed that individuals who violate this sexual ruling not only become ill but may have numerous accidents, such as cutting themselves with a machete or falling from a tree, or they may become barren or have poor crops. While this supernatural retribution is thought in the first instance to fall on the "sinners," it sometimes spreads to other lineage members, a fact discovered by the lineage elders when they consult a diviner to find out the cause of the trouble. There is a great deal of group concern over adultery or possible adultery, and it is the task of the lineage elders, aided by young men of the descent group, to ferret out the guilty.

The ruling forbids a married woman from having sexual relations with any man but her husband. Lineage elders fine women who violate the rule a goat (the woman's husband usually pays for it) which is sacrificed at the ancestral shrine, but mainly eaten by the priest and lineage elders. Similarly, men are liable to punishment for having sexual intercourse with women who have married into the lineage. This ruling is extended to all married women living in the compound, whether of the major patrilineage or not. The law further prohibits any man of the compound from having sexual relations with a woman once married into the compound who has left to live or to marry elsewhere. Such a woman cannot remarry in the compound of her former husband.

If both violators are from the same compound, they each

provide a goat. If pressed by the elders, one of them often confesses if suspicion is thrown on the person. When the woman is from a compound and the man from outside, it is normally she who is fined; the lineage elders of the compound have no controls over the man in this case. They may report the matter to his major patrilineage, but this group is not likely to take any action. Unless the woman had once been married into the man's descent group that lineage is not concerned with punishing him—and in fact illicit relations outside a compound are common and are an important way in which men acquire wives.

Should the accused deny the charge, he or she is tried by that person's lineage elders. If the case is unclear the individual—usually a woman—takes an oath at an Afikpo shrine designed especially for swearing (see p. 165), where she states that she did not have the forbidden sexual relations, and that she has not used special magic to ward off the power of the ancestral shrine or the swearing itself. The Afikpo believe that if she is guilty she will become ill or die within a year as a result of action by the shrine spirit, but that if she is innocent no harm will come to her.

While many men feel that the primary purpose of the sexual regulations of *Mma obu* is to control women, some educated males, some persons who have lived away from Afikpo for a time, and the few wives who have been to school, do not want to perform the ceremony that binds them to *Mma obu*. They do not believe in the power of the ancestors, and consider the annual ritual a waste of food. The elders, wishing to respect the ancestors and suspecting that the wives of educated men, as well as educated women, are promiscuous—otherwise they would not refuse to bind themselves to the shrine—are not anxious to have these women bound. They fear that it might anger the shrine spirits and cause illness or other troubles as a result of these persons' behavior, and they do not encourage such women to perform the customary rituals. Thus while marriage normally means that sexual rights over the wife are exclusively for the husband and not for his patrilineage (this is confirmed by the rules of remarriage exogamy discussed below), a man may allow his wife freedom from the rule, though not from the moral view under-lying it, by refusing to "bind" her. Therefore, the husband's sexual rights over his wife include the right of nonexclusiveness over her.

A strict rule of remarriage exogamy applies to spouses of lineage men, and is extended to women married to nonlineage males living in the compound. In short, a woman who has ever been married to a man in the compound may never marry there again once he dies or she has been divorced, unless she remarries him. Should she marry again in the compound it would be said that she, or her new husband, had poisoned or otherwise killed the first one if he has died, or had employed magic if they were divorced. It is believed to make the ancestors extremely angry. This tradition minimizes conflict and prevents wife-stealing within the residential group. It confirms the point already made that marriage vests sexual rights over the wife in her husband and not in his patrilineage, and that the woman does not become property of the lineage. A widow who is still of childbearing age ordinarily leaves to remarry, though if she has borne children she may remain, and then no man of the compound may enter her house or have sexual relations with her. However, a woman of child-bearing age is likely to marry again, especially if she has had children—finding a new husband and leaving the compound will normally be no serious hardship for her. If a woman has passed the menopause when her husband dies, she is likely to remain and be cared for by one of his brothers, or a son. These regulations are essentially major patrilineage rules applied to a residential area, the compound.

The rulings on sexual behavior and remarriage operate to minimize conflicts between lineage males over married women, and prevent accusations of wife-stealing among them. They turn personal sexual interests, anxieties, or problems of married per-sons outward from the residential group into other lineages and dwelling areas. In so doing the lineage harmony is maintained at the expense of producing some interlineage friction over sexual matters.

Members of a major patrilineage are not bound by rules of exogamy. However, marriage of certain close patrilineal relatives is forbidden as an offense against the ancestors, though the Afikpo usually say simply that such persons are "too close" to marry. These are that a man may not marry daughters of his father (whether adopted or not), daughters of his father's sons (whether or not the sons are adopted), or agnatic half-sisters. By remarriage rules we have seen that a man may not marry any of his father's wives or former wives or those of a brother. Matrilineal exogamy exists, as we shall see, so that patrilineal relatives who are also matrikinsmen may not marry (see "The Matrilineal Clan" in chap. iii).

Aside from these, a man may marry a woman of the minor patrilineage, but such marriages are rare. For example, in the genealogy of one minor lineage, in Ndɛ Akputa, Mgbom Village, seventy-eight marriages of male members covering a span of six generations were recorded. Of these, six marriages were with women of the three other minor lineages which form the major patrilineage, and one marriage was within the minor lineage. In the latter instance, however, the woman was the daughter of a man who had been adopted into the compound, thus not a true patrilineal relation of her husband. If a girl is exceptionally hard-working and able, members of her major patrilineage may wish to keep her within the group, or if a girl becomes pregnant, and the father is from the major lineage, they may marry, but it is not necessary for her to marry him or anyone in the major patrilineage. In general, however, marriage outside of her patrilineal grouping either brings increased contacts to her lineage or is an expression of existing contacts, and this form of marriage is the commonest.

The ancestors and the ancestral shrine are thus involved in the regulation of sexual activities and marriage in the residential area of the lineage. As we shall see, punishment of sexual violation is done by lineage elders, in cooperation with the lineage age grade of young men, who together administer the secular aspects of lineage affairs. We now turn to this sphere of patrilineal life.

SECULAR ASPECTS

The *ukɛ ɛkpɛ* grade is the executive arm of the lineage elders. It carries out their orders, reports violations of lineage regulations, and suggests needed tasks. Some of its functions are executed by its leaders, who assume that the members will support them. At times the leaders act after consultation with the lineage elders. Decisions are proclaimed by a member who beats the iron gong (*ɛgɛlɛ*) of the grade, hangs a few leaves of the *ogirisi* tree from any house roof at the compound public meeting place as a sign of the pronouncement, and states the decision to any persons present, who pass the information on to others.

The grade is responsible for supplying materials for sacrifices done on behalf of the major patrilineage. In cases of general lineage illness or other troubles it arranges to call and to pay a diviner, whom the elders consult. It also provides some foods for annual feasts in the compound and sees that they are properly organized. When the time for a feast is not set by groups outside the compound, such as by the village, it decides the date with the approval of the elders, and reminds them of approaching feast days. The grade has the authority to fine persons within the compound who do not take their proper part in these festivities, often a penalty of 2s 6d. It also arranges for the collection of dues from lineage males when it needs special funds for some activity.

Ukɛ ɛkpɛ is also responsible for the maintenance of peace and order in the compound. If there is a sexual offense of the types already discussed it is this grade which seizes the goat to be held for sacrifice, or until the elders try the case. In this and any other important matters it is the grade's responsibility to bring the problem to the lineage elders' attention. The grade will keep watch for an adulterer if a diviner indicates that there is one in the compound.

An important function of *ukɛ ɛkpɛ* is to control intracompound disputes. These may be over personal property or shares of food, between husbands and wives, or between cowives over some domestic matter. The grade can force the disputants to pay a temporary fine and come before the lineage elders for judgment. The grade also brings accusations of stealing to the elders and collects the fines levied for theft or for false accusations of theft.

Perhaps the duty of this age grade which the men consider most important is to keep the women living in the compound under control. If a woman argues with a male of that residential unit, the latter may summon any *ukɛ ɛkpɛ* members he can find, who will impose a fine on her. If he is an *ukɛ ɛkpɛ* member, he can fine her directly unless he is her husband. A man who quarrels with a woman is rarely fined; the assumption is that the woman caused the dispute. However, when the case is taken to the compound elders for judgment, as it will be if any party objects to the penalty, the elders can fine him. Many disputes leading to *ukɛ ɛkpɛ* action also occur between cowives over property and other rights in relation to their husband (P. Ottenberg, 1958, chap. vi). A woman who is fined by the grade may refuse to pay if she feels that she is not at fault or if she is very angry. If this occurs, the grade members seize her cooking pots in lieu of the fine, storing them in the house of their leader. The matter is then taken to the compound elders, and after the case has been decided and the fine paid the pots will be returned.

The elders judge cases at the compound public meeting place, where *ukɛ ɛkpɛ* members and disputants testify. The only women present are those who are directly involved, their friends, and perhaps some close patrilineal and matrilineal female relatives, but any man may attend. The women are treated with respect and given an opportunity to present their views without interruption. After presenting the case, the litigants leave and the elders discuss the matter, calling those concerned back when they have arrived at a decision. The verdict is reached after a full discussion, in which younger men, including *ukɛ ɛkpɛ* members if they are concerned with the case, may take part. Debate continues until a satisfactory solution is agreed on, when a sound of approval (*eheee!*), the characteristic sign that a conclusion has been reached, is given by those present. The lineage man who normally summarizes decisions, or another good speaker, announces the findings, sometimes citing past cases and rebuking violators. All fines and collections are kept by *ukɛ ɛkpɛ*. The money is divided equally among its sets, or among the members grouped by minor lineages, to avoid concentration in one person's hands and consequent temptation to steal it. This is characteristic banking pattern used by groups in Afikpo. The money is collected again by the grade leaders for diviners' fees, to purchase sacrificial materials, or for other activities for which the grade is responsible.

If a person refuses to pay a fine to *ukɛ ɛkpɛ* after his case has been judged, the grade will seize and keep a goat or some other property of his until it is paid. In earlier times the grade would kill and eat the goat, which would then be forfeited, though the fine still had to be paid, but this is no longer done. If a person is not satisfied with the lineage elders' decision he may appeal to the village elders, or, particularly in cases of theft or sexual offenses, he may swear his innocence at an Afikpo shrine. Or he may take the case to the Native Authority Court to have it retried, or even call in elders from outside the village to help settle the matter. For intracompound disputes these steps are not often taken since the cost is frequently higher than the original fine, and it is considered bad form to question the decision of the lineage elders, or to air lineage disputes in public. This is said only to lead to further friction between the disputants.[9]

If, after a man's goat or other property has been seized, he still refuses to pay his fine and is a continuing source of dispute in the compound, he is likely as a last resort to be ostracized by the lineage elders, though this occurs only after bitter trouble. No one in the compound associates with him, and his wives are dissuaded from doing anything for him except meeting his minimal needs. He will still receive his share of any benefits of title societies in the compound, but he cannot take part in title ceremonies or take any new titles involving his lineage. He is permit-

[9] For cases involving intravillage disputes between major patrilineages, see pp. 152–53.

ted to perform the burial and secondary funeral ceremonies for his parents, but cannot take certain titles associated with these rites. Such a man cannot sponsor his sons' initiation into the village men's society, which is an honor for himself as well as a transition from boyhood to manhood for a child. He may offer sacrifices and perform certain of the necessary *rites de passage* for his children, including the ceremony of "bringing out" a new child into the compound four days after its birth and the circumcision ceremony. He will be assisted in these activities by his fellow lineage members, if necessary. He may also engage in activities that do not involve the lineage, such as trading. Ostracism continues until he pays his fines and shows evidence of good will. While one has no trouble learning of cases of ostracism, as they are well known, they are not too prevalent. Lineage elders are reluctant to so condemn a person. They fear that he may leave the group, and an isolated state is avoided or terminated by them whenever possible. Ostracism creates a situation where the lineage and persons involved are subject to public song and comment at certain village feasts, a matter of which no lineage is likely to be proud.[10]

Ostracism does not normally apply to women, though when twins are born, or there is a breech birth, both believed to "spoil the ground" of the compound (see p. 67), the mother and her children may be driven out, in former times for a long period of time or even permanently. This is the principal situation in which a major lineage banishes a woman, and though a man's patrilineal relatives may urge him to dismiss a wife who is a constant troublemaker, the authority to do so lies with him. A woman's husband is ultimately responsible for paying penalties levied against her; thus the pressures over a misbehaving wife fall largely on her spouse.

When the lineage is involved in a dispute with another group in Afikpo, perhaps another major patrilineage, or a matrilineal

[10] In precolonial times ostracism might be followed by selling the person into slavery if he were still recalcitrant.

grouping, the *ukɛ ɛkpɛ* grade is expected to see that lineage members lend support to it. The grade can levy dues to fight the case, fine members who support the opposition or who fail to uphold the lineage, and direct members to appear as witnesses in the matter. While the lineage elders are in charge of the case, the age grade plays a strong supportive role in maintaining the unity of the group against outsiders.

Thus in many situations the young men's grade of the major patrilineage has authority to levy dues and fines, seize property, and bring matters to the elders. Its authority extends to those who are senior to them in age, something quite unusual in this age-ranked society. In fact, this only exists because they are supported by the lineage elders, in whose name they act.

The *ukɛ ɛkpɛ* does not itself perform much of the communal labor for the lineage, but supervises younger men and women whom it appoints or persons named by the elders. In the compound these are usually organized into sets or groupings on the basis of age, again according to the ward and village organization. The grade is responsible for keeping fences and other compound property in good condition, and for the general cleanliness of the residential area. It sees that firewood is provided for the ancestral rest house so that the priest and elders may cook and keep warm there. It is responsible for determining what junior age groupings will carry out housebuilding, a complicated communal affair in which young persons of certain ages are assigned specific tasks in the building of homes, such as roofing, procuring mud, and mudding down the walls. If a lineage member becomes a diviner, the grade also directs the erection of a special house for him where he carries out his work. It is responsible for rebuilding the ancestral shrine house—the fashion nowdays is to use cement blocks and galvanized iron roofs, but only after receiving assurances from a diviner that the ancestral spirits will not be offended by this bit of modernity. The *ukɛ ɛkpɛ* sees that the necessary communal work is carried out, that any contractor involved is paid, and that sacrifices to the appropriate shrines are performed so that the ancestral spirits will not be upset by the rebuilding.

A characteristic feature of the major patrilineage is its lack of extensive holdings of productive property. Such property as is found is largely administered by the *ukɛ ɛkpɛ* under the ultimate guidance of the lineage elders.

While most farmland in Afikpo is matrilineally controlled, a small amount, about 15 per cent, is patrilineal. The controls take one of four forms: (1) control by a single major patrilineage, (2) joint control by two related major patrilineages in the same village or in different villages, (3) joint control by a number of contiguous, often unrelated, major patrilineages, in different compounds which make up a residential ward of the village, and (4) control by minor patrilineages. Only the first is discussed here.[11]

Before proceeding something of a general nature should be said concerning farmland. Although most farmland is owned by matrilineal and patrilineal groupings and not the village, the latter has certain controls over it, and the land lies outside village areas and is identified with these settlements. Thus for each village there are six land sections, one farmed each year, and in the succeeding year as well, usually in rotation, successively going out from the settlement in one direction from it. The village elders determine which section to farm each year, perform certain rituals, and have some general farming regulations, but have no further controls over this land. The farmland nearest the village, called *ebo*, is outside of this six-block system and can be farmed any year, and similarly the land bordering the Afikpo Village-Group is largely beyond village controls and can be used at will. Both *ebo* and this distant land are also controlled by matrilineal and patrilineal descent groups and sometimes wards. Thus patrilineal land holdings are found in the six-block sections, in *ebo* land, and in the border land. In addition, the land most immediately in back of each compound, *osohɔ*, where new houses

[11] See p. 85 for land controlled by two major patrilineages, p. 147 for ward land, and pp. 81–82 for minor patrilineage land. The origins of these forms of land are discussed on pp. 204–5. Cf. Obi (1963, chap. ix); Chubb (1948:22).

are built, and where a garbage dump, latrines, and pot-burning field may be located, are owned by the major patrilineage residing there. However, this is not considered farmland and only a little planting is done there.

The right to use land of a major patrilineage is open to any male lineage member who is an initiate of the village secret society, that is, all adult males. Before each farming season it is divided according to relationship, age (the older the man the larger the share), and willingness to use the land. Interested men help to clear the bush, particularly the section they expect to farm, on days set by the lineage elders.[12] When the land is divided, each man usually receives the same portion he had when this land was last farmed, with some changes to account for increased age, death, illness, and the presence of new farmers. Young sons are often given small shares which their father farms for them and which become theirs on his death. The father's main portion often goes to his eldest son upon his death if the son is a full adult and needs land, but it sometimes goes to full or half-brothers, depending upon age and need. A man may share some of his land with his wives, giving them poorer land to plant cassava, and letting them plant vegetable crops among his yams. He may let nonlineage friends and matrilineal relatives from outside the compound use all or part of the land, the lineage being mainly concerned that it is not neglected. If it is unused, which is rare, he may receive a smaller share at the next division of the land.

The land is divided for farming in the first year of its use in the farming cycle by the *ukɛ ɛkpɛ* grade; users retain the same shares for the second year. Grade leaders report on the division to the lineage elders, who have the authority to redivide the land if they

---

[12] A man may send a representative to clear for him, as he is likely to be busy with other farmland at this time of year. It is particularly important for friends or matrilineal relatives of patrilineal compound members who want small portions of the land to help in its clearing and to contribute to the expense of sacrifices made by the lineage for the land. Failure to do either is an indication of lack of serious interest in the land.

are not satisfied. In some lineages the elders divide it, or a prominent lineage member makes the division. Unlike the case of matrilineal land holdings, there is little disagreement concerning the allocation; this is frowned upon by the patrilineage. Further, the amount of this land available to any individual is often so small that there is little point in quarreling over it. The conflicts that occur over patrilineal land are with outside groupings, particularly matrilineal ones, for whole sections (see "Farmland" in chap. v).

Before farming a section of major patrilineage land, the elders and ancestral priest consult a diviner to determine what sacrifices should be made, in a ceremony called *egbeja*, in which the *ukε ɛkpε* grade calls the diviner. The suggestions vary from time to time, and from specialist to specialist, but they usually involve the sacrifice of a small chicken at the ancestral shrine by its priest, sometimes with a promise to sacrifice a larger one if the harvest is good. At this ritual the priest tells the founding ancestor that such-and-such land is to be farmed and asks that the crops be good. The diviner sometimes also suggests a sacrifice called *ɔhoha ɛkwu ukwɔ* (squeeze-leaf-heap) to the spirit of the ground (*ale*), performed at the land itself by the elders and a diviner. If the land has a shrine to the Aro Chuku oracle, *Ibini ɔkpabe*, associated with it, the elders see that the ancestral priest or a responsible senior person sacrifices to it, for this shrine is specifically to prevent the land from being seized or otherwise obtained by nonmembers. If the land is held in pledge only the ancestral sacrifice may be done, if any at all. As one Afikpo said, "Why should you be happy over this land? Tomorrow the original owners might take it back from you." Individual patrilineal members offer sacrifices at various shrines before farming to ask for good crops, but not usually for specific sections of patrilineal land, rather for general success.

Only occasionally does a major patrilineage own a grove of trees or a water area. If it has a palm grove this is usually in *ebo* land, and the young men's grade sees that it is rented out or that young men of the lineage collect the fruits at the proper times and turn at least part of the profits back to the grade. In either case the funds become lineage property under the ultimate control of its elders. Individual lineage members sometimes own or control raffia groves, but the grade can pre-empt their use if this material is needed for repairing or rebuilding the ancestral shrine house. A major patrilineage may occasionally control a section of a stream that passes near its living quarters; this is used for washing and as a water supply, and young girls of the lineage usually keep it cleaned up. Occasionally the lineage may control a section of a stream somewhere in the farmland areas which is reserved for seasonal communal fishing.

LINEAGE SHRINES AND ACTIVITIES

A distinguishing feature of the major patrilineage, in contrast to matrilineal groupings, is the presence of a large number of spirit shrines. Some of these are characteristic of nearly all major patrilineages, while others are specific to certain ones, and are associated with specialized functions (see "Agnation in the Village-Group Structure" in chap. iv).

The shrines common to *all* major patrilineages serve a wide variety of functions: the fertility of crops and of women, sexual control of married persons and adolescents, success of warfare and wrestling contests, guarantee of good health for patrilineal members, protection of the residential area against evil, and so on. Two broad categories of functions are involved: (1) those which promote the general prosperity and welfare of the lineage, and (2) those which are concerned with social controls over lineage members. These functions are the concern of the patrilineal elders and shrine priests; they are part of the administrative aspect of the descent grouping.

The most important of the major patrilineages' shrines other than the ancestral one, which we have already discussed, is ɔma ɛzi (good-compound), also called *aja ale ɛzi*. It is a raised circular structure, lined on the outside with hard wood, located just inside the entrance gate of every Afikpo compound. It must exist before a residential area is considered organized as living quarters for a major patrilineage, and the lineage founder is usually believed to have established it. Its spirit, that of the earth (*ale*), both of the compound and the ground in general, protects the lineage against evil entering the compound and within it. It is of great importance because of its association with the earth. Sacrifices are given at it to "keep the ground cool"; anyone who angers its spirit or violates its taboos is said to be one who "spoiled the ground," *onyɛ ɔrθ ale* (person-spoil-ground).[13] Its priest is chosen by the elders in a like manner to the ancestral shrine priest, and in some lineages he is the same person. He should have similar personal qualities, and is in a like relation of authority to the elders.

The shrine is for the general welfare of the major patrilineage. A regular sacrifice at it is made before yam planting begins, to insure good crops and the general welfare of lineage members for the period ahead, and a second one involving its spirit may be performed at the farms as well. Sacrifices are also made on behalf of the whole lineage at the suggestion of a diviner whom the elders consult when illness, decline in the birth rate, or poor crops trouble the group.[14] Sometimes a sacrifice to insure continual prosperity will be made without consulting a diviner and this also can be made for individual men to remedy almost any trouble. Boys and men who go away for fishing or trading frequently give a minor sacrifice at *ɔma ɛzi* to insure success and offer a larger one on their return if all has gone well. Thus in its general protective and supportive functions it is similar to the ancestral shrine, though the appeal here is to the spirit of the ground, not to ancestors.

The shrine has specific functions relating to sexual controls

[13] It is the Afikpo equivalent of the earth shrines, *ale, ala,* or *ane,* found in Igbo areas to the west, though it does not play as dominating a role as in other Igbo areas. See Meek (1937:24–33); Forde and Jones (1950:25). It also seems to be related to a spirit, *ɔma ɛzi,* which in other Igbo areas is a compound shrine, owned by the compound head, and which refers to the compound as a physical element.

[14] In one case the diviner recommended a sacrifice in order to bring back the lineage men who were living away from the compound.

over young persons, abnormal births or unusual conditions in children, and barrenness in women. If an uncircumcised boy is discovered to have had sexual intercourse an extensive sacrifice, generally known as ɔgwugwa ale (bless-ground), or omumɛ ale (perform-ground) is done at the shrine in the boy's compound. This varies in content from situation to situation, but involves considerable expense and some sacrificial materials which are difficult to obtain, and which are considered essential to "cool the ground." In former times one of the boy's ears would be cut off; today it is nicked so that blood drops on the shrine, a public reminder of the sin. Formerly boys were circumcised in adolescence, and the pattern of sexual restraint was related to warfare and wrestling, as it was believed that intercourse could weaken an uncircumcised boy. Today circumcision is usually done between the ages of one and five, and this sacrifice rarely needs to be made. Following circumcision there is a great deal of sexual freedom for boys, providing they do not have intercourse with married women of the compound, with women formerly married into this residential area, or with matrilineal relations. Sexual conflicts within a major patrilineage among unmarried persons seem rare. There is little feeling that such relations are essentially disruptive to lineage life, perhaps because no contractual relationship is involved.

Formerly a girl detected having intercourse before her clitoridectomy performed a similar ceremony, though an ear was not cut off. If she became pregnant she, and often her parents and lover, fled for their lives, for this was considered a terrible abomination, a disgrace to the major patrilineage. In some cases the girl was killed, and her parents' houses destroyed or damaged. In the bush she underwent a severe form of clitoridectomy, and the special sacrifice was performed. Songs of derision concerning such girls were and still are sung in the farm and bush before the New Yam Festival. Both in the case of boys and girls the sacrifices are performed by the ɔma ɛzi priest and elders in the compound of birth, regardless of where the person is living. It is clearly an affront to the major patrilineage to which the child belongs.

While clitoridectomy formerly was done after puberty, today it is carried out before, so that the cases described above are rare. The Afikpo say that this is to prevent shame falling on the girl and the brutal consequences from occurring.

In former times if a woman bore twins or had a breech birth, these were considered terrible offenses against the ground. The woman was banished to the bush area surrounding the village for seven Igbo weeks. The compound and its patrilineal members were considered contaminated; on the day of birth a special ceremony to the ground was performed, the same "squeeze-leaf" ceremony done before planting on patrilineal land (see p. 63). A special sacrifice at the shrine of the ground was also given. Usually one and sometimes both twins were killed, or the breech-born child. Such a woman was ritually suspect forever after; priests as well as others feared to touch her or to eat food she prepared. Major patrilineages with special and important shrines forbade her in their compounds, and her female friendships were often limited to other women in a like condition. These rules have largely broken down today by the pressure of "progressive" Afikpo and the advent of effective police protection, but the stigma still lingers on, and the sacrifices are usually done (see Anon., 1957).

If a child cuts its upper teeth first this is again considered an unnatural condition and a special sacrifice will have to be done. This is also so if a female climbs up on the roof of a house, or touches its symbolic extension, any object leaning against a roof. The reasons for this are not clearly stated by Afikpo, but roof construction and repairing are definitely the work of males. Perhaps a more important factor is that climbing of any kind is likely to expose a female's sexual organs to view.

If a woman is barren, or bears children who continually die, and she consults a diviner, he may attribute this to the fact that she angered the ground in any of the above ways at some time in the past and this was not detected, or that she had touched the ɔma ɛzi shrine by accident.[15] When a woman has a normal birth her husband often offers a piece of chalk to the shrine in his compound as a thank-offering and she may have this done in her compound of birth as well.

As in the case of the sexual relations and the patrilineal ancestral shrine, the association with the ground shrine places an emphasis on women and their violations. It is not the male but the woman who "spoils the ground," and it is usually believed that the female has misbehaved sexually. While sexual controls associated with this shrine concern young children before social maturity, in contrast to the ancestral shrine, which is linked to the sexual rights and restrictions of married persons, in both cases violation is likely to be linked with childlessness.

Another important major patrilineage shrine is *Nsi omɔmɔ* (medicine-birth), primarily for fertility, but also concerned with general welfare. Though occasionally controlled by a minor patrilineage said to have founded it rather than the major patrilineage, it is for the whole lineage. The controlling group selects the priest, who may also be the ancestral shrine priest, in the usual manner.

Two like major fertility feasts, *Nri Nsi omɔmɔ* (food-medicine-birth) are given annually, one by men during the yam-planting season, the other by women before the New Yam Festival. The main fare is the hens given by the women at the latter and the cocks given by the men at the former, symbolic of their sexes. These fowl are killed by the shrine priest, who sprinkles blood and feathers on the shrine; his wife then cooks them and returns them to him so that he may offer some of their organs to it. The priest gives one wing, the breast, and one leg of each fowl to the women, and the rest to the men. The rites are believed to bring fertility to those who eat of the fowl. Women who have married away from the compound may return and take part, but

---

[15] Diviners often attribute barrenness to other factors as well, adultery causing anger to ancestors, violations against learning about the secret society annoying the spirit of the society, and so on.

this is not compulsory. The feast given by the women is organized by the female elders, who collect funds from the compound women to purchase food and who see that each of them cooks food. The men's feast is usually under the direction of the *ukɛ ɛkpɛ* age group.

When there is a general lack of fertility in the patrilineage the shrine may be sacrificed at by the priest and elders. Individual women perform sacrifices with the aid of the priest if they are barren or have other troubles. A woman may give a small offering to the shrine, promising its spirit a large hen or cock if she bears a child, or she may simply make a thank-offering after giving birth, at her husband's compound shrine, and sometimes in her own as well. At the direction of a diviner men sometimes offer sacrifices here because of illness, but not for lack of fertility, a subject of considerable sensitivity among them.

There are other shrines of lesser importance in the compound of every major patrilineage. These include one to the Aro oracle, *Ibini ɔkpabe*, generally located in front of the ancestral rest house, which is sacrificed at by the ancestral shrine priest or an elder at irregular intervals for general welfare. Another, *Ngwo*, and a related one, *ɔbase ɔha*, are associated with success in wrestling and warfare. There is also a protective shrine, *ɛgbo*, a cylindrical bundle hanging from the top of each compound entrance, which guards against evil entering the compound (S. Ottenberg, 1968b).

It is evident that the beliefs and rituals associated with these religious objects are important in the major lineage, in terms of social control and the carrying out of group or individual activities in a positive manner. These shrines supplement the ancestral shrine, diffusing the ritual focus somewhat, but covering areas of concern not handled through that major religious object. As in the case of that shrine it is the elders and the shrine priests who share the administrative control for the sake of the whole lineage. The shrine priests do not form an organized special group; each plays his role with reference to the elders and the lineage as occasion demands. In fact, as we have seen, in some cases one male may act as priest of all or a number of the lineage shrines; if so, his role in each case is distinct and separate.

About one-third of the major patrilineages in Afikpo carry out some specialized activity—often involving not only members of their own lineage but other Afikpo as well—which is associated with control of a special shrine. The shrine itself is frequently considered a powerful one and sometimes thought to be unique. In some cases, it overshadows the role of the ancestral shrine, and the lineage members, especially males, are involved in important rituals associated with it. The priest of a special shrine, sometimes a different person from the ancestral priest, is a significant sacred figure in the lineage, particularly since the shrine and lineage are often involved in specialized relationships with other Afikpo. As in the case of the ancestral priest, this second priest cooperates with lineage elders, rather than dominating them, and there seems to be no conflict between the two sacred officials. Otherwise the internal administration of a specialized lineage does not differ from that of other lineages, though external relations do.

There are special shrines which are for the welfare of the village in which the patrilineage resides and others that are connected with the welfare of Afikpo as a whole. Among the important specialized shrines are two general yam shrines, and another associated with the Afikpo Rain Controller. There are also the so-called *amadi* lineages, of which there are about thirty-five in Afikpo, peoples of ancient Aro Chuku stock who formerly held special legal rights. There are also a number of blacksmith lineages with shrines associated with this work, and other lineages whose shrines are concerned with persons swearing oaths of innocence. Other major patrilineages have men practice special cures associated with particular shrines, including the treatment of madness, broken bones, deafness, blindness, and smallpox. There are also lineages whose ritual specialists perform the ceremonies at the shrine of ɔma ɛzi for violations of the spirit of the ground, *ale* (see pp. 64–65). Finally it should be noted that diviners tend to come from certain patrilineages in Afikpo.

Because these lineage specialties involve single villages or Afikpo as a whole and orient the descent groups concerned to other groups in Afikpo, they are discussed in Chapter IV. We mention them here to indicate that there is variation in the organization and activities of major patrilineages in the religious sphere.

MALE LINEAGE ASSOCIATIONS

We have now discussed the major positions for males in the patrilineage: the elders, the young men's grade, and the role of certain priests, around which the administration of the lineage is carried out. There are two other types of male groupings in the lineage, both forms of economic organizations. Membership in them, open to males within the lineage, is usually extended to other men regularly living in the compound regardless of the nature of their affiliation with the agnatic group. These are the title societies and a loan organization.

Every major patrilineage has about ten different titles (*mɛmɛ*), each associated with a title society in the lineage. The number and nature of the titles vary greatly from group to group, and there are also other titles organized on the basis of the village and village-group. Some lineage titles are mainly for prestige, some are associated with second funeral ceremonies, and some with the village secret society. Most of them bring financial rewards to their members.

A man joins a title society by feasting the title holders and paying them a sum of money. The size of the feast and the amount of the payment vary from one title and society to another, and are determined by the members who may change these as they wish. They divide the money equally among themselves and use it as they please. After a person has joined a society he is entitled to take part in future feasts, and to share the payments, though in some cases he must wait one year for the latter. The society only meets when a member takes a title; it has no other activity. Title members are not addressed in any special way, nor do they have any special costume or insignia. Titles are variously ranked, and the titles lineage members have taken are common knowledge among the adult males of the descent group. Pressures will be put on wealthy men to join title societies and so increase the income of members and the number of feasts they enjoy. Some poor men borrow money when they are young in order to join these societies, repaying the loans as they receive shares of money paid by later aspirants.

Most men join at least the less expensive lower title societies, and those connected with second funerals; this is expected of a good lineage member in order to have standing in his descent group. The title societies do not limit the number of members, in fact they encourage joining. Title members, not the major patri-lineages as a whole, control them, and the elders do not pass rulings on them.

Within the lineage the title societies are important symbols of prestige, and a man's wealth and status are in part measured in terms of the societies to which he belongs. They serve as a form of wealth distribution, minimizing disparities of income, while at the same time increasing prestige differentials. We have already indicated that being a member of title societies is a secondary factor in lineage leadership (see "The Lineage Elders" in chap. ii), and this is so for titles taken on a lineage basis as well as those organized by village or village-group. The societies them-selves are not political units and have no formal role in lineage administration.

In many compounds, particularly the middle- and large-sized ones, there is a form of loan association, usually called a "union" or "meeting" (*isusu* or *mitini*). These started in some of the larger major patrilineages in Afikpo in the early 1950's emulat-ing the village unions already in existence (S. Ottenberg, 1955b, 1968a), which had themselves only recently developed. By the mid-1950's this type of organization had spread to the matrilineal clans.[16]

The unions do not seem to exist in the smallest major patriline-

[16] See S. Ottenberg (1968a) for a general discussion of loan organiza-tions at Afikpo, and for references to their earlier growth elsewhere.

ages since they need at least ten or so young men who are willing to take part. Where they are found they meet on one Sunday a month, usually when this day falls on the Afikpo market day, *ɛkɛ*, when persons will have time to attend. Members pay small monthly dues, normally a shilling or two. Once a year, usually in December, loans are made on a yearly basis to members, usually between two and five pounds, for trade, marriage, to buy yams for farming, and so on. A few unions give scholarship aid to a student of the major patrilineage, or are concerned with improving the physical appearance of the compound, but generally they act as loan associations, providing a means for an individual to acquire a lump sum for some enterprise. Their members are mainly young and middle-aged men. In some cases the unions are entirely voluntary, while in others all the men of certain of the younger sets must join, by lineage rule, whether they take loans every year or not. In either case they are viewed as assisting the welfare of the lineage. Few elders are interested, or view their economic situation in terms of the need for such loans, having been brought up in a different economic world, using title societies as a source of income. But if there is organizational or financial trouble the union may be subject, it is said, to the authority of the lineage elders, though no such case was encountered.

WOMEN'S GROUPINGS

The majority of the females of a major patrilineage marry outside of the compound, into other parts of the village or into other villages. They return home to take part in an occasional sacrifice, to visit during feasting times, or as a permanent or temporary refuge during marital difficulties. There is no organization for such lineage women at all, though, of course, they are still considered members of the group, but in essence, they have left it behind. To put the matter in another way the females living in the compound comprise the wives of lineage members, only a few of whom are likely to be of their husband's lineage, and the unmarried girls of the descent group.

The married women in the compound are not organized into a formal grouping, but they usually have as their head a senior woman. The leadership seems to fall to one who was born into the lineage and who lives in the compound, but there is insufficient evidence to confirm this in many cases. The head and other adult women try to keep peace among themselves, preventing petty disputes between women in the compound, particularly cowives, from reaching the ears of the young men's age grade, *ukɛ ɛkpɛ*. They fear this organization, and dislike its fines and its authority over them.

In addition, many compounds have a pot-burning field (*ɔhoho;* some share this with neighboring compounds) under the direction of the senior women of the compound. Pot firing is done on an open circular ground area behind the quarters, using dried grass and brush. The breakage of pots at Afikpo in the burning process is high and there is a mystical air surrounding the success or failure of the firing process. The burning grounds are forbidden to men by lineage rules, and women until recently did not wear cloths during the firing. If pots continually break, the senior compound women consult a diviner and he may perform a sacrifice at the field or indicate a shrine at which this should be done.

The women also consult diviners if there is sickness, lack of children, or other trouble among them; for this and subsequent sacrifices they impose small dues upon themselves. In the past five to ten years the married women in many compounds have organized unions or "meetings" similar to those of the men, but for the collection of money for group sacrifices or rituals rather than for loans.

On the whole, however, the women married to the men of a major patrilineage are not well organized, and over them always looms the superior authority of men. When they meet they chatter a great deal without apparently listening to one another, and have great difficulty in reaching even minor decisions. The dignity and well-developed techniques of debate which characterize the male elders' deliberations are rarely present. Since they are of different origins within Afikpo, some only recently come to the compound, some to stay only a short time, and many bound up in cowife hostilities and allegiances, there is not much unity to their life. Though their role as an organized group in relationship to the major patrilineage is minimal, there are important rules concerning their sexual behavior and other activities made by men, the lineage elders. This is typical of Afikpo as a whole; the government is very much concerned in regulating their behavior but they have little to say in it.

Among the unmarried lineage daughters of the compound there is usually an organization, *okpo Ntu* (gathering-ashes), which maintains the latrines and the garbage dump behind the compound. Generally consisting of girls from about six or seven years of age up to the time of marriage, *okpo Ntu* is also called upon by the men's age grade to perform communal labor in housebuilding and other tasks. The girls fine their own members for failure to take part in work activities. In addition, many of these organizations form dancing societies, giving performances in the village and sometimes at the schools, and traveling to the houses of prominent persons at the Government Station area at Christmas and New Year's to dance for gifts of money. Called by such names as "The Girls Union," or "The Dancing Association," they wear brightly colored costumes. Some carry banners, for example, one read:

> "Ezi Agbi Girls Dancing Association
> Quality Is Better than Quantity
> That's the Children of God Dancing
> Happiness Is the Key of Life."

The girls are instructed in dancing and singing by their mothers or other adult women who are interested and who help to arrange for their costumes. While the type of dress and song has changed greatly in recent years, for they now use many Igbo steps and songs from areas west of Afikpo, this form of association is old. There are close ties between these females who grow up together in the lineage, and they probably have a stronger sense of common identity than do married women in the compound. As an organized group they may be advised and guided by the latter but they are relatively autonomous of them in their dancing activities, if not in their more domestic duties.

ADMINISTRATION OF THE MAJOR PATRILINEAGE

The major patrilineage is a highly cooperative structure, whose core consists of males living together. Decision-making is largely through consensus rather than the authority of a few individuals. Controls placed on persons through moral beliefs, associated with supernatural sanctions, and through the needs of living together in close face-to-face relationships, play a basic role in the life of the descent group.

The lineage moves around the interdependent activities of its priests, its elders, and young men's grade; each has well-defined duties. The priests perform the necessary sacrifices and act as intermediaries between the living and the ancestral and other spirits. The elders adjudicate and legislate, forming the ultimate decision-making body. The young men, acting as police, see that the routine of lineage life is maintained, carry out the elders' rulings, and are responsible for the financial needs of the group. They supply sacrificial materials for the priest and elders. The priests and elders cooperate on a friendly and equal basis: neither dominates the other. The government of the major patrilineage, through these three arms, is mainly concerned with administrative problems; political questions are secondary, there is relatively little factionalism within the agnatic group or with other groups. The roots of dissent and discord lie elsewhere at Afikpo.

There are differences between the priestly roles and the more secular ones of elders and young men. The sacred roles are single, filled by single persons, even though there may be three or four priests for different lineage shrines. They are achieved in the sense that they are filled by selection, but there is an element of prescription to them in that they are partly chosen through divination. They are not strongly authoritarian positions, and are often complemented through the elders in decision-making in ritual matters, as well as by diviners, who may be external to the lineage.

The roles of elders and young men are multiple and ascribed. Any male of the proper age has the right to take part, and all men who live long enough do so, as a rule, so that sex and age are the prime criteria. Within both the elders' and *ukɛ ɛkpɛ* grades personal qualities are important in determining the extent of leadership roles. There is no dominant head of the elders, and no authoritarian leader of *ukɛ ɛkpɛ* though here there exists a distinct role of head.

Leadership roles in lineage administration thus are blends of ascription and achievement; neither pattern is universal. There is little centralization of authority in the hands of a single person, or even of a few; authority in the lineage is broadly based.

The role of beliefs in automatic supernatural sanctions resulting from the actions of spirits as a result of misconduct is important in the regulation of lineage behavior. The notion that misbehavior by a person may bring supernatural retribution to other lineage members and even nonlineage persons, as well as to himself, acts as a deterrent to misconduct, as well as an explanation of unfortunate occurrences. Here the sense of group identification in and with the lineage is strong, especially for males. We note to what a large extent lineage administration is concerned with matters that are handled through ritual and in the context of supernatural belief. Health, welfare, the solution of problems, and a whole variety of troubles, either involving the lineage as a whole or its individual members, are controlled through ritual actions by the lineage administration.

The role of women in the administration of the lineage is negligible in the sense that females take little part in it, either those born to it or married to its members. Lineage government is very much concerned with controlling females, particularly in sexual matters but also their general conduct. While women are usually given a fair hearing in judicial matters they play only a small judicial role, handling minor matters concerning their own sex.

In all of these aspects—structure, role, and behavior—the administration of the major lineage resembles that of the ward, the village, and the village-group, and to a limited degree that of the matrilineal clans. The basic pattern of government in Afikpo is learned by the child in the context of the residential setting of his major patrilineage, and the government of Afikpo is, to a large extent, a projection of its organization.

THE MINOR LINEAGE

Internal solidarity of the major patrilineage is high, and while frictions occur between persons and families in the descent group they do not normally lead to factionalism, but are adjudicated by the lineage elders. We have seen how distinctions between adopted and indigenous lineage members and their ancestors are not bruited about; rather there is an attempt to maintain the fiction of common origin. Again, we have noted that competition within the lineage for control or domination of its administrative machinery is virtually nonexistent, due to its broad membership base, and because there is not much property or other wealth to be gained through administrative control. Yet, despite all of these factors, internal segmentation, as well as the processes of fission, accretion, and extinction, occur within the major patrilineage.

The minor patrilineages of the major lineage, which form its fundamental internal division, are considered by Afikpo to be natural divisions, peacefully developed through the first son of each wife of the lineage founder, rather than divisions which have grown out of hostilities among sons. The number of minor patrilineages that comprise a major patrilineage normally varies between two and four as we have seen. A few of the smaller major patrilineages show no division at all, and in the absence of minor lineages their usual activities are carried out by the major lineage. Where minor lineages exist, and this is in virtually all of the medium-sized and larger major patrilineages in Afikpo, they are named, corporate groups, although not highly organized. Al-

5. Sacrifice at patrilineage fertility shrine, *Nsi omɔmɔ*, by its priest

6. The main village rest house in the central common, Mgbom Village

7. Chalk sellers at the Afikpo market (one woman is also selling cassava)

8. Above: Boys eating mashed yam at
   a ritual before constructing a new
   ancestral shrine house

9. Right: The senior Afikpo diviner,
   holding a tortoise shell and an ante-
   lope horn. Other divination materials
   are in front of him.

though they may control a little farmland, occasionally own groves, have some connection with certain shrines, and play a role in house ownership, their property interests are unimportant, compared to other Afikpo descent groups. They are characterized by being actively involved in the *rites de passage* and other ceremonial activities of their members.

The rank order of minor lineages within a major patrilineage is genealogically known. The senior minor lineage may occasionally control a shrine which the other lines do not (usually for the benefit of the whole major patrilineage), but no serious rank distinction is made among minor segments. A good example of this is the practice of sharing food, drink, or money by the major patrilineage elders on the basis of age rather than minor lineage membership. However, each minor lineage is conscious of its size in relation to others in the larger descent group. Since these lineage segments often trace their origin to the same generation of ancestors, size denotes prosperity. The larger groups are proud of their position, while smaller ones are concerned with their lack of growth and take ritual steps to increase it. It is not at all rare to find that one or more minor groupings have died out during the course of the development of the major patrilineage. But rivalries over size among minor lineages do not lead to serious friction; there is a lack of sense of distinctiveness and hostility among them. Disputes between them are rare, though separation may result when this occurs. Rather, strong emphasis is placed on the unity of the segments of the larger major patrilineage.

Within the minor patrilineage agnatic descent lines are often recognized, generally tracing descent from sons of the founder of the minor patrilineage, and from sons of his full brothers, though sometimes from a prominent man of a later generation or from an adopted male. These seem to be rarely more than a few such lines in a minor patrilineage. For example, the four minor patrilineages that comprise the major patrilineage of Ndε Akputa have a total of seven such descent lines among them (see Chart 1), plus some others that are a result of adoptions. The living members of any one of these lines within the minor patrilineage, closely related agnatically, share a sense of competition over the size of their line in comparison to other lines in the minor patrilineage, and are highly supportive of their members in rituals and *rites de passage*, but they are not corporately organized as groups.

The minor patrilineage has no special meeting place. Its elders discuss lineage matters when they gather for some ceremony, or they may meet at the house of a senior member when there is a specific problem at hand. The eldest male nominally heads the group. Whether he actually acts in this capacity, or whether other elders of the minor lineage also play a leadership role, depends to a certain extent on his ability as a leader in terms of the leadership qualities for the major patrilineage (see "The Lineage Elders" in chap. ii). In any case he will be respected and treated with deference. As we have seen, any elder can represent his minor patrilineage at meetings of the major patrilineage, and if the eldest man present he is expected to do so. As a result of the dearth of senior men, middle-aged men play a greater leadership role here than in major patrilineages. Leadership in the minor lineage is intermediate between that of the agnatically oriented extended family, with its single head, and the major lineage, with its body of elders.

Since the focus of common interest of the minor lineage lies in the important ceremonies and *rites de passage* of its members, it is not surprising that it is represented on such occasions by its senior members, who must take part to validate the rituals. These men receive shares of food in the feasting, and sometimes sums of money which are said to be for the minor lineage, and which they divide among themselves. In any title a man takes in which his wives each give him money in a public ceremony—something done only for the most important titles—the minor lineage usually receives a small amount from each wife as a token of respect. At the feasts which mark burial and funeral rites, seniors of the minor patrilineage receive important shares of food.

These senior men take part in the feasts given when a man acquires certain individual shrines (see "Shrines" in chap. v), receive a share of bride price payments, and participate in divorce proceedings involving members of their lineage (P. Ottenberg, 1958). They are concerned with the welfare of the group and are expected to support its members when difficulties arise. While the head of the extended family is supposed to concern himself with disputes involving its members, the minor patrilineages, and in certain cases the major patrilineage, are always to be looked to for support and advice. Senior members of a minor patrilineage may help provide for an orphan under the care of a lineage member, and they are supposed to aid their members financially if the extended family cannot do so.

The farmland of a minor patrilineage—and most minor lineages do not control much farmland—is a product of its permanent division by the major lineage. There are numerous reasons why the major lineage may so act. In some cases the founder shared the land among his sons and it fell, through descent, to the minor lineages. Occasionally there has been ill feeling among the minor lineages, and this is a technique for cutting down potential disputes among them. For example, there was a notorious thief in one major patrilineage, and the descent group divided its land holdings among its minor lines to prevent him from passing away its land—all he could pledge was that of his own minor lineage. In other cases persons say that it is simply a more convenient way of handling the actual division of the land for farming. The Afikpo do have a penchant for dealing in very small pieces of land. It is rare for a minor lineage to acquire land on its own, or to have land while its related minor lineages do not.

The farmland is controlled by the elders of the minor lineage, who divide it, or have the younger men of the descent group do so for them. The minor lineages of a major patrilineage may arrange to have their land cleared at the same time, since their land sections are usually next to one another. Consultation with a diviner and the subsequent sacrifices are usually under the control of the major patrilineage, which performs these ceremonies once for all patrilineal lands rather than each group doing its own. Outside of the saving in expenses, this indicates that the major lineage still retains a general interest in the land, and will defend it against acquisition by outsiders, and arrange for its return to the original owners if it is held in pledge and they wish it back. Controls over groves, if minor lineages possess them, which is not common, are similar to those of a major lineage.

New houses in the compound are constructed for a person by young age sets in the major lineage under the watchful eye of the *uke ekpe* grade and the major lineage elders; the latter perform a sacrifice at the site to bless the new structure. Any male member, or any independent woman [17] associated with a minor patrilineage may erect a house on unused compound land.[18] Once built, the house and the land on which it stands become the property of the minor patrilineage. If a man's dwelling is vacated, other members of this lineage have first call on it, priority going to a close male agnatic relative of the last holder, normally the eldest son or next younger brother.[19] If repairs are needed, the house is rebuilt for a member of the minor patrilineage. Houses can be used by members of other minor lineages in the compound with the permission of the owner or, in the event of his death, of close patrikinsmen. Usually no fee is paid and no special ritual obligations are undertaken, but such a tenant may be removed if a member of the minor lineage, particularly a close patrilineal relative of a deceased or absent owner, wants the house for himself or for a wife. Widows are rarely thus moved, however. Wives have no control over houses, being placed in them by their husbands. A man who fails to find a house for a wife and has her live with him, with his mother, with another of his wives, or with

[17] That is, a woman who is divorced, separated from her husband, or widowed, and lives alone in her compound of birth, or perhaps in the case of a widow in the compound of her husband.

[18] Wives do not usually arrange for the construction of their houses; their husbands do this. A close patrilineal relative of a deceased man will arrange for the widow's house, if she remains in the compound and should need one. Independent women who have returned to the compound of their birth are often assisted by a brother.

[19] A younger brother will frequently have a house of his own already so that the eldest son of the former owner will usually take over or designate another patrilineal relative to do so.

a female relative, is likely to be considered "lazy" and to be publicly ridiculed in song by the young men of the compound during house-building season. If a compound has a number of such "lazy" men, its major lineage elders have the right to order each one to see that a house is erected for each wife by a certain time under threat of fine, though no such ruling was known to be given during the course of the research.

Houses are continually occupied by members of the same sex. Those for males have in many cases been occupied by priests; for a woman to live in them might anger the spirits of the shrines concerned. This is particularly true of houses in older sections of the compound. Disputes over occupancy or control of houses are rare, perhaps because the communal aspect of house-building inhibits strong feelings about ownership. If a minor lineage is dying out its houses can be taken over by other minor lineages in the compound or left to decay. There is virtually no friction in the compound over the control and transfer of houses.

Each compound has a number of structures, called *ulote*, where boys who no longer live with their mothers play and sleep (see "The Domestic Groupings" in chap. v). These houses, ultimately under the control of a minor patrilineage, are usually looked after by a male patrilineal relative of the former owner or builder, frequently an eldest son, who lives near by. While unmarried boys of his extended family and minor lineage use them, they are also open to other compound boys. The man in charge has the right to turn the *ulote* over to an adult to use, but he is not likely to, since it is convenient to have the boys run errands and convey messages. Some *ulote* are not under the special care of any persons, having been long abandoned as private homes.

In the past ten years, the Afikpo have been building dwelling places and small shops outside the compound in increasing numbers, along roads and near the markets (S. and P. Ottenberg, 1962). These houses, of mud or cement blocks with galvanized iron or aluminum roofs, are not usually constructed by the communal labor of the major patrilineage but by the owner, often with hired contractors and carpenters. Such houses are considered to be individual property, not under patrilineal control. A few homes of this kind are also being built in the compounds, but this is not usually preferred, as space there is limited. Customary rules of inheritance for these new dwellings are still being established, but they seem to pass from father to eldest son. Nevertheless, a great deal of traditional house-building in the compound is still carried out.

Several shrines are associated with minor patrilineages, though they are rarely used by the lineage as a whole, being rather for individual members. In some cases the ancestral shrine of the major patrilineage is divided into sections by minor patrilineages, though the minor patrilineage rarely performs rituals to its section as a group. The fertility shrine for women, *Nsi omɔmɔ*, is sometimes controlled by a minor rather than a major patrilineage. However, the minor patrilineage lacks a major shrine in contrast to the situation in the major patrilineage.

In general, then, the minor patrilineage is not a highly distinctive or visible descent grouping. It is more a convenient way of reckoning lines of descent within the major patrilineage, without giving these lines a highly organized structure or many specialized functions.

FISSION, ACCRETION, AND EXTINCTION

The most typical situation at Afikpo is one in which a major patrilineage and its minor segments occupy a single compound. But there are other conditions which indicate that the processes of growth and decay are at work.

Several instances occur in the village-group where an agnatic grouping resides in a separate compound beside a larger patrilineal grouping to which it is related, the two groups carrying out some activities jointly and others separately. This is one stage in the process of major patrilineage fission.

In two cases where detailed information was gathered, involving a minor lineage in a small compound next to its parent major patrilineage, there was some disagreement leading to the separation. However, the presence of available land near the original compound, and probably other factors, restrained the fissioning group from moving further away.

In both instances each descent group has its separate ancestral shrine, compound gate with its protective shrine, *ɛgbo,* and shrine to the ground, *ale,* and neither may build on the other's houseland. They join to uphold the laws of adultery and remarriage exogamy. When a newly married woman is "bound" to her husband's ancestral shrine this is extended to include persons associated with the other ancestral shrine. The two descent groups, in both cases, join together in other activities, including title-taking, and accept the action of the combined elders and of a unified young men's grade as the fundamental authority.

There are also cases where major patrilineages, once agnatically related, and living side by side in neighboring compounds, are almost totally separated. They do not join together except in matters in which they would unite in any case as segments of a village or a ward. This final stage normally occurs when the group which has broken away becomes large enough to have its own title groups and a separate system of internal authority. But even here the separation is not always final. The rule of remarriage exogamy may still apply ("We are too close to marry each other's wives"), and the two descent groups may still share farmland or groves. This type of arrangement seems relatively permanent.

In cases of a more distant physical separation, whether within the same village or not, the two major patrilineages do not share common authority or title societies. They have rapidly reached a state of distinctiveness, again except for the rule of remarriage exogamy, and sometimes of common control of farmland or groves. But the group remaining behind may in anger force those who have left off the land; the latter lose interest in it, having acquired resources in their new settlement area. But rules of remarriage exogamy often apply for many generations. In all these cases of fission the genealogical tie between the two groups is known, though members of one rarely are familiar with the specific details of the other's descent line.

Thus, whether the separated major patrilineages live side by side, further apart in the village, or in separate villages, there is sometimes a continuing link between them. They form a type of agnatic structure beyond the major patrilineage which we will call *linked major patrilineages.* In terms of everyday activities, these linked lineages have little to do with each other, and are relatively unimportant in the total perspective of patrilineal organization. If one group is involved in a dispute its related descent group may come to its aid if asked, regardless of where the two groups are located, and the ties between linked groups form an irregular network among persons in different residential areas in Afikpo. Probably as many as one-fifth of the Afikpo patrilineages show linkage of this kind, while others simply know that they were once related but have no ties at all. On the whole, however, the links are more historical than functional.

Reasons for the separation of patrilineal groupings are difficult to explore as the Afikpo do not like to discuss them in detail—it is not something to be proud of—and stories as to the causes of fission are often vague. Frequently they involve a dispute between brothers over failure of one to interact in a customary manner toward the other, or over jealousy concerning their relative status and authority. It is generally the younger brother who leaves. Separation does not seem associated with any specific size of the major patrilineage, though it sometimes is connected with a shortage of living space in the immediate area of the lineage. It occurs in patrilineal groupings of various populations, and a maximum size beyond which fission must occur is difficult to postulate. This seems reasonable, since productive farmlands are not usually held to any great extent by these groupings. Yet difficulties apparently arise as the lineages of a village increase in size and readily available farmland runs short in the area. Persons may then think of resettling where land is more freely at hand. This is not usually a result of the growth of a single major patrilineage, however, but of a number of them in the same settlement.

Fission often begins with one man and his family, or with two or more brothers and their domestic kin. After successful resettlement, other members of the minor patrilineage or of the agnatic line within it that is most directly involved may also move. If matters go well, the remaining members of the lineage or line may in time join up. Whether the separation involves settlement nearby or at a distance, with another lineage or not, seems to depend on (1) the availability of nearby households to start a separate compound, (2) the degree of hostility leading to separation, and (3) external lures to settlement at a distance, such as available virgin land, matrilateral or matrilineal ties in other areas, strong friendships with members of other patrilineages, or the reputation of other lineages for being wealthy and influential.

Patrilineal fission rarely seems to cut across minor patrilineages of a major lineage, but rather to involve only members of a minor segment. Sometimes there is consultation with a diviner before movement. He determines whether separation is propitious, and assists in establishing the necessary shrines in the new compound. If there is illness or other trouble after resettlement a diviner may recommend return to the original group, and this may be done. The pattern of movement or expansion of patrilineages in Afikpo apparently takes no single geographical direction. Movement, in the past, was common. It was expected, and is to some extent related to the high esteem placed on achievement. While lineages usually made every effort to retain members or to effect their return and to hold strangers who had joined them, it was understood that defections would occur, and that lineage members would leave to form their own residential groups and develop their own identities. It should be emphasized, however, that some resettlements were due more to the lure of better economic opportunities than a result of frictions in the home descent group.

Turning now to accretion, we have indicated how persons from within and without Afikpo are readily absorbed or involved, to varying degrees, in patrilineal groupings other than their own. This probably forms the bulk of the cases of accretion, particularly of individuals and families. In addition, there is the instance of one compound in which adoption commenced with the founding generation of the descent group. Here a compound was formed by a man known as the founder and his good friend, forming the two minor lineage lines in the major patrilineage. The members of both lineages use the same ancestral shrine, which incorporates the pots of the dead of both groups, and they share as one major lineage in other properties and activities. It is a pseudo-male sibling tie, developed, it is said, because of the close friendship of the two men. While such a case is exceptional it illustrates the degree to which adoption can go. In another case, that of Ameta village, five separate agnatic lines—small in size and originating in another village—form one loosely organized compound for many activities. This is clearly a necessity as each lineage is quite small. Such a compound is unusual in Afikpo.

Accretion may result when members of a lineage leave because of a dispute or other friction but do not start their own lineage. Or it is a result of the decline in size of an agnatic group. Which lineage is joined depends on such factors as matrilateral and matrilineal links, friendship ties, and the wealth and influence of the lineage which may be joined.

Evidence gathered during a survey of the patrilineal groupings at Afikpo indicates that in addition to the approximately 195 compounds there exist at least seventeen identifiable extinct ones. These lineages have in most cases disappeared through the death of the members, or this plus their movement to other patrilineages. The process is still occurring; a number of small major lineages are now disappearing. Extinction is usually an accelerating process; once a lineage declines in size, or fails to grow over a period of time, its members tend to leave and join one or more other lineages. The Afikpo say that they do not like to live in small compounds. Lack of growth is usually associated with supernatural disapproval or hostility, a matter confirmed by a diviner, who states that the ground of the compound has been "spoiled," that the lineage ancestors are annoyed; relief may only be achieved by amalgamation into a more prosperous group.

Sometimes full extinction is avoided, at least for a time, by joining with a larger lineage neighbor in certain activities which the smaller group has difficulty in carrying out alone, or by two or three small neighboring major lineages joining together for certain purposes. This usually involves a common system of title societies for the unrelated lineages, a combined *ukɛ ɛkpɛ* grade, and a common communal system of labor and house-building. In some cases cooperating lineages, although originally unrelated, eventually merge.

Two cases were noted—there are probably more—where the amalgamation of a small lineage into a larger one appears indefinitely arrested. In both instances, one group holds a special shrine which it does not share with the other, and this prevents full union. This possessive feeling over special shrines is strong at Afikpo. In one case, the Afikpo Rain Controller's small but separate patrilineage abandoned its own compound sometime in the past and joined a larger major patrilineage for protection, since the Rain Controller had had trouble with the Afikpo over the quality of his work. This special lineage retains its ancestral and rainmaking shrines in what is now a bush area, but its members join the compound of adoption in title activities, in matters of general authority and social control, in elders' and young men's grade activities, and in common rituals.

In the other case, members of a dying major patrilineage are gradually moving into a nearby compound in the same village. This compound is composed of a major patrilineage, with three minor segments. It possesses a blacksmith shrine (its males formerly practiced this art) which is still used for general protection, and which it does not share with the newcomers. Each major patrilineage has its own ancestral shrine in the compound, that of the original descent group being the meeting place of the elders of both groups for matters of common interest. The two lineages share a common entrance and protective shrine, *ɛgbo*, the ground shrine, *ɔma ɛzi*, and other shrines. Adultery and remarriage exogamy rules hold for all compound members. Activities of the elders, the young men's grade, and of title groupings involve both groups, and both share farmland belonging to the original major lineage in the compound, the right to its use being extended to the new compound members. This movement into the compound has been facilitated since some of the blacksmith lineage members are moving out to form a new compound in a village in nearby Edda Village-Group, leaving room for persons to move in.

Those who have moved into the blacksmith's compound still share adultery and remarriage exogamy rules with their agnatic relatives who remain behind. The latter still maintain an ancestral shrine in the original compound, and are pushing off the patrilineal land those who moved away, feeling that those who have deserted the lineage and formed another ancestral shrine should not share in the patrilineal land.

Though some lineages and compounds are clearly dying out, there seems to be no more founding of new ones today in Afikpo. The most recently created separate patrilineages in new compounds were formed about thirty to forty years ago. Some Afikpo have, however, moved to form lineages in nearby Ɔkpoma Village, in Edda Village-Group. There is little new farmland available, and the sense of going out to create a new community, even to start a new village, is thus lost or is now directed to trade and other Western economic pursuits, as well as to educational goals, as avenues for advancement. The prestige associated with developing one's own settlement is still found in the quasi-historical accounts of the founding of patrilineages and villages, but it does not excite persons today to go and do likewise. As a result of the extinction of some lineages without the founding of others, as well as the general increase in population, major patrilineages and their compound areas are growing in size. This is partially offset by the absence of many persons, particularly young males, for work or other reasons. Further, as we have seen, educated and wealthy Afikpo living at home tend to dwell in modern-style houses outside their compound, and not to take part in some lineage activities. There is no immediate likelihood of the breakdown of the patrilineal groups, and many Afikpo recognize them as large and significant organizations, but their future, particularly since they do not control much farmland or other property which would tend to hold their members together, will probably be one of gradual dissolution into a complex of semi-urban organizations. This pattern is already developing in the areas nearest the Government Station and the main Afikpo market (S. and P. Ottenberg, 1962; Livingston Booth, 1955; S. Ottenberg, 1956).

RESIDENCE AND PATRILINEALITY

The discussion of fission and accretion suggests that some closing remarks concerning residence are necessary. Among those elements very closely identified with patrilineal groupings are certain shrines including the ancestral shrine and its basic rituals; special shrines not common to all agnatic groupings in Afikpo; the support of patrilineal relatives in the *rites de passage* and other ceremonials of its members; and the controls over wives and children of lineage members. The control of farmlands and groves and the ownership of homes are strongly patrilineal, as is the identity of the major patrilineage with the ground upon which it stands.

But there are also aspects of patrilineal existence that though fundamentally unilineal in nature are readily extended to other persons residing in the compound on any regular basis, regardless of their patrilineal affiliations. These include adultery laws and remarriage regulations, the usufruct of farmland and groves, and availability of shrines and charms, such as the protective charm *ɛgbo*, and the fertility shrine *Nsi omɔmɔ*, to the service of all living in the dwelling area. Although these and other sacred objects are controlled by major patrilineage elders, they are open to all living in the compound, while the ancestral shrine is somewhat more restricted.

Another set of categories of patrilineal affairs seems to be, while still basically agnatic, even more heavily residential in appearance. Included here are the age grade organization and its activities, the elders of the compound as a judicial and legislative body, the title societies, and the informal organization of married women. We have seen how small major patrilineages may join neighboring unrelated lineages in some or all of these, rather than attempting to handle them separately. Most elements in the third category, unlike those in the first and second, require some population base in order to function properly, thus the presence of nonagnates may be crucial.

In an analysis based on the first period of field research, it was argued that two separate organizations really existed, one patrilineal, the major patrilineage, and one residential, the compound (S. Ottenberg, 1957, chaps. iii–vii). Ancestral shrines and rites; control of farmland, groves, and houses; and certain ceremonial activities were seen as fundamentally patrilineal, but many of the other elements listed above were basically of another form of grouping, the compound as a residential unit. The argument was that since in most instances there was but a single major patrilineage in a single compound, these two aspects of organization were normally fused. Their distinctiveness only appeared in a few cases, where two separate major lineages lived in one compound, or one major lineage in two contiguous compounds.

Something may still be said for this point of view, but since restudy indicates that in over 95 per cent of the cases a single major patrilineage is associated with a single compound, the aspects discussed above are basically unilineal in character, the concern of the lineage and its elders. The "exceptions" are lineages in fission or accretion, or in some other special relationship. This view has been confirmed on the second field trip by a closer examination of the Afikpo's attitudes toward the lineage and the compound. They conceive the patrilineage as primary, its physical setting as important but of a secondary nature.

The patrilineages, unlike the matrilineal groupings, nevertheless have significant tendencies toward the development of a residential organization. This is reinforced since the fundamental form of organization of authority in the compound is largely duplicated in the wards, villages, and village-group, where unrelated patrilineal groupings join in common identity. The projection of the village age set and grade organization—fundamentally a residential, not a descent structure—into the major patrilineage organization as a basis of its authority system also indicates the significance of the residential aspects of major patrilineage organization.

We conclude that the role of the major patrilineage in the compound is a dominating one. It forms the basic locality group to which nonmembers attach themselves, and it cooperates with other patrilineal lineages in common activities on the basis either of contiguity of residence or agnatic ties. But there is an underlying aspect of the organization of the lineage in terms of locality that is extremely important in the administration of its affairs.[20]

[20] See Ardener (1954) for comments on locality in a patrilineal Igbo group. The problem of the relative importance of residence and kinship is by no means settled. See Kroeber (1938); Lowie (1927); Fortes (1953:36).

III. THE MATRILINEAL GROUPINGS

WHILE many Afikpo recognize the importance of patrilineality, they commonly hold that matrilineal ties are primary.
Precisely what this means varies from person to person, but
emphasis is usually placed on the fact that most productive
property is matrilineally controlled and inherited and that this is
more basic than the residential aspects of life and the ancestral
beliefs of patrilineal ties. There is a traditional tale which states
the feelings of Afikpo concerning the relative strength of matrilineal and patrilineal ties. It has many variants, but all possess a
common theme: descent was at one time patrilineal and property
passed from a man to his sons. One man killed another and was
expected to give up one of his sons to be killed by the dead man's
relatives. He asked each of his wives in turn to give up a son, but
they all refused, and the sons hid themselves. His sister then
offered her son. From that day the Afikpo decided that property
should pass in a matrilineal way.

Regardless of the accuracy of the tale, its emphasis on the close
tie of a man with his sister and her children and on the matrilineal aspect of property accurately expresses the weight given by
the Afikpo to descent through the female line. The term for any

matrilineal relative, regardless of the nature of the relationship, is *ikwu*. In other Igbo areas it may mean any relative on the mother's side, or have other meanings (Henderson, 1967: 39–40), but in Afikpo and the neighboring Igbo village-groups it is used specifically for matrilineal descent. Thus an Afikpo refers to his matrilineal relative as *ikwum* (my matrilineal relative), or *ikwu Nnɛ* (matrilineal relative-mother), to his father's matrilineal relative as *ikwu Nna* (matrilineal relative-father), and so on.

THE MATRILINEAL CLAN

The two basic forms of matrilineal groups in Afikpo are the large-scale clan and the small lineages which are its segments. The clan [1] is a named, nontotemic, corporate descent group, nonresidential in character and exogamic in marriage. Its members do not form a compound or other residential unit. They are widely dispersed throughout the village-group, and the persons dwelling in any compound belong to a wide range of clans, though, as we have seen, usually to a single major patrilineage. Because of the widespread location of their members in the village-group, as well as other field work difficulties, it was impossible to obtain a complete listing of all the clans, but there are about thirty-five and possibly one or two more. It also proved impractical to take a total census of any single clan, but on the basis of membership lists of young men's clan improvement associations and other evidence, they vary in size from several hundred to over two thousand members, with the average size being close to a thousand persons.

The clans, with one exception (see "The Slave Matriclan," in this chapter), are unranked. While some persons consider that their clan is the oldest, largest, or wealthiest in Afikpo, there is little agreement on these beliefs. Unlike the major patrilineages and the villages a real sense of historical priority is lacking in the clans. They also exhibit a high degree of autonomy from one another.

[1] When the term clan is used in this book it will always refer to the matrilineal clan. There is no patrilineal clan in Afikpo.

Each clan has a name prefixed by *ibε* (side or part), such as *ibε aja isu*. The remainder of the term may be the name of the clan founder, of a prominent member, or in some cases a name whose meaning has been forgotten. There is no other symbol of clanship, such as scarification patterns or dress. Clans claim descent from a female founder, but there is relatively little interest in the founder, and no ancestor cult. The clan as a whole has no genealogy. While genealogies of its numerous small unranked segments exist, none of them seem able to trace specific genealogical lines to the founder though all claim matrilineal descent from her. Consistent with this, specific tales describing the founding of a clan are rare, in contrast to the case of patrilineal descent, and most clans have only a vague story of origin. Sometimes this is the same tale as the one explaining matrilineal descent in general, to which is added, "this is how our clan was founded." The vagueness of the origin tales and genealogies is in keeping with the clans' less significant governmental role in the total structure of Afikpo than that of patrilineages, and probably their greater antiquity. Their members do not have to justify a political presence through history or legend.

Not only are clan persons widely dispersed throughout Afikpo, but a clan controls land and other property in many parts of the village-group, though most clans concentrate members and property in one or more areas, that is, a group of neighboring villages. The members frequently are acquainted from having taken part in common clan activities, and they greet one another using the clan name even though they may not know their specific relationship.

A rule of clan exogamy is strictly enforced in Afikpo; it is said that a marriage between two members of a clan would anger the spirit of the clan shrine. The offenders would have to make sacrifices to appease it, and the marriage would be dissolved. However, no such case was recorded, and neither the clan elders nor the families of the persons involved would permit such a marriage. Sexual relations between members of a clan are also forbidden, and each offender offers sacrifices at the clan shrine, with the aid of its priest. Until this is done the miscreants cannot take part in matrilineal activities.

Once born into an Afikpo clan, a person does not change his membership, unlike the case of the patrilineages. The four neighboring Igbo village-groups of Unwana, Edda, Amaseri, and Okpoha have independent but, as a rule, like-named clans, and a person from one of these areas who settles in Afikpo takes part in the activities of his like group without adoption. He may retain ties with his home matrilineal groupings if he desires, or may become affiliated with a matrilineage in Afikpo which has members where he lives, mainly to gain access to land rights.

Adoption in Afikpo is accomplished by symbolically kissing or touching the breast of a woman who then becomes the person's mother. It is done only for a person from outside of these five village-groups. The adopted individual has equal rights in the clan and matrilineage of the mother, though he would probably never be chosen clan priest or head of the matrilineage. There are even records of adoption in the past of *ohu* slaves into their master's clan. Matrilineal groupings characteristically have not been as free to incorporate persons, nor to develop as many types of close associations with outsiders, as have the patrilineal groupings. This is undoubtedly due to the lack of a residential organization, and also because, as the major property-holding groups in Afikpo, they are not anxious to open their farmlands to the direct use and possible control of strangers.

CLAN LEADERSHIP

Control of clan affairs, as in the case of the major patrilineage, is in the hands of its elders and the priest of its major shrine. The central meeting place of a clan is the compound of its priest, who is guardian of its shrine, *Nja*, located in his compound. This consists of a small hut containing rocks and pots. *Nja* is also the term for the spirit associated with the shrine, which is vague in form and not ancestral in nature. Most clan shrines are found in the more centrally located villages in Afikpo. The shrine is moved to a new priest's village and compound when he is selected. The central location is probably a function of convenience rather than an indication that the central villages are necessarily the oldest in the village-group. Here the elders and shrine priest meet at irregular intervals, as the need arises.

The shrine is the central symbol of the matrilineal clan. Its control rests with the priest and the clan elders. The latter are those clan males who have reached the degree of seniority so that they belong to age groupings which have been organized on a village-group basis; that is, they are roughly over fifty-five years of age, the same as elders of the major patrilineages and the villages. Some of those who live in villages more distant from the shrine and some who simply are not very interested in guiding the clan's affairs do not take an active part among the elders. There is thus a core of perhaps ten to twenty elders who, with the priest, dominate clan leadership.

Lineages in the clan are not represented in this elders' group by specific individuals. If a lineage contains no elders, no member will attend the leaders' meetings unless a matter especially concerning that lineage is being discussed. If a single lineage contains several elders, all may attend the leaders' activities, though the most senior may have more influence. The primary qualities of leadership in this elders' group are similar to those already discussed for the major patrilineages: interest, and the ability to speak well and to cite precedents (see "The Lineage Elders," in chap. ii). Since lineages within the clan are unranked by historical priority, genealogical fiction, or any other device, it is not surprising that formal ranking among the clan leaders is also absent. The secondary qualities associated with patrilineal leadership are also important in the matriclan, except that the titles which bring prestige and leadership are those taken on the broad base of the village-group or its subgroups rather than in the compound. Further, whether a man's father was a leader or not is of less importance than in the patrilineal setting. It is also not of much assistance to a man if a mother's brother was a prominent leader: it does not improve his leadership position. There seems to be little rivalry within the matriclan over its control, but the same cannot be said of leadership in the matrilineages.

The priest stands out among the leaders by virtue of his special status and ritual activities, but he does not rule the elders. Rather, they make decisions cooperatively, the latter assisting the priest in the performance of the important clan rituals. Together they determine policy and action in clan affairs. Like the patrilineal ancestral priest, the clan priest is generally a quiet, unaggressive elder who "stays close to home" so that he may be present to give sacrifices. He does not have any special privileges with regard to clan land or other properties, but there are certain taboos and other restrictions that he must be careful to follow. As the clan ritual leader, the intermediary between the shrine spirit and clan members, he may refuse to offer sacrifices with an individual who he thinks is violating certain restrictions imposed on the annual feasting day of the clan,[2] to skeptics who he thinks do not believe in the power of the shrine spirit, or to anyone he feels is harming the clan.[3]

Most clans also possess a charm, *ɛkikɛ* (tie), about a foot and a half long and six inches thick, and made of wrapped twigs, medicines, charms, and other materials, which is controlled by the priest and usually found in his home or in the shrine hut.[4] It protects the priest and the clan members from harm, particularly from the divisive or disruptive effects of fighting and killing involving a clansman. The priest sacrifices at it for the whole clan on the annual meeting day and again before the planting season. Individuals do not carry out sacrifices here as they do at *Nja* except when a clansman kills or harms someone. The charm is an

[2] The most important restriction is that no one should touch any coco yams or the coco yam plant on that day.

[3] This includes those trying to turn matrilineal land over to other social groups, and those who side against the clan in disputes even though they belong to it. These actions are said to anger the shrine spirit and to cause illness, and possibly death, to its priest.

[4] This type of charm is also owned by individuals, patrilineal groupings, and residential organizations. The protective charm, *ɛgbo*, which guards the gate of every Afikpo compound, belongs to this class of religious objects (S. Ottenberg, 1968b).

adjunct to the clan shrine; it acts as a protection against evil while *Nja* functions more to promote positive action.

In contrast to the major patrilineage, the matriclan has few other shrines or charms, and only one priest. There are shrines on matrilineal land, particularly to the Aro oracle *Ibini ɔkpabe*, and a few individual shrines such as *adudɔ*, which are controlled by women and pass matrilineally from mother to daughter (see "Other Lineage Activities" in chap. iii). Unlike the patrilineal case there are very few matrilineal shrines which are concerned with Afikpo as a whole. Even one associated with a pond which is publicly fished seems connected with land or property. Generally, the uterine shrines concern their members (and their affines), not the public at large, and not matters associated with the *rites de passage* of individuals, in contrast to patrilineal and residential shrines.

A new *Nja* priest is selected only when the existing one dies. The clan elders then choose a diviner, who provides the name of the new ritual leader. The diviner can be anyone that the elders desire to hire, and often is not a clan member. Sometimes the famous Aro Chuku oracle, *Ibini ɔkpabe*, is consulted to confirm the choice, to indicate what rituals should be performed by the new priest and the leaders to insure his welfare, and the successful moving of the shrine to the new priest's compound. Such a move is often necessary since the new priest is frequently from a different major patrilineage and village than his predecessor. The new priest is almost invariably one of the leaders among the elders or occasionally a slightly younger man who interests himself in clan affairs. The role of the elders in selection is similar to their role in the choice of the patrilineal ancestral priest. The successor need not come from the same matrilineage as his predecessor, or from any specific descent line within the clan, an indication of the lack of lineage ranking within this group. During the period between the death of a priest and the selection of his successor, the shrine is usually cared for by a son of the deceased, though he is not himself a clan member; thus there is no problem in maintaining ritual continuity.

Although younger persons occasionally join the elders and priest in their discussions, they take a less active part in clan affairs than do young and middle-aged men in the major patrilineages. This is partly because the clans are generally larger and there are more elders to take the initiative. Also, while patrilineal groupings often carry out communal tasks which require young men as leaders as well as workers, the clan rarely undertakes such projects.

Until the early 1950's, young men had no grouping which brought them together on a clan basis for any common activity. At that time men started organizing clan improvement associations modeled after existing village unions (S. Ottenberg, 1955b; 1968a), and after similar ones which were developing in many Afikpo patrilineages; virtually all the clans today have these associations. The motive for their creation varied, but it was partly to develop a basis for securing loans—a major function of these unions—and, particularly on the part of some educated and acculturated Afikpo, to try to take from the clan elders some of the control of clan affairs. Behind this reason has been a growing feeling among some young Afikpo that the elders are wasting clan funds on too many rituals, too many trips to Aro Chuku to consult the oracle, and on foolish gifts in land litigation cases. However, once these meetings became well organized they served primarily as a basis for loans and conviviality; they have had little effect on the actions of the clan elders.

Most unions share a common pattern. They are called "Family," thus *Ibɛ ɔkwu Family*, and meet once a month at a regular and central meeting place. They exclude clan elders from membership, except sometimes one well-liked man who acts as advisor or guide. His presence reduces suspicion on the part of the elders as to what occurs at the meetings, and he serves as a channel of communication with them. The union generally has a secretary, who is either a member or the son of a member, who keeps record of the monthly dues, which form the basis of the loans. The elders have no control over these funds, generally a working capital of several hundred pounds. A union usually has a membership list of several hundred, the majority of the clan males who are not elders, but the active members, those who live at home and in the more central villages, comprise roughly between 10 and 20 per cent of the total clan membership. Members are bound by rules to help each other in times of trouble or in court cases.

These meetings provide the younger clan males with an earlier opportunity to join together and to become familiar with one another than in former times. They strengthen the clan concept, and present an as-yet-undeveloped opportunity to challenge the traditional leadership in the descent group.

INTERNAL CLAN ACTIVITIES

For the elders the most important clan rituals center around its shrine. Though a member can offer sacrifice at it with the assistance of the priest at any time during the year, there is an annual day on which the clan members meet there, during the New Yam Festival, two days after the first of the new yam crop is eaten (late August or early September). The elders feast on the sacrificial foods brought to the shrine by individual members, and the older clan women feast separately. Young male and female members come and greet the clan elders, but they do not usually take part in the feasting or in the discussions of clan affairs which the elders carry on.

Individual sacrifices are offered at this gathering with the priest's aid, by persons of any age and either sex who have poor crops, have failed to produce children, are ill, or have other troubles. Whether individuals perform sacrifices at the shrine or not on this day, they lick chalk which has touched the shrine to insure their health and welfare. The priest also performs a sacrifice for the welfare of the whole clan.

This gathering affords clan members an opportunity to renew old ties and meet younger members coming to the shrine for the first time, and it helps give a sense of social solidarity to this geographically dispersed group. On this day a man usually also visits his father's clan shrine, those of his wives, and, more rarely, that of the clan of an intended wife. A woman, in addition to visiting her own shrine and perhaps offering sacrifices at it, visits her husband's or future husband's shrine, and sometimes that of her husband's father. While persons normally perform sacrifices only at their own shrines, the visits to others are for greeting relatives and to show an interest in them and in their clans. It is particularly important for a man to do this. He receives land and various kinds of aid from both his father's and his wives' matrilineal relatives, and he should show them this courtesy.

No division of the feasting groups according to lineages within the clan occurs at this gathering, the idea of clan solidarity being strongly maintained. The elders discuss the welfare of the clan: whether it is growing, whether its members have produced good crops during the year, whether there is any serious dispute involving it. They may arrange to try a dispute with another grouping, to consult a diviner over some problem, to visit the Aro Chuku oracle for advice, or some member may announce that he is planning a ceremony in which the clan members will want to take part. They may decide that assessments from all members must be made to pay the expenses of a visit to the Aro oracle, to consult a diviner, to perform a ritual, to help settle a disagreement, or to give a present to a clansman taking a title. This right of taxation on the part of the clan elders—and those who refuse to pay can be fined by them—is essential to the carrying out of clan activities, something of which the elders are certainly cognizant.

The productive property of the matriclan is extremely important, and the elders spend a considerable amount of time over it. The clan controls several kinds of property but its most important corporate interest is in farmland. About 85 per cent of the Afikpo farmland is matrilineally controlled. The clan land is found within the farmland areas of the various Afikpo villages, interspersed with that of other clans and with agnatically and residentially controlled land (see pp. 61–62). It is under the direct control of the individual matrilineages which comprise it, the clan functioning as general overseer. Clan leaders and priest perform rituals to insure its fertility; they are concerned with the pledging or redemption of portions of it. If there is a dispute among its lineage owners over the usufruct of a piece of land, these leaders will try to settle it if those directly concerned cannot. If there is a disagreement with another clan or a patrilineal group over land, the clan leaders will represent its members in the case. Under normal conditions, the lineages control the apportionment and use of their lands and the clan does not interfere.

A similar relationship of clan and lineage exists for matrilineally controlled groves, mainly palm and raffia, which are generally located in the areas about the Afikpo villages, and ponds and sections of streams.

The clan elders insure that the property of a deceased member is inherited according to custom, and they send representatives to see that this is done (see "Death and Inheritance" in chap. v; S. Ottenberg, 1965). The crux of the clan's interest here is the movable wealth of the deceased, especially coin or traditional forms of money and trade goods, which pass matrilineally and which, in the case of the death of a man, will be mainly shared by the clan elders. They often seem to be involved in litigation over the inheritance of these movable items. Other property of the deceased, such as farmland, stays under the control of the matrilineage which owns it.

In the case of a dispute involving matrilineage land, groves, water areas, or inheritance, the lineage head, if he cannot resolve the matter himself, meets with the clan leaders and priest at the latter's compound. If it is an internal dispute involving the members of a matrilineage or between two or more of them, the elders call for those concerned to meet with them. This same procedure is used if it is a question of improper behavior of one clan member toward another, for example, failure to support a close matrikinsman who is taking an important title, or failure of a man to greet his clan elders with wine and food after returning from abroad. As in the case of the patrilineages, the clan elders are reluctant to let internal matters be settled outside the clan if this can be avoided, and such cases rarely reach the village-group elders or the Native Authority Court. The authority of the leaders is taken as final, and whatever punishment—usually fines—accepted. There is not much other choice as failure to acquiesce means ostracism for an individual, loss of farmland and other rights, and no other clan in Afikpo will take him in. They will tell him to make his peace with his brothers.

If the case involves a lineage or a clan with another matrilineal group, or with patrilineal or residential groups, each side follows the usual procedure of asking selected Afikpo elders to try it (see pp. 214–15). Such disputes over land are especially common between harvest and planting season (from about October to February) when Afikpo begin to think of their rights to sections of land that they will farm the coming year. The clan elders spend much time in litigation during this period. These cases may involve swearing to an Afikpo shrine and consultation with the Aro Chuku oracle over the original ownership of the property, and the clan leaders can levy a head tax on all adult males of the clan to help pay the expenses involved. In addition, the clan priest may sacrifice at the clan shrine to ask for a successful settlement. If the case is won, the clan elders who played a prominent role in it often receive portions of the land to farm as a reward, even though they are not members of the matrilineage which controls it.

In pre-British times the clans were involved in murder cases, blood revenge being characteristic, and in cases of theft. These matters are no longer so directly their concern, and are more fittingly discussed in the chapter on the role of descent groups in the village and village-group (see "The Matrilineal Clans in the Village-Group" in chap. iv).

Women know little about clan affairs administration and are mainly concerned with the activities of their immediate matrilineal relatives. Nevertheless, the senior women who meet and feast together on the annual day at the shrine discuss the welfare of the clan women, how to increase their fertility, means of ending disputes among themselves, and the particular fortunes of individual members. As in the case of the men they gather to talk over clan affairs at other times of the year when necessary. It is common for the senior women to ask the male elders to consult a diviner as to why the clan is not producing enough children. This sometimes leads to a visit with the Aro oracle and to heavy expenses before the necessary rituals are completed. Both male and female members are very much concerned over the fertility of the clan; in some cases "anxious" would be the better word to describe their feelings.

During the mid-1950's women formed clan meetings similar to those of the young men. Unlike the latter, who excluded most senior men, the women included female elders. They were not greatly concerned with loans or social change, but rather with collecting money for consulting with diviners and for rituals to insure clan prosperity. Several years later the village-group age grades, despite the women's protests, banned these meetings on the grounds that they kept the women away from home until too late to cook for their husbands and to perform household duties. There was also suspicion that these meetings led to adulterous behavior. This is one of those very rare cases where the Afikpo elders took steps which interfered with the internal autonomy of clans.

THE SLAVE MATRICLAN

There is one matrilineal clan, the *ibɛ osim,* that differs from the others. Afikpo consider it an outcast or slave clan, to which belong a type of person known throughout Igbo country as *osu.*[5] It has some attributes of a low caste and some of a despised class. Some of the members of the *ibɛ osim* maintain that their ancestors were the original inhabitants of Afikpo, though this is disputed.[6] The

---

[5] See J. Harris (1942); Leith-Ross (1937); Meek (1937); Offonry (1951). In other areas of Igbo country *osu* trace descent patrilineally. *Osu* should not be confused with another type of slave, called *ohu.*

[6] As one nonslave put it, "Why should an *osu* own Afikpo?" i.e., why should a man of slave status claim that his relatives originally inhabited Afikpo? In Igbo country early settlement in an area is frequently one basis for a claim to political authority.

tale of this group's origin is as follows: One day the men of Afikpo were hunting and found a woman in the bush. They asked her who she was and where she came from, but she could not say. They decided to make her public property and took her to the Aro Chuku oracle, where a ceremony was performed to protect her in this way. Then they took her to all the important Afikpo shrines and performed rites so that the spirits would protect her and would harm any man attempting to own her privately. Then the men began to sleep with her, she bore children, and the clan developed.

The *osu* are exogamous, and live scattered about Afikpo, as do members of other clans, and have no distinguishing peculiarities of dress or costume. Their total number is said to be small but this was impossible to determine for reasons that will soon be clear. They were traditionally characterized by certain restrictions in social behavior. They could not control or own land, though individual members could farm. Males obtained land to use through a spouse belonging to another clan, through their father's matrilineage, through their own patrilineage and ward, and from friends. Women obtained plots from their nonslave husbands, or through other relatives outside of their clan. On the whole, members of this clan did not have as much farmland at their disposal as others did. They were also forbidden to play any leadership role in the patrilineages, villages, or village-group. Despite these factors some *osim* men have become wealthy. Some have taken the highest titles, the wealth being accumulated through trade within and outside of Afikpo, particularly in recent years.

The slave clan did not possess the usual clan shrine—this was forbidden by the Afikpo elders—but had its own, *ugwu eho*, the name of the bush in Amaizu village where it was located. The eldest clan female acted as its priest and lived in a special house in her own small compound in Amuro village, not too far from the shrine. This compound was considered to be a separate village which had its regular place in certain rotational feastings in Afikpo. The shrine was to insure not only the welfare of the clan members, as do the usual *Nja* shrines of other clans, but *osu* carried out rituals there for the benefit of Afikpo as a whole.

Numerous religious restrictions were placed on clan members. Women could not perform ceremonies at the patrilineal ancestral shrine, *Mma obu*. Neither men nor women could sacrifice at *Nsi omɔmɔ*, the compound fertility shrine, though they could take part in the festivals associated with it. However, some family and personal shrines, including *Njɔku*, the one for yams, and *Nkamalo*, an individual man's shrine for general welfare, were accessible to them, and they could consult diviners and perform burial and funeral rites.

Clan women, married or not, were sexually available to any man in the same manner as was the clan founder according to the traditional tale of origin. It was particularly common for young men to pursue them, and while these women might attempt to resist such advances, they had no legal recourse. Some became prostitutes, and they have the reputation of being the most beautiful and desirable of all Afikpo women.

No bride price was paid by a man who married a woman of this clan, and the presents that a man normally gave a girl while courting were omitted. He merely took her to his compound, and they were considered married, though she was still sexually available to others and might leave her husband for another, the marriage being considered a rather casual matter. The women were, and still are, forbidden to perform the ceremony to the patrilineal ancestral shrine which would bind them to follow its sexual rules.

Clan exogamy was enforced, and normal matrilineal descent rules existed, though the father of a slave woman's child did not have to acknowledge it as his own, nor did a man "married" to her if he did not wish to. Children of a slave mother and a free father were slaves and subject to the restrictions placed on all *osu*. Children of a free mother and a slave father were free, and no *osu* limitations were imposed upon them.

Among nonslaves it was considered a very poor match for a free person of either sex to "marry" an *osu*. Some Afikpo major patrilineages forbade this and did not allow *osu* to live in their residential area. Where not forbidden, it was strongly discouraged by invoking such social sanctions as ridicule.[7] The patrilineal elders sometimes offered to arrange a marriage with a freeborn woman instead.

The property of *osu* could no more be seized than that of freeborn persons, and *osu* males could join the village men's secret society. At a gathering of men where palm wine was served the eldest poured the last drop on the ground for the ancestors, but an *osu* could not do this. It would be performed instead by the eldest freeborn present. As one Afikpo said, "Could a slave say blessing for free men?"

Members of the slave clan were formerly subject to capture and sale by freeborn persons, especially by the *amadi* and Aro. No retribution was possible, though some escaped or fought free during the capture attempt. Slave-catching was particularly carried out with *osu* children and was a means of obtaining money to perform an important title or ceremony. Freeborn men could sell their children by a slave wife, one reason for marrying such a woman. Blood revenge was not allowed for the killing of a member of this clan.

While according to Nigerian law *osu* now exercise full equality with freeborn persons, and while their social position has improved, they are still in an inferior status. After the arrival of the British in 1902 the eldest woman of this clan on several occasions refused to act as clan priest and was dragged to its shrine by direction of the Afikpo elders, who insisted that the shrine be maintained. The members of the clan at times refused to lead her to the shrine because they desired to be freed of their lowly

[7] In addition to lowering the prestige of the major patrilineage in the eyes of others, if a slave woman married into a compound this might arouse sexual tensions there since she would not be bound by its sexual rules. In the case of a free woman marrying a slave man her patrilineage would put pressure on her not to do so. Although the man would have to pay bride price, since she would not be of slave origin, her agnatic kin would object as he would be viewed as beneath her in status. Her matrilineal relatives would object to the marriage.

position. By about 1940 British controls became so strong that attempts to maintain the shrine ceased, and it no longer exists. A few years ago this clan tried to establish its own *Nja* shrine, but the village where the attempt was made forbade its being placed there and the clan still lacks a shrine. Some *osu* feel that having their own shrine would be a major step toward equality with others.

Slave women are not as freely available sexually to freeborn men as formerly, since they can file a complaint in the Native Authority Court or with the police. There are now freeborn persons who think that the sexual pattern involved should be abolished and who come to the protection of *osu* in such cases. Nevertheless it is still common for freeborn males to attempt to make free with girls of this clan, and many patrilineages still forbid *osu* to live in or to marry into their compounds.

An important device of the *osu* in their attempts to improve their status is to claim that they are members of another clan, and not really *ibɛ osim* at all. There are two important groups of this kind, each with a distinctive clan name. In recent years disputes over their origin have arisen, particularly over the subject of bride wealth. Men with slave daughters are anxious to obtain the bride price for them, as for any other daughter. The technique of claiming membership in some supposed clan may eventually be successful, for the dispersion of clans makes it difficult to prove the identity and matrilineal associations of Afikpo persons. For example, a married woman, apparently an *osu,* claimed membership in another clan, and the husband paid bride price on her before his suspicions were aroused. The Afikpo elders who judged the case decided against the woman, not by proving her exact matrilineal ties, but on the fact that they had never heard of the clan she claimed. It is interesting to note that the Afikpo elders have much greater authority in matters involving the *ibɛ osim* clan than the other Afikpo clans, which they claim is proper under the mantle of maintaining native law and custom (see p. 171).

Other restrictions on the clan still apply, though *osu* are no longer sold into slavery. Some have prospered through the increased trading opportunities brought about by European culture contact, while still others would like to own land but cannot obtain it. Though *osu* men are among the wealthiest in Afikpo, they are afraid to participate in public affairs or its government. They know that others are aware of their status and may publicly question their right to do so. It is likely, however, that they will eventually exert greater authority because of their economic position.

THE MATRILINEAL LINEAGE

In contrast to the general supportive and protective role of the matrilineal clans, the matrilineages have much greater specific concern with personal uterine interrelationships, are most directly involved with property controls, and have a quite distinctive structure of authority. These differences are much greater, in many ways, than those between the major and minor patrilineal groupings.

The matrilineages are unnamed, corporate, uterine groupings which trace descent to a female ancestor roughly three to seven generations in depth. The number of living members varies from about ten to seventy persons. The senior matrilineage members are able to trace all descent ties within the group, but other matrilineage persons usually do not know the full genealogy. Fictitious genealogical relations are virtually absent from the genealogies, possibly because many matrilineages are shallow in generational depth, and because adoption into them is not very frequent, as we have seen.

There is usually a recognition by some senior matrilineage members of a distinct uterine kin tie with some other matrilineage or lineages of the clan, usually through sisters of the founder of their own group. There is little knowledge of the genealogy of such matrilineages, however, beyond the awareness that within the clan their members are more closely related than persons of other uterine lines in the clan. Such remotely linked uterine groups act independently within the larger descent group.

The husband of the matrilineage founder and his other wives are usually not remembered by the group's members, nor are children of male members in generations other than the previous and present ones always recalled. The amount of genealogical data on the matrilineages is sparse compared to that of patrilineal groupings. Persons know little of the genealogy of matrilineages other than their own, and clan elders are not always fully aware of the number of matrilineages in their clan. Some of the larger clans probably contain nearly one hundred of them, while the smaller ones have considerably fewer.

Matrilineages lack specific names to distinguish them from one another, and it is considered unwise publicly to make distinctions between them if it can be avoided. A strong sense of clan solidarity exists, and he who speaks publicly about his lineage or another in a distinguishing way is said to speak against the cohesiveness of the clan. One does not usually refer to a matrilineage by its founder's name, as in the case of patrilineal groupings. In discussing matrilineage land in public, it is referred to as clan land which a certain person founded, and a person greets a fellow member of his matrilineage by the clan name and not by reference to the matrilineage. These actions help to maintain unity among the clan segments in the face of geographical dispersal. Yet everyone recognizes that matrilineage distinctions do exist, and if they must be referred to in public an expression such as *ɔnu θzom* (entrance-road), "those of my way," can be used. The most common term for the matrilineage, however, is *ɔnum era* (my mouth-breast), those who feed at the same breast. Some persons use the term *ikwu era* (matrilineal-breast) though it does not seem to be as commonly heard. The matrilineages of a clan are completely unranked with reference to one another.

The members of a matrilineage do not live in a compact residential group, but are spread about in a number of villages, sometimes as many as ten, or as few as two or three; they are practically never found within a single settlement, although there may be a concentration of them in one village. Even those who live within one village often reside in different compounds and wards. Nor does the matrilineage have a shrine or meeting place in which to center its activities. It is rather in the personage of the matrilineage head, wherever he may live, that the focus is found. The membership of any Afikpo village will be found to contain persons from many matrilineages of different clans, and one clan may have representatives from as many as eight or ten of its matrilineages living within a single large village. Reference to a fairly typical matrilineage genealogy [8] in terms of the map of Afikpo shows this distribution in some detail (see Map 2).

In this genealogy the matrilineage is six generations in depth, having a total of forty-eight remembered persons. Of these, thirty-eight are living, fifteen males and twenty-three females. The core of the lineage is in the village of Mgbom, where fourteen live, seven male, seven female. In addition, ten (four male, six female) live in the three nearby Afikpo villages of Ugwuago, Amuro, and Amachara, where they form potential segments of the lineage. Considerable mobility outside of the village-group is evident from the fact that fourteen lineage members (four male, ten female) live away from it, in six widely separated areas, and seven of these over fifty miles from home. The marriages of persons of the older generations tend to be within the same village; for younger generations there are more frequent marriages of women into neighboring villages. This pattern, reflected in other genealogies and marriage data, mirrors the greater mobility within the village-group which came about during the colonial period, and it indicates that the matrilineage was probably more localized in earlier times than it is today.

This locality arrangement can be understood only in terms of

[8] See Chart 2. In this genealogy, and those in charts 3 and 4, only the marriages of female lineage members are shown. The name under the symbol of a person is his or her place of residence. This is not shown for a married woman, whose birthplace is that of her father and whose adult residence that of her husband, unless she is not living with her husband. If the place of residence is italicized this indicates that it is outside of Afikpo. In these genealogies there are many dead children and some deceased childless adults who are not listed, as Afikpo are extremely reluctant to admit that such individuals existed, and to provide specific information concerning them.

Chart II. The Matrilineage of Ibe (1960)

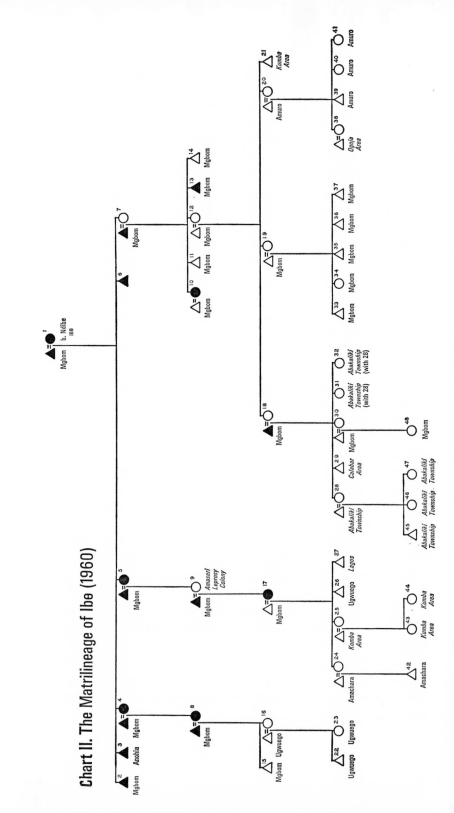

the Afikpo marriage patterns. An analysis of over two hundred marriages, culled from the author's and Phoebe Ottenberg's records, indicates that in somewhat less than half of the cases the women have married within the village in which they were born, though only a few within their compound of birth. To this extent marriages tend to localize matrilineage dispersal. In the majority of the nonvillage marriages, the women went to settlements within a radius of about five miles of their own. There are, however, a fair number of cases where marriage takes place to or from the more outlying villages. The reasons for the choice of marriage residence are complex and have been discussed elsewhere (P. Ottenberg, 1958); the fact is that there is no single dominating reason which determines this pattern. In some cases it results from an arrangement between friends who are fathers of the spouses, sometimes it is through contacts a woman has made by trade or through her matrilineal relations in another village. The fact that persons have a variety of sources of land means that a woman is not compelled to marry into a village in which land of her matrilineage is located. She can farm its land in nearby villages, and may make use of other land resources: those of her husband, those of agnatic half-siblings, or through other ties. We will show later she may, conversly, be deliberately married into a village where her matrilineage has land but where no lineage member exists at the time to use it, the land being in danger of falling into other hands. These and other factors lead to a condition in which matrilineage dispersal in the village-group is considered normal by the Afikpo (cf. R. Harris, 1926b: 95–98).

Authority over the matrilineage, its land and other properties, rests in its senior male member whether or not he is the closest in genealogical ties to the founding ancestor of the lineage. For example, a son of the third daughter of the founder will be the head if older than a son of the first daughter. The principle of seniority of age within a descent group as a basis of authority is similar to that within the matriclan and the patrilineages. It is, in fact, a characteristic feature of Afikpo leadership. The head may be young or middle-aged, unlike the clan leaders. While personality factors are important in his success, and he is expected to exhibit the general qualities of leadership which are vital in the clan and major patrilineages, personality has nothing to do with his choice as head. Leadership here, as in the case of the minor patrilineage, is essentially the right of a single person. He holds strong controls over most matrilineage land and his decisions as to its allocation are more or less final. He is an authoritarian figure, acting with little reliance on a council or group of advisors, having few checks on his authority. There is no matrilineage priest or other ritual specialist in his group, though he does rely on the advice of diviners, Aro agents, and clan elders to some extent. There is, however, sometimes a subhead for the matrilineage, the senior male member living in an area of Afikpo at some distance from the head. This subhead may have considerable autonomy and local control, and his presence is usually related to the process of segmentation within the lineage, as we shall see.

There may also be occasions when there are no adult males alive in a matrilineage. In this case the oldest female or a senior one may play the role of the head, and at least to some extent is in charge of matrilineage land and rituals. But she will be replaced by a male matrilineage member when he reaches maturity, even if he is younger than she.

PRODUCTIVE PROPERTY

It is the duty of the matrilineage head to maintain control over the lineage land, to see to the performance of the required general sacrifices to it, and he often does these himself. He allocates the land for use before farming. If some land is far away and he is not interested in it, he allows the senior male lineage member near the land, or the subhead, to allocate it, but this person is responsible to him. Females have virtually no authority or control over matrilineal lands, though, of course, it descends through them.

Most matrilineages hold land in a number of village areas, from two to as many as six or seven. The historical reasons for this complex system of tenure cannot be explained here though some comments on its dynamics may be made. Matrilineage members are not restricted to farming lineage land within their own village, and many farm in other village areas than their own. This is not difficult to do, as a fair number of the Afikpo villages are within a few miles of one another. Since the land that is farmed is mainly in the block sections of the village farmland (see pp. 61–62), different matrilineages develop different tenure patterns. A matrilineage may have land to farm in one village in certain years only, and in another village in different or overlapping years. There are cases where a matrilineage lacks farmland for a whole year, and its members must rely on their spouses, fathers, half-siblings, and other persons and groups for land. Individual sections of matrilineage land holdings are small. The Afikpo measure land in terms of heaps, and a man who has one hundred heaps to farm in one section is farming a good-sized portion of land. One heap can hold five to ten yams if it is large and as few as one to two yams if small in size.

Matrilineal land open to all lineage members[9] is allocated for farming on the same basis as patrilineal land, that is, in terms of lineage membership, seniority of age, and interest in farming. It is given mainly to men, though widowed, divorced, or separated women have a high claim to land of their matrilineage, and men share some of their portions with their spouses. Persons usually receive about the same portions each time it is divided, with changes to account for deaths, increasing age, and the presence of new members who farm. Sons of a lineage member receive shares when their father is alive and continue to use the land after his death, but they do not control its division and cannot pass it on to their sons.

Portions are given out only once for the two years that the land is to be farmed before it lies fallow again. Those who want land must notify the matrilineage head or other allocator that he appoints; the person dividing the land does not seek others to ask whether they wish to farm. Failure to ask for land indicates lack

[9] The control of more restricted forms of matrilineal land is discussed below in this section.

of interest, and this is true for close uterine relatives of the divider as well as for others. Land is not usually divided until after the bush is cleared, and those who want to farm it must aid in the clearing, have a friend or relative work for them, or pay another person to help clear the land. In addition, those who farm are expected to help in paying for rituals and sacrifices to insure the success of the crops. One who fails to do any of these things is considered to have no interest in the land, and the allocator will be reluctant to give him a share. Persons concentrate on clearing the portion of land they hope to farm themselves, former users clearing the section they used before, new hopefuls working on sections that others do not seem to be clearing. If there is a potential difference of opinion over land shares it becomes evident at this time, and the allocator will be prepared to handle the matter at the time of the actual division. He will not usually try to settle it beforehand, however.

Persons who are not members of the matrilineage but who are friends of its head or allocator bring him small amounts of palm wine and food before the division to request land. Strangers who want to use lineage land can buy temporary rights from the allocator if there is sufficient land. Called *awata*, this is common practice of both male and female farmers, particularly those who want upland areas for cassava as a cash crop.

The land is divided at the farm, in a meeting of the interested persons which may take all day and involve extensive discussions over their rights and privileges. The pattern of division varies somewhat among matrilineages, but usually the first portions given out are to male matrilineage members by seniority of age. The allocator gets the largest share if he wants it. Female matrilineage members who are widowed, divorced, or who are separated from their husband also usually get shares at this time. In addition, any clan members of other matrilineages who are interested in the land, particularly those who are prominent or have helped the lineage in some way, will be given a share, though not as a rule a large one. Next to be provided for is a category of relatives by birth or marriage which the Afikpo call ɔgo. Among these are the husbands of matrilineage members, their wives rarely being given land directly. Grown sons of matrilineage members are also included, although they belong to different uterine groups than that which controls the land. Agnatic half-brothers of matrilineage members, particularly of the lineage head, will also receive shares and may reciprocate in the allocation of their own matrilineage lands. Last, friends of the allocator, prominent persons, and strangers who make arrangements to use the land, will receive shares, as will an occasional close patrilineal relative of his. Shares in this category are usually not large.

The matrilineage allocator must be a skillful diplomat to balance all these demands without causing anger or resentment. By the same token, he may, through land allocations, make allies of men outside the matrilineage who will support him when he becomes engaged in political activities of some kind, or in a dispute or case. For example, a nonclansman might fear to oppose the matrilineage head in a case involving this man if he were using land which the head controlled, for fear of being removed from the land at the next distribution. A matrilineage head, particularly if young or middle-aged, often gains valuable experience in the administration of lineage land which will be useful to him when he becomes a clan elder.

The actual farming needs of those who receive land are not important, except insofar as they are reflected in whether or not persons are interested enough to ask for land. Arguments as to whether a person has other sources of land to farm, whether he is starving or is rich in food and land, are quite unimportant, no attempt being made by the allocator or other persons to evaluate personal subsistence needs except in the case of self-supporting women. Similarly, the number of children or other persons that an individual supports is irrelevant; a wife with one child does not get less than a wife with four children because of the number of her offspring.

There are, however, exceptions to this pattern of division of open matrilineage land. If the whole clan has been involved in fighting for a piece of land and the case is won, clan elders may ask for shares of it and it may thus become dominated by them rather than the lineage, which normally controls it. Again, a matrilineage sometimes throws a section of its land open to the clan as a whole when the lineage members of the descent group are unwilling or uninterested in making full use of the land: because it is relatively unproductive, it is at a great distance from the Afikpo villages, or the matrilineage has insufficient members to use it. While in all of these cases the group in theory still controls it, the land may become dominated by nonlineage clan members, becoming in effect open clan land. Many clans seem to have one or two sections of this type of land, and controls over it are minimal. Clan members use shares they previously farmed, and any other clan member may use unfarmed sections.

Those who receive land may do whatever they wish with it so long as it is farmed. They can rent it out in *awata* or give it to anyone to farm, as they wish. This is no longer the business of the matrilineage head or of the lineage as a whole. It is assumed that the receiver is a responsible person and will use it to his best advantage. This is also so with patrilineal land holdings. Only in the case where the receiver does not use the land at all will the matrilineage head question the matter; such a person may find his share smaller at the next land division. Such negligence is not common, since a person can usually rent or give the land to someone else to use if he finds he cannot use it.

What appears to be a simple arrangement of matrilineal controls over land is actually quite complex, involving land transfer, land conflicts, and secrecy in land transactions. For not all matrilineage land is so readily open to all of its members; there is some which is more tightly controlled by a single person. This may come about through the transfer of land from a dying matrilineage within the clan, when land is transferred to a matrilineage from a matrilineage in another clan as a compensation for murder, through the opportunistic seizure of land by individuals, or through individuals redeeming pledged land.[10] In theory all such lands should become open to the matrilineage of the individual or individuals involved in its acquisition, but in practice lands obtained in these ways are often tightly controlled by their acquirers for their own benefit at the expense of the matrilineage. In the case of a redemption its mere acquisition may even be kept a secret. At times the controller simply refuses to "show the land" to his uterine relatives or otherwise share it. His justification is that he has played the major role in its acquisition and he may do what he wishes with it. Such a person may be the matrilineage head, or he could be another matrilineage member. After a generation or two such land, which at any rate generally passes matrilineally, may become open to the whole matrilineage.

Serious disputes sometimes arise among members of a clan as a result of attempts at land acquisition or over failure to allocate it fairly. The clan elders usually attempt to settle these to keep the peace. The matter is tried in a manner similar to adjudication in the major patrilineage. Each side brings witnesses, there is full discussion, and the elders try to reach consensus. The land in question may also be examined if the elders are not familiar with it. Their decision is as much the voice of moral authority as of legal sanction. If litigants are unsatisfied, they may go to the Afikpo Native Authority Court, or even to the Magistrate's Court, though clan members are reluctant to have internal disputes made public. Sometimes the matter continues to drag on until one side simply gives up. There are many cases where the dispute never reaches the clan elders, persons simply accepting that someone has gained control of uterine land holdings which they feel entitled to control or to share. Almost any adult male Afikpo can recount stories of how he was "done out" of land by some matrikinsman. This is partly due to the difficulty of acquiring knowledge of the history of land and of proving one's claim to it. It also seems to be because individuals are often resigned to a

---

[10] See "Farmland" in chap. v for a discussion of the origin of matrilineal land.

constant condition of friction over land and are not always willing to take the trouble to prevent what they consider to be land
seizure.

It is clear that, while the Afikpo say that the land of a matrilineage should be controlled by its head, they are very much
aware that in many lineages individuals control land in a private
or semiprivate way in addition to the land open to all its members. While the head may ask for and be given portions of such
land to farm, he really has little control over its dispensation at
farming time. He himself may have acquired land in a like
fashion which he withholds from his matrilineage. There is a
strong element of individual possessiveness and secrecy over
matrilineage land. This sometimes leads to friction and hard
feelings between members and, as we shall see, plays an important role in segmentation within this uterine descent group.

The interests of the members of a matrilineage in land overshadows their concern with the control of groves and of water areas;
these are nowhere as extensive as farmland holdings. The groves,
usually small and near the Afikpo villages, are either of palm
trees, raffia, or bamboo, a recent introduction to Afikpo. They are
subject to pledging and redemption and the types of litigation
and transfer of ownership which are common to farmland,
though there is no division of a grove for a season's use. Palm
groves, which produce cash crops in the form of fruits or wine,
are generally under the control of a matrilineage male who lives
nearby, and he is also said to control the land on which the trees
stand. If the trees are fruit-bearing, they may be used commu-
nally by the matrilineage, but frequently they, as well as groves
of wine trees or mixed groves, are rented for a year. The rent is
shared among the male matrilineage members by age, lineage
women getting smaller shares, if any. Raffia and bamboo groves,
which are located in swampy areas or along stream banks, and
whose products are mainly used in housebuilding and not sold for
cash, are normally controlled and used by a single male lineage
member, passing to a younger uterine brother or a sister's son
upon his death. But they are considered by the Afikpo to be

matrilineage, not personal, property. As a rule, women do not control groves.

Ponds or sections of streams controlled by matrilineages are said to be subject to the same kinds of transactions as land, though no such case was actually noted during field work. They are not a common form of property. Few matrilineages have them, and they usually do not contain enough fish for steady sale. They are under the control of the matrilineage head, who determines when they should be fished and if a stream section should be dammed or not for better fishing, and they are usually open to the use of all members of the controlling descent group.

OTHER LINEAGE ACTIVITIES

The male matrilineage members rarely meet together as a group to discuss an issue, but there are numerous occasions in which the members join for some ritual or activity. They play important roles in rites associated with death, such as funerals, second funerals, and inheritance, and in title ceremonies and marriage proceedings. Since all of these also involve patrilineal ties, they will be discussed in the context of the role relations of descent in Chapter V. Here we indicate only that it is the matrilineage head's responsibility to see that his lineage kinsmen play their proper part in these ceremonies and to advise them in such matters if they need assistance. The lineage and its head were also formerly very much involved in blood revenge concerning a member of their group (see "The Matrilineal Clans in the Village-Group" in chap. iv).

While individuals and groups may perform sacrifices at various shrines to insure their prosperity in farming, there are sacrifices and rituals associated with the specific sections of matrilineal land controlled by the head or by other matrilineage members. If the plot is small, some or all of these may be omitted, but for one or more good farmland sections the controller usually calls in a diviner to ask what should be done to insure success in farming, usually between the clearing and planting periods. The diviner almost invariably suggests that the "squeeze-leaf" ceremony (*ɔhoha ɛkwu ukwɔ*: squeeze-leaf-heap) be performed, a ritual which he usually directs. This sacrifice, carried out on the land itself or at the path leading to where the land is located, must be done before the yam heaps are made, and is to the ground, *ale*. The leaves and other sacrificial materials are thought to make the crops, especially yams, grow well. In addition, the diviner may suggest that a sacrifice be performed at the patrilineal ancestral shrine of the uterine relative who originally obtained the land. This is done by the controller or his representative with the aid of the shrine priest, in whichever compound the shrine for this ancestor is located. This is to inform the ancestor that the land is to be farmed again and to ask his aid in producing good crops. If there is a shrine to *Ibini ɔkpabe*, the Aro oracle, protecting the land, the diviner indicates that the land controller should sacrifice to it as well. Thus the influence of three of the most powerful supernatural agencies, the ground, the ancestors, and the Aro oracle are brought to bear by the controller. Sometimes the diviner suggests further sacrifices, for example to the controller's matriclan shrine. These consultations and sacrifices do not need to be done again the second year of planting.

At the consultation with the diviner those present sometimes also take the opportunity to ask for help over personal problems such as their own illness or illness in their polygynous households. Those who expect substantial shares of land from the controller sometimes come to this consultation, but under any condition they are expected to contribute to its costs and the subsequent sacrifices.

The head of the matrilineage acts as general advisor to all members. Males usually first consult the immediate senior male uterine relative, an elder brother or the mother's eldest brother, but if these cannot resolve a problem, or live far away, the matter will be taken to the head. If it is a question of illness or other trouble, the person consulted may suggest that a diviner be visited, but a diviner may be seen without first asking someone's approval. If there is a dispute between a matrilineage member and her husband, the head may try to negotiate with the spouse on her behalf if the brother or mother's brother is away or does not succeed. Matrilineal male relatives are more likely to act as her representatives in such a dispute than are her patrilineal relatives since the former are considered more closely related to her and more concerned with her needs. A person involved in a property dispute will also seek his matrilineage head's advice. Of course, the head tries to settle disagreements among members.

There is a similar pattern of leadership among the matrilineage females, where the eldest acts as informal head. As in the case of males, there may be a female subhead, a senior female living in a different area of Afikpo. The female leaders are advisors to the married women, help them perform sacrifices at their individual shrines, and back them in disputes with their husbands or cowives. If a serious disagreement arises they will generally refer it to the male lineage head, who may eventually pass it on to the clan elders.

These female leaders help matrilineage women perform rituals, give funerals, take titles, and aid them in ceremonies involving their husbands. They may even help them to leave a husband secretly and find another one. If a woman has a "bad birth," that is, twins or a breech presentation, it is the responsibility of a senior lineage female past the menopause to look after her.[11] If a woman cannot nurse a child, a lineage mate will generally do so for her. In the case of a female child it is done by a member of her lineage, or at least of her clan, but in the case of a male it can be by any woman. When a woman gives birth it is her matrilineage mates who stay close to her and help care for the child for the first four days, until the child is first brought into public view at a prescribed ritual. The bond between lineage females is very strong and surrounds the activities of marriage, birth, and family life (P. Ottenberg, 1958). There is little conflict between matrilineage women of the sort that occurs among men. The women are much less personally involved in matrilineage segmentation

[11] So that contamination from the "bad birth" will not make her infertile.

than are males; they may continue to cooperate and act together even after segmentation within the descent group is in full swing. Paradoxically, though the pattern of marrying away from home is a primary factor in this segmentation, the hostility and ill-feelings surrounding this process are mainly found among the males, who are concerned with the control of authority amongst themselves.

Although men and women of a matrilineage have individual shrines which they use for themselves and their families (see "Shrines" in chap. v), there is one shrine for females which is particularly associated with matrilineality. Called *adudɔ*, it is a small pot erected for a dead woman by her eldest daughter,[12] and is similar in some ways to *Mma obu*, the patrilineal ancestral shrine. However, it has no priest, and the shrine pot is placed in the house of the eldest daughter, or a close senior female matrilineal relative, of the deceased. It may be used as a shrine for several generations, passing within the uterine line, and it is moved from house to house as deaths or marriages make this necessary. After each such move a woman associated with it sacrifices to its spirit so that it will not be angry (S. Ottenberg, 1969).

The shrine representing the ancestral spirit is for the welfare of her daughters and granddaughters. Offerings are made during the New Yam Festival and at other feasts by whoever is in charge of it to insure the prosperity of relatives of the deceased. Any daughter, granddaughter, or greatgranddaughter may offer sacrifice at it if a diviner indicates that the ancestor is troubling her. But after three or four generations, as the ancestor is forgotten, the pot becomes lost. A person in whom the spirit of the ancestor is reincarnated, and this does not have to be a matrilineal relative of the ancestor, may also sacrifice at the shrine if a diviner indicates that this ancestor is "troubling her." Men are not usually affected by the shrine, though women are sometimes

---

[12] If the eldest daughter fails to erect it the female matrilineage head or another senior lineage woman does it for her to avoid angering the spirit of the dead woman.

troubled by the ancestral spirits of *Mma obu,* the male patrilineal shrine.

THE MATRILINEAL LOCALITY GROUP

There will be in a village, or in a few neighboring villages, a very loose grouping of all the matrilineal relatives of a clan who live there, larger than any single lineage as a rule and, of course, smaller than the clan as a whole. It is a matrilineal locality group, without formal organization or leadership, whose members generally know each other though they often belong to distinct matrilineages of the clan. In many activities involving an individual, such as title ceremonies, marriage, and funerals, members of this group take part as a matter of courtesy and interest even if they do not belong to the person's matrilineage. If the title is a very important one, or if the burial is of a prominent person, clan members from other areas join as well, but otherwise they may not be sufficiently interested to come. While local matrikinsmen appear at such rituals of fellow members as a courtesy, the person performing the ceremony is expected to show his respect for them by inviting them.

Similarly, we have seen how a clan member, especially a senior or prominent person, can ask for and receive land to farm from matrilineages other than his own which have land in the local area. Again, the collection of clan funds is frequently broken down on a village basis, with one responsible clan member in each village being designated by the clan elders to raise dues from the members there.[13] Finally, this local group is a channel of communication through which members in a village keep in touch with clan affairs. For example, a matrilineage head who is not an elder, and thus does not go to meetings of the clan elders, will learn of clan matters through one of its elders living in his village. This diffuse, noncorporate grouping of matrikinsmen has no special name and is not recognized as a specific group by the

---

[13] This is probably done in this way rather than through matrilineage heads because of the dispersion of lineages, and perhaps also because some are having internal conflicts.

Afikpo. It is a collectivity of clan members who live in the same area and cooperate and show courtesy toward one another because of common descent ties within a clan.

FISSION, SEGMENTATION, AND ACCRETION

The matrilineal clans and lineages are not static organizations; there is always growth and decay. At Afikpo there are three main processes which have been or are at work. There are the fission and the accretion of clans. At the same time there is segmentation: the continual breaking up and reforming of matrilineages within the clan without losing their attachment to their larger organization. The reasons why these processes occur differ, but relate to the structure of the clans and lineages, the facts of geographic dispersal, and the particular activities that each form of uterine group carries out.

Fission was characteristic of Afikpo clans in precolonial times, in contrast to their tendency to regroup today. About half the clans, particularly the larger ones, have histories of division. Information, some of it incomplete, gathered on thirty-five clans shows that fifteen had no record of fission, ten had divided into two clans each, four into three each, two into four each, and one into seven. This has ceased in the last thirty years, and the majority of the divided units are now united.

In most cases, fission occurred between lineages and not across them. It did not usually involve a division of the clan into halves, but rather the separation of one matrilineage and its properties from the rest of the clan. The group that separated often merely added another name or term to its original name or dropped part of the original. Thus *ibɛ ɛnyi ɛnyum* split into *ibɛ ɛnyi ɛnyum*, *ibɛ ugwu ɛnyi*, and *ibɛ ɛnyi*, though some took completely separate names. The effect of the split was to create separate clan shrines, each with its own priest, to permit marriage between the two groups, and to put rules of blood revenge into effect between them. They became autonomous units, associated only by the knowledge that they were once together and stemmed from a common ancestor and that merging was possible at some future time. This seems to have been rare previous to British contact, however. A group which separated would have all the features of a clan as we have outlined them, but it usually was a matrilineage at the time of the division, in that all members could trace their uterine relationship to one another. It would remain so for some time, but would evolve gradually into the status of a clan as it grew, with its own internal matrilineage segments. All its members then could no longer trace specific uterine ties with one another.

Two types of incidents have acted as catalysts in fission. In one, a particular matrilineage continually caused trouble through the murders, thefts, or other crimes of its members, especially those carried out against members of other clans. Murder particularly threatened the whole clan, not just the matrilineage of the killer, in terms of the pattern of blood revenge. The second type involved killings within the clan, apparently a result of internal conflict over farmland controls, which led to continuing, unresolved disputes. In either case the separation was determined by the clan leaders, who would announce it by walking through the Afikpo market, hitting two machetes together and stating that persons of such-and-such a uterine line were no longer part of the clan.

It was also possible to cast individuals out of the clan, for example, a long-time thief. This was rare, however, and did not lead to the formation of a new grouping unless the outcast was a female, or, if a male, he could persuade a sister or other matrilineage female to join him. It was more likely that the clan leaders would sell such an individual into slavery to get rid of him. This form of fission does not occur today.

In turn, a man or a woman could quit a clan by publicly cutting a yam with a machete and stating that he or she was no longer a member. Rarely was a permanent separation intended; rather, this was a device to force the clan to come to terms with whatever lay behind the defection, generally a quarrel. Such a person was simply self-ostracized until a *rapprochement* was arranged. This form of separation still occasionally occurs today. It is men who have married into the matriclan who take the initiative in settling the matter, for clan members feel they should not stoop to this for someone who has behaved badly toward them.

It is difficult to tell, since fission no longer occurs, but fission may have been related to some maximum effective size for clan operation, though today there seem to be no upper limits. In former times there was much less contact between clan members in different parts of Afikpo, as a result of intermittent fighting in the village-group and surrounding region and the possibility of being seized and sold into slavery by the Aro or others. As a clan grew and its members dispersed, it probably became harder for them to meet. Divisions may have been spurred by this, though the more immediate causes were as outlined above. Conversely, the amalgamation of these clans since about 1900 is related to increasing contact between residential units, the gradual cessation of warfare, and the changing manner of handling murder cases and troublesome persons.

The procedure for accretion is for a smaller unit to seek to join the larger one of which it was once a part rather than the reverse. It does this for its own protection, since small clans are particularly vulnerable in disputes over land and other rights, lacking funds, as many influential leaders, and numerous political contacts. Unlike unrelated patrilineal groupings, unrelated clans never join together.

Before reuniting, the elders of the groups concerned consult a diviner to ask whether they may do so since they are all "brothers." He usually suggests that they consult the Aro Chuku oracle, which generally accedes and indicates who will be the priest of the joined groupings. This is usually the priest of the larger or wealthier clan; the smaller group joins its shrine to the other. When this is done all clan regulations and traditions hold for members of both groups. Property held by the various matrilineages in both clans remains under lineage control, though the enlarged clan now has the over-all authority.

The rule of exogamy applies in the newly amalgamated clans, and existing marriages which violate it must be dissolved. If the wife is still of childbearing age, she should leave her husband's compound and reside elsewhere.[14] She will probably remarry, particularly if she has children and is thus considered fertile. Bride price is not paid by the new husband to the former one, as would normally be the case.[15] The children, if they are young, will go with their mother, the daughters remaining with her until they marry. Older sons stay with their father or may eventually return to live in his compound, as is the case with sons of divorced parents. A wife past childbearing age may remain in the compound but not near her husband. He will continue to support her and she will continue to care for their children, who are not particularly at a disadvantage. Whether the mother remarries or not her children will still have their matrilineage from which to inherit property and land rights, and will be affiliated with a patrilineal grouping, either of the father or stepfather.

The effect of culture contact has been to strengthen the internal solidarity and increase the size of the Afikpo clans, creating more effective matrilineal support groups than probably ever existed before.

In the case of the matrilineages segmentation is a characteristic feature and also occurred in the pre-British period. It is not primarily the result of fighting or murder within the lineage but is related to the residential location of matrilineage members and the system of matrilineal land controls.

Unlike clan fission, which probably was often sudden and traumatic, matrilineage segmentation proceeds gradually over two or three generations. It is not as upsetting, though there are

[14] In several cases where the wife refused to do this or the husband would not allow her, the clan did not force them to separate but denied them the use of clan land and other clan properties and forbade them to take part in clan rituals and activities.

[15] In remarriage the new husband generally pays the former one the bride price or a portion of it as settlement to dissolve the first marriage. In this case the former husband would not accept such money because it would be bad form to take money for his "sister," as his former wife now becomes. He would, however, accept bride wealth for daughters of such a marriage.

strains involved, and there is no distinct ritual of separation. The process begins two or three generations after a matrilineage has itself formed as a separate unit. At this point the matrilineage members are characteristically, through marriage of female members, spread about in the village-group in the manner already indicated. The lineage head, unless he is an extremely energetic farmer, has neither the interest nor time to farm those matrilineage lands which are not near his particular village, and he will not be very interested in these distant lands. As we have indicated in discussing land division, he delegates their control to the senior male matrilineage member in the area where they are found. Thus a sort of localized sublineage develops with its own subhead, still under the authority of the lineage head in the event of trouble. The procedure of delegating authority may occur more than once in a single matrilineage if the lands are quite widespread; that is, there may be more than one subhead at one time. A subhead himself will be less interested in land near where the head lives than in that near his own village. Strong commitment to one's patrilineal and residential groupings make the movement of the matrilineage head's residence to an intermediate point where he could control all lineage lands extremely unlikely: this does not seem to occur.

In the second stage of segmentation, perhaps a generation later, we find that the senior male uterine descendant of the subhead living near the distant land is now in charge of the former subhead's land, and that a coolness between him and the present head is likely to have developed.[16] This subhead feels that the matrilineage head is stingy, that he is keeping the subhead and his close matrilineal relatives off land other than in the latter's local area. The present head or his immediate predecessor quite likely has acquired new land on his own (see "Farmland"

[16] Unless the present head of the lineage now lives near the subhead's area. In this case he will have charge of the former subhead's land and the distinction between them may disappear, but other subheads may arise elsewhere in the meantime; the process seems inevitable.

in chap. v), and does not wish to share it with his subhead or other matrikinsmen who live away from him. This may be so even if the land is located near enough for the subhead or his close relatives to farm it. The subhead and other members of his particular uterine line may also have obtained land and kept it from the head. This kind of secrecy over land transactions in a segmenting matrilineage is common; the extent to which such land is kept from open use of the lineage as a whole seems to be the extent to which the whole process of segmentation is accelerated.

At this stage we find the beginning of a loss of genealogical knowledge between the head's close matrilineal relatives and those of the subhead. The head, mainly because of his age and position, has greater knowledge than do members of segmenting sections of the matrilineage. At this stage matrilineage members still cooperate in rituals and other matters.

A generation or two later matters have reached full segmentation. The genealogical ties of the two groupings are obscure; their members know they are related to each other more closely than to other clansmen but they are no longer sure of the exact genealogical details. The head of the older matrilineage will have greater knowledge, but he withholds it. He is unwilling to divulge the information and avoids the issue if possible, for to explain the genealogical links is to recognize that persons may have rights to his matrilineage land. The subgrouping, now a separate matrilineage, takes as its founding ancestress the mother or a sister of the first subhead. Since there are no separate matrilineage shrines or other lineage symbols to be established, there is no formal ritual to mark this separation such as exists in the case of clan fission. The eldest member of the new lineage is its head. He does not cooperate with the head of the former lineage in farm rituals or most other matters, but directs his own rituals and guides his own members.

As the new lineage develops, its localization soon begins to disappear as females marry out and bear children. Members of the lineage begin to acquire land through redemption, transfer, or seizure in various parts of Afikpo. Soon the whole process of segmentation commences again.

There is a variant form of segmentation which may occur when an energetic and enterprising farmer who is neither a head nor a subhead acquires land but keeps it secret or under very tight control, refusing to share it with other matrilineage members. If he obtains sufficient land for himself and his most immediate relations he is less concerned with other matrilineage land. Other lineage members, resenting his action, begin to discourage him from using matrilineage land. Gradually, the same process as outlined above occurs. Here it is not geographical distance which leads to the separation but the activity of a person in acquiring land for himself. While Afikpo lament such practices many carry them out, though in some cases not to a sufficient degree to lead to segmentation. But it is not rare for a man to hold a piece or two of land which he does not share freely with other matrikinsmen. But if individuals engage in full-scale land acquisition without sharing the land with matrilineage relatives it is difficult to avoid the development of a divison.

The pattern of segmentation and its relation to land holding may be clarified by two examples. The first concerns a segment of a full matrilineage which is in the early stages of separation. This segment, founded by (3),[17] has a genealogy of twenty-three remembered members through five generations, of whom eleven are still living. Of these nine live in three nearby villages: Amuro, Mgbom, and Ngodo. Two male members are working away from home, at a considerable distance from Afikpo.

The full matrilineage is actually dividing into three separate segments, based on the founder (3) and her two sisters (2, 4). The head, Ogbonnia Echem (17), of the full matrilineage is also the head of the segment in question here. Relationships among all the members of the full matrilineage are good and the land is generally open and not secret, perhaps because most of the matrilineage members live near one another.

[17] The numbers refer to persons on the genealogical chart. See Chart 3.

There is a great deal of the full matrilineage's land in the Mgbom Village farming area, some for every year of the seven-year farming cycle. This is land originally cleared by a brother of the three sisters (5), and it is under Echem's direction and for the entire lineage, though used mainly by the senior members. In addition, each of the three developing segments has control of land which some of its members acquired, and to which other members of the full lineage have only limited access. The lineage segment whose genealogy is given here has a piece of land in Mgbom village redeemed by the head's mother's brother (11),

Chart III. The Matrilineage Segment of Ogbonnia Edem (1952)

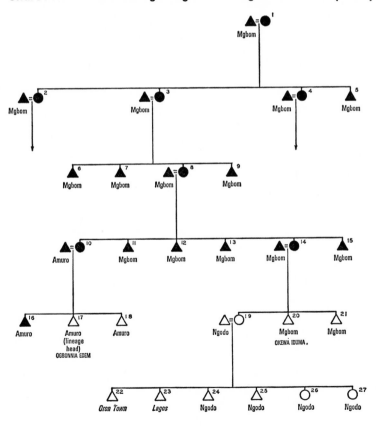

and two sections redeemed by a mother's mother's brother of the head (6). These lands belong primarily to this segment; while Echem still is in charge, he leaves their actual division to Okewa Iduma (20) and others of the lineage. When Echem dies, Okewa Iduma, as the senior male member of the segment of the full matrilineage, will probably take control of these three pieces of land. He already has complete control of another piece of land which was pledged to his patrilineage many years ago in lieu of payment of a fine levied on a matrilineage man for assaulting a member of the agnatic group. The origin of the land apparently became lost to the original matrilineal owners; Okewa Iduma's father knew of it and redeemed it for him, though the father used most of it himself while he was alive. Okewa Iduma now controls this land, which he shares with his younger uterine siblings. Other members of the segment and of the whole matrilineage receive small shares, the land being under restricted control.

Okewa Iduma thus represents the point around which a separate matrilineage may eventually form. He is already acquiring land controls which are restrictive in terms of the total matrilineage. While Echem knows most of the genealogies of the three segments of the lineage, Okewa Iduma knows only his own well and probably never will know the others in detail. But Echem has no sisters and thus no uterine line to outlast him while Okewa Iduma does. Segmentation is slowed in this particular case because the lineage members live fairly close together and there is no energetic land speculator among them to create hostility.

A second genealogy (see Chart 4), that of Nnachi Enwo (9), exemplifies the final stage of segmentation. The matrilineage has a remembered genealogy of thirty-two members, twenty-two of whom are living, and extends over six generations. Of the living, fourteen are in Afikpo. They are divided evenly between Mgbom village in the central area, where the head, a middle-aged man, lives, and the Ozizza villages of Afikpo some distance away to the northeast. The remaining members, except for one female who has no permanent home, live away from Afikpo. None of the matrilineage members at Ozizza do much farming except the head's eldest sister. If they did, they would probably attempt to acquire land there and the senior male member (17) would be in charge of it.

The major land holdings involved are as follows.

First, land in the Ukpa village farming area which the first husband of the head's eldest sister (7) redeemed for her after their marriage. He pledged the land away when they were divorced, but she reported the matter to the matrilineage head, who redeemed it. The head lets the former husband farm it, but the sons living in Ozizza would have priority if they wished to use it.

Second, the lineage founder (1) was given by her husband a piece of land in Mgbom which eventually fell to the head's mother (3). When the head's mother died the head was away from Afikpo, and it was used by his two elder sisters (7, 8) particularly the one living in Mgbom (8), as the other (7) lived in another village. This other sister, senior of the two, could have been in charge of the land had she been interested, for at this time the males of the lineage in Afikpo were young and she was thus effective head of the uterine group. However, she left it for the younger sister, who used most of it. On his return the head took over the land and he refuses to reveal its location to matrilineal relatives outside his matrilineage, though they are aware of its existence. He fears that some of them, being much older than he, will attempt to gain control over it if he does.

Third, the head has also acquired, and keeps personal control of, a valuable section of land in Mkpoghoro village which a clan member had pledged away, resulting in a series of court cases that went to the Supreme Court in Enugu in the Eastern Region.

Fourth, the head gained control of a piece of land belonging to his father's matrilineage. His father had redeemed it many years after it had originally been pledged away, knowledge of the land having been lost to other matrilineage members. The father kept tight control over this land, permitting only a few matrilineage members to share in it, but letting his wives and some close patrilineal relatives join him in its use. When the father died the head claimed it and has dominated it since, though his father's

Chart IV. The Matrilineage of Nnachi Enwo (1952)

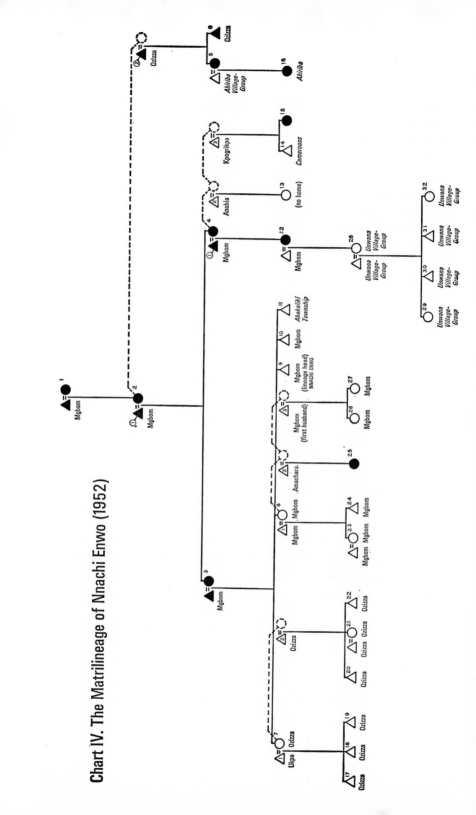

matrilineal relatives also claim it and are trying to win it back. The head is also trying to acquire other lands of his father's matrilineal grouping in a similar fashion.

The head has little to do with the lands of the once larger matrilineage of which his descent line was a part; his segment is now effectively a separate matrilineage. He and his matrilineage mates have little contact with their more distant matrikinsmen. They are separated by distance as well as genealogy, for these persons live all over Afikpo, though mainly in the central villages. He gives them only small shares of the land he controls and they act in kind toward him. He does not know the details of his genealogical connections with most of them. He performs the necessary farm rituals for the land he controls and heads his matrilineage in other activities. He has shown considerable enterprise in land matters and will probably increase his holdings in the future.

His newly developed lineage shows no sign of segmentation despite its genealogical depth, possibly because he is the only mature male of the lineage who is interested in the land and in living at Afikpo. If the adult males living at Ozizza (17, 18, 19, 20) were farmers rather than traders, it is likely that segmentation would be occurring on the basis of their descent from the head's eldest sister (7), in point of cleavage against his other sister (8), but these men do not threaten the head's land interests. Other than himself, the most enterprising member of his lineage is this second eldest sister (8) who, as we have seen, was active in lineage land matters when he was away, and who is a hard-working farmer. She illustrates how a woman may play an active role in matrilineage matters in the absence of the male head.

Since matrilineal genealogies from the last century are not remembered it is difficult to say whether or not matrilineal segmentation has accelerated since the advent of the British. Although we are unable to arrive at definite conclusions, several observations should be made. Certainly the greater contact and freedom of movement within Afikpo since precolonial times has made it easier for a matrilineage head to maintain contact with its members within the village-group, as well as permitting persons, particularly women, who used to be quite restricted, to farm land outside of their own villages more easily. The physical freedom for women is reflected in the evidence that they now marry further away from home than formerly (see Chart 2, above in this chap.). This creates greater matrilineage dispersion than before, which accelerates segmentation, though greater contact among lineage members acts to slow it down.

There are other important changes from former times. Many young and middle-aged men are away from Afikpo trading and working, some with wives and children. These men lose track of their matrilineal relations and of potential land rights within their matrilineage. When they return to live at Afikpo, as many do, it is difficult for them to gain access to their matrilineal land. Other matrilineage members are reluctant to cut down their share so that kinsmen may join them. If there is tightly controlled or secretly held land within the lineage they will certainly be the last to know of it. If their matrilineage is in the second stage of the segmentation process, they may be caught in the mutual distrust of the lineage head and the leader of the segmenting section. Though such persons often have difficulty in obtaining their matrilineal land they have ready access to their patrilineal holdings, which are open. An example is the story of the man who lost genealogical knowledge of and contact with the rest of his lineage after being abroad for a number of years. Upon his return as a middle-aged man, he found himself the head of a matrilineage segment of which he was the only adult male at home. He knew of only one section of land, in a village about three miles from his home, which his close matrilineal relatives were using and which he might control. He cast about for other land of his former larger matrilineage to farm, or land to redeem, but his matrikinsmen were in no hurry to "show him" land. This problem is common. Those who stay at home keep an eye on matrilineal land matters, on the pledging and redeeming of land, and on the allocation of land during its division for farming, and they reap the rewards of the intricate game of land politics. To be away is to be excluded, to have others seize and use land that one is entitled to.

The departure from Afikpo of male members of a matrilineage for trade, education, and other reasons, so common today, seems to lead to a slowing down of lineage segmentation. Since this process occurs around males who acquire land within the lineage, their absence reduces potential land conflicts, and the normal pattern of geographic separation of matrikinsmen does not operate as strongly as it otherwise would. This can be seen from Nnachi Enwo's lineage.

Finally, the accidents of life and fortune lead to the disappearance of some matrilineages. They are small in scale and some have few females. The females may not reproduce, or the children who live to adulthood may all be males. There is no device of bringing an outside female into the descent group as a fictional relative to produce children for a dying matrilineage.

IV. DESCENT GROUPS WITHIN
THE LARGER STRUCTURE

THE agnatic and uterine groupings do not stand apart from the social life of the village and the village-group; the unilineal organizations are interconnected with those larger structures. It is the residentially based patrilineal groupings which are most directly integrated, especially into the village, while the uterine groups are more autonomous and isolated. But double descent does not by any means totally dominate social life at Afikpo. The role of association groupings and other organizations in the village and village-group looms large, sufficiently so to be the subject of a separate study (S. Ottenberg, n.d.). These nondescent groupings unite persons in common activities regardless of unilineal ties. They cut across the forces that pull persons in varying directions through unilineality. The descent structures at Afikpo are only a part of a total society. They form an underlying base of orientation, sustenance, and ritual activity, beyond which are found these larger elements.

We first consider the descent groups' roles in the village, then the village-group, and then beyond, in terms of other village-groups. The organization of Afikpo is complex, and dominated by age groupings and secret societies. We are interested in how the descent groups are arranged and interconnect with village and village-group organizations, the degree to which they are autonomous or are under the guidance and control of these larger structures, and the reasons for the particular types of interrelationships that occur.

PATRILINEAL GROUPINGS IN THE VILLAGE

The Afikpo village is variable in size, ranging from 183 to 3,662 persons,[1] but its fundamental structure is generally the same. It consists of a grouping of major patrilineages, often divided into wards, around a central common or several commons. The compounds are located side by side, the village being relatively compact. The number of major patrilineages in a village range from one to thirty-two. In the larger villages some of the compounds may be located at a short distance from the rest, perhaps half a mile, forming one or more wards which have considerable autonomy from the main village. But these are extremes. In the majority of cases the village consists of from roughly three to ten compounds, each with its major patrilineage, grouped into two or three wards. Some of these agnatic groupings in the village are related to one another, others are not. The Afikpo do not seem to feel that they have to be and view the village as a collectivity of major patrilineages which are more or less equal in stature, with full rights regardless of their origin or their relationship to other major patrilineages in or outside of it.

The history of any village is essentially the history of the growth and development of its separate major patrilineages. It is generally known which patrilineages arrived first and which came last, but the order for the middle period is often confused, different persons from different patrilineages providing varying accounts. Historical priority is of some importance in the village, as we will see. In fact, there is some doubt that in a good number of cases the patrilineage which today is fully accepted as the first

[1] According to the 1953 Census. See Nigeria, Census Superintendent (1953–54, Pt. IV, pp. 25–26). The actual figures are probably about 20 per cent higher.

in the village actually was so. Most of these unsure cases seem to involve persons of Aro Chuku descent, the *amadi* patrilineages, and what probably is meant is that they early came to play a dominating role in the village.

Most villages are of quite mixed origin, as we might expect from the history of Afikpo (see "Setting" in chap. i). There are, in some, remnants of two early indigenous peoples, called Ego and Nkalo by the Afikpo, and of a group of unknown origin, the Ebiri. Many villages have one or more major patrilineages which were founded by persons from Aro Chuku, and which settled at Afikpo following a series of movements, through several generations, from the Ohaffia area to the south. Other Igbo come from Okposi to the northwest, Enugu, Okigwi, Owerri to the west, and from other areas. There is also evidence of the movement into the area of non-Igbo Cross River peoples, such as the Enna and the Ekumeru, who founded certain patrilineages. Sometimes the agnatic groupings came directly to their present site, and in other cases they first settled elsewhere at Afikpo. Generally a new group received permission from an existing one to settle beside it but today it is not in a position of obligation because of this. The histories do not discuss matrilineal matters at all. Though sometimes a full brother of the founder of the patrilineage is mentioned this is invariably in the agnatic and not the uterine context.

Afikpo has been an area of immigration rather than emigration. At least for several hundred years patrilineal groupings have been moving in. The migration seems to have been by families, often a single one, sometimes with brothers or friends and their domestic groupings, to start their own major patrilineages. Two major patrilineages in the village which are related are often believed to have been so founded by brothers, by a father and a son, or by friends. Some of these patrilineages are still separating but are linked by rules of remarriage exogamy and by common controls over productive property (see "Fission, Accretion, and Extinction" in chap. ii). Other related ones have totally separated. In either case they are not necessarily living side by side in the village, or even in the same ward, and they do not automatically join together in opposition to other major patrilineages in village politics. A village is therefore a collection of major patrilineages of diverse origin, some of which are related to others, but others that are not, which unite in common activities through a common organization.

The major structure that joins the patrilineages in this form of community is a system of male age sets and grades. There are between fifteen and twenty age sets in every village, each with about a three-year age span. They are formed when men reach the age of about twenty-eight to thirty years, are compulsory and last the life of their members. They are the basis for the major authority distinctions in the village as well as the means of reckoning age. Each set has its own organization, leader, and internal rules. The sets are grouped into grades, there being two important ones in every village, an executive grade of two or three sets of men, of roughly thirty-five to forty-five years, and an elders' grade of the senior sets, or males roughly fifty-five years and over. The executive grade is appointed by the elders, but the membership in the elders' grade occurs when sets in the village join like sets in the other Afikpo villages to form the elders' grade for the entire village-group. These village-group elders are the elders of the villages as well.

The executive grade carries out the orders of the elders, who in this egalitarian gerontocracy control village affairs. It directs communal work, collects and holds village funds, acts as a village police, and assists the elders in carrying out rituals and sacrifices. The elders, meeting as the need arises, are responsible for the village properties, which include the farmland areas where the various patrilineal and matrilineal descent groups hold land, and also sometimes a village palm grove and a pond and stream. They carry out rituals at various village shrines to insure the health of the villagers and the prosperity of their crops. They direct the annual village feasts and ceremonies. They prepare sacrifices and rituals, they keep the peace among villagers by settling disputes among its members and its patrilineages, and they legislate as necessary, though this is not frequent. They represent the village to the outside world of Afikpo. The qualities of leadership are much the same as in the case of those who direct the major patrilineages, and often they are the same persons.

All of these activities draw individuals in the community together regardless of patrilineal affiliation. In all they are more or less on a common footing in terms of these patrilineal affiliations —it is age which is the major distinguishing feature rather than descent. The village poses a face of unity and equality. As within the major patrilineage, where the stress is on the nonranking of its segments, so it is likewise in the village. To make distinctions publicly other than by age is to create a sense of division, which is abhorred.

Among the village elders decision-making is largely through consensus, unanimity being important. There is no specific representative among the elders from each major patrilineage. If it has ten elders all can take part in directing the village. If there is none, none take part, though in this case if a matter specifically concerning that agnatic group arises its senior male members represent it to the elders. However elders who are prominent in their major patrilineages often come to voice feelings of its members in the village scene. They are thus likely to be influential among the village elders. The patrilineages form the governmental blocks of the village. They are the basic units of a consensus form of village organization and of a government based on age distinctions.

There is therefore a continuity of pattern between the organization of the major patrilineage and the village, and, as we shall see, the village-group. The major patrilineage is where the basic procedures of authority and politics, of government, and of ritual, are learned by the growing individual; it is the place of socialization for adult life in the village and the village-group. He then moves to the village sphere as a young man and as a senior person into the organization of the village-group. If for no other reason the major patrilineage plays an important role vis-à-vis the larger structures.

Between the level of the village and its major patrilineage lie the wards. They are local groupings of contiguous compounds, dividing the village into major sections. Each is composed of from roughly one to five major patrilineages. Each has a men's rest house and a common, and in each those persons who represent the two major grades in the village generally also form grades there as its basis of organization and authority. Every ward has a few shrines of its own, and some control a few sections of farmland—apportioned much as a major patrilineage does when it is farmed. Wards form the basis of the separation of persons for intravillage competition, especially wrestling and whipping contests. But in general the ward is not a very active organization. The major focus lies on the village.

There is another major organization which unites the members of the various patrilineages in the village. This is the secret society. Compulsory for all adult males, it is secret only to women and children. It is the focus of a series of rituals and plays produced in the village, some of which are public. It is also a source of prestige, mainly through a series of ranked titles within it which all secret society members are eligible to take. The title societies are actually formed separately in each major patrilineage where they are taken, each society being independent (see "Male Lineage Associations" in chap. ii). However, they give the title-taker the appropriate rank in the village secret society. There are shrines associated with these titles which are said to be "owned" by the lineage title societies; yet they also involve the secret society. The holders of the more senior secret society titles in the village form a separate organization, a titled group, which reinforces the authority structure of the village. When any village organization, and this may be a major patrilineage, as well as a ward, an age set, or the executive or elders' grade, passes a very important ruling there is a procedure whereby this titled group can be invoked so as to play a role in determining the punishment of any infraction. But in general the secret society performs ritual and prestige functions.

In some villages the society is led by a priest and an assistant priest, though in others there are no such persons. In all cases a small group of middle-aged men and elders, volunteers who can be from any of the patrilineages in the village, lead and direct its initiation ceremonies and other rituals. The principle of participation of all villagers regardless of agnatic affiliation which exists in the village at large is also found in its secret society. The distinctions here are largely on the basis of age, title society membership, and interest, rather than on patrilineal ties.

While there is a strong sense of equality of the descent groups which comprise the village, there are also some crucial, if rarely stated, differences. We have already noted that villages are aware that some lineages or compounds are the oldest in the settlement, and some the youngest. There is a feeling that the oldest ones form the heart of the village. It is usually in the rest house in the common of the ward containing the oldest lineage or lineages that the elders meet to discuss village matters. Here or in the compound of the senior major patrilineage there is generally one or more shrines, said to be brought by the founder of the first major patrilineage, who is also considered the founder of the village. And here annual rituals and sacrifices are carried out by these elders, perhaps with the assistance of a priest who is from that agnatic group. Further, the village elders in some villages perform an annual sacrifice at the ancestral shrine of this founder in his honor during the New Yam Festival. There is thus a special ritual focus in the settlement around the senior major patrilineage.

There is other evidence of differentiation. In theory the leader of each age set in the village is chosen, on the basis of interest and popularity, by the set members at the time this group forms. This is as the Afikpo generally will state the matter. In practice there is a strong tendency for such a person to come from the older lineages of the community, from its first ward. This may not seem like a very crucial matter, but the leaders of these sets have a unique opportunity to gain leadership experience. When sets form the executive grade it is they who lead it, especially the head of the senior set of the two or three sets which make up this grade. And, in fact, by the time we come to the ruling group of village elders it is clear that there is a tendency for leadership to come from these persons who have had this special position in the past, thus from the older village patrilineages. The same condition occurs in the ritual priests' group which controls the secret society. If there is a priest and assistant priest for this society, as in some villages, they often come from the older village patrilineages, as do some other members of this group. Further, many of the older patrilineages claim to be of ancient Aro Chuku origin, the *amadi* patrilineages who formerly held an important position in Afikpo, both in the village and the village-group, by virtue of their right to try certain serious crimes and because of their role in the slave trade. These matters are better discussed in the context of the village-group than the village (see "Agnation in the Village-Group Structure," below in this chap.), but it is necessary to say here that in terms of leadership potential this quality still slightly enhances their position in the village vis-à-vis persons from other major patrilineages.

There is no formal rule in any of these matters of leadership selection. It is said that if they were stated they would cause divisions in the village, much as in the case of the major patrilineage. And in every village there are prominent men from patrilineages other than the earliest ones. But there is a predominance of leadership from the older descent groups, and it is more difficult for a person from a younger patrilineage to gain the necessary experience and acquire recognition. Only one type of male in the village is formally excluded from leadership position and from priesthood, the members of the matrilineal slave clan, *ibɛ osim*, regardless of their patrilineal affiliation.

Two opposing principles operate here. There is the belief in equality of opportunity for individuals, and that all agnatic groups have a common share in village activities. Contrariwise there is the sense that historical priority is important in village matters. The seniority accorded living individuals by their age is also accorded descent groups in keeping with their antiquity. Both are key principles. Compared to other Igbo groupings [2] the egalitarian motif seems dominant, but the differentiating factors are also extremely important.

As the patrilineal descent groupings form the basic units of the village, the latter's organization permeates and effects them. The system of age sets and grades which originates in the village as a whole forms the groundwork of authority and leadership in the agnatic groupings; the executive grade members and the elders are generally the same in both. It is probably for this reason that genealogy plays a less important role in the determination of positions of authority in the major patrilineage than in the case of agnatic descent groupings in other Igbo areas, where the village organization is not so tightly associated with formalized age categories, though they often exist (Meek, 1937, chap. ix; Forde and Jones, 1950:18–19). Similarly, the locating of the organization of the title societies within the major patrilineages, rather than on the basis of the village as a whole, links these lineages to the village prestige system and to the secret society in a direct manner.

Some shrines are found in a village which are owned by major patrilineages but are for the welfare of the village as a whole.[3] These are said to have been brought to the village by the founders of the major patrilineages which control them and which appoint their priests, and they have, through some unknown process, become generalized to the village at large. Often they are located in the village commons. At important village feasts, such as the New Yam Festival, or on the occasion of important activities, such as wrestling contests, they are sacrificed at by their

[2] See, for example, Meek (1937) ; Henderson (1963) ; Forde and Jones (1950:15–21).

[3] To be differentiated from shrines in the village owned and controlled by wards, and still others by the village elders. There are also shrines located in the village which are owned by major patrilineages but which are for the welfare of Afikpo as a whole, such as the Yam Shrine and the Rain Controller's shrine. See "Agnation in the Village-Group Structure," below in this chapter.

priest for the sake of the whole village. The village elders can request that such a sacrifice be made but this is usually unnecessary as the priest will usually do so on his own. Such a shrine is also said to bring welfare to its own major patrilineage and may also be used for the sake of the lineage. Its priest is selected by this descent group in the manner of the ancestral shrine priest.

There are other connections between major patrilineages and the village at large. As we have seen, the patrilineal land holdings, as well as matrilineal ones, are located in the blocks of farmland said to belong to the village. The village elders perform rituals to insure the fertility of this land. They also pass rulings through which young sets in the village, or men of each ward, perform communal labor to maintain the farm paths, erect rest shelters at the farms, prepare the village yam racks (located between the farms and the village) for yam storage. The village elders also fine persons who fight or otherwise disturb the peace of the farms, including persons from other villages, and determine which block of land will be used in a given year. This is usually routine, the blocks being farmed in rotation, but the elders have the right to change this at will. There is usually no strict rule that one cannot farm a section outside of the block for the year, or the past year, as land is farmed two years in a row. However, a person doing so farms in isolation, surrounded in some cases by high bush and hungry crop-eating animals. Only in some of the swampier areas where the soil is richer are farms usually made out of season. Thus the village elders determine what land is to be used by the descent groups for farming at a given time, while at the same time acting in a variety of ritual and secular ways to insure the maximum success in crop production.

The elders are also concerned with resolving serious internal conflicts within the major patrilineages and with settling disputes in the village between these groupings. Their role in both is minimal, though for differing reasons. In the first instance, as we have seen, the descent groups are generally able to resolve their own affairs and do not take pride in bringing them to the village elders for public purview. In fact, many Afikpo prefer to take such matters to the Native Authority Court. But if matters go to the village elders it generally means that a serious internal division is in the making in the major patrilineage. In one case, already mentioned in another context, a man who lacked sons refused to initiate a surrogate son into the secret society as he should do by custom and was fined by his major patrilineage and later informally ostracized by this group. This led to a division of feeling and sentiment between his minor patrilineage and the rest of the descent group, and a state of noncooperation developed between the two. The leaders of the major patrilineage finally brought the matter to the attention of the village elders, who reviewed the case, hearing the evidence on both sides, and who supported these leaders with an additional fine. But the man refused to pay and the matter still dragged on at the termination of field work. This illustrates a number of points. The elders rarely interfere in internal affairs of the major patrilineage, and when they do it is generally at the behest of this group, not on their own initiative. While they can add to the pressure on recalcitrants their ultimate authority is not great. They have the power in such a case as this to ostracize the offender from village life itself, but they cannot force him to make amends. But most matters which the elders try in the village involve the violation of village rules by individuals; they are not matters which involve the culprit's major patrilineage as a whole.

Conflicts between single major patrilineages of a village are rare. There is little for them to quarrel over. The leadership of the village is not at stake, and they are not essentially in competition over productive property—here the tension is between patrilineal and matrilineal groupings and among the matrilineal ones. One type of case that occasionally occurs is when a major patrilineage grows faster than a neighboring one, expanding into the latter's back yard area and cutting down its future housebuilding space. This can be serious and the village elders will take a hand in settling the matter, for it leads to hostile feelings between the groups involved. Another situation involves two linked major patrilineages that share farmland. Sometimes in the process of final fission they quarrel over the ownership of the land. The village elders will attempt to settle the case if the descent groups are from the same village; if from different villages, it will go to the special Afikpo elders' court or the Native Authority Court. Again, when patrilineages diverge their title societies usually split and quarrels may arise over this. This is particularly so in the case of the secret society titles, for the ownership of shrines associated with the titles are involved and each group claims them. Here the matter is settled by the senior title members in the village or villages concerned rather than by village elders.

Otherwise the affairs of the agnatic descent groups are carried out without external interference. By far the vast majority of disputes within the compound are settled there. Some between major patrilineages are resolved without recourse to outside agencies. The activities associated with the ancestral shrine are not the elders' concern, nor are the means by which each descent group controls its members, divides its farmland for use, or its house site for building. In domestic affairs the village elders stay as aloof as possible. The autonomy of the agnatic groupings is highly respected.

In the case of the smaller villages in Afikpo, those with only one to five compounds and one or two wards, the village organization tends to resemble a condition of cooperating independent patrilineages without a great deal of authority over them at all. The small population makes it difficult for these settlements to have a full-fledged and extensive age system and the secret society is not as active or as functional as in the medium-sized and large villages. And here we generally find that the agnatic rule of remarriage exogamy is applied to the whole village, although not all patrilineal groupings within it are related to one another. In these smaller villages the autonomy of the major patrilineages with respect to the elders, the age structure, and the secret society, seems even greater than in the larger settlements. This appears also to be so for the small subvillages which exist as part of most of the larger villages, located a half a mile or so from the main settlement. These are usually wards of the larger village. They do not take as great a part in village affairs as the main village sections; many have their own special shrines and some even their own farmland divided into six sections. They tend to arrange matters among themselves in a rather informal manner without reference to the larger settlement.

MATRILINEALITY AND THE VILLAGE

The relationship of the matrilineal groupings to the village structure is considerably more limited. While every village contains members of numerous matrilineages and matriclans there is no formal integration of these groupings in the village, and there is no direct relationship involved. This may seem paradoxical since the majority of the land in the village farming area is actually owned and controlled by uterine groups. The rituals performed by the village for success in farming and the other village activities associated with agriculture that we have just mentioned are carried out for this land as well as for patrilineal holdings—they are the same acts. But persons often farm matrilineal land in a number of villages other than their own, frequently neighboring ones. The village rituals are believed, by a principle of extension, to be efficacious to its villagers in all their farming activities, whether the land involved is in that village or another. Further, these rituals and activities also cover village land farmed by persons from other villages. The Afikpo are ritually generous. The general supportive role of the village in matrilineal land holdings is extremely important, although the village does not take part in the numerous disputes or disagreements concerning its actual ownership, or is it concerned with its division for use at the beginning of the farming season.

In turn there is, as in the case of agnatic units, the penetration of the leadership structure and authority pattern in the matrilineal clan of the age set and grade system of the villages, insofar as the clan's elders and leaders are concerned. The basis of clan leadership is eldership in the villages (and the village-group), regardless of what villages the individual belongs to. This is also true in the matrilineages with regard to the head, where authority goes to the senior person by age. The age system of organizing authority thus enters the uterine groupings despite the lack of a formal association between these descent organizations and the village.

Beyond the matters of land and of age organization there is little direct connection between the two forms of groupings. Members of the slave matriclan, *ibɛ osim,* are restricted in the village, as we have seen, but they can join age groupings and the secret society, can take titles, and today they can even farm land in the village area if they have access to it through their agnatic or ward ties.

Matrilineal groupings do not, as a rule, control shrines which are for village welfare. Membership in a well-known or prominent matrilineal clan does not automatically give a person special prestige or leadership in his village—this has nothing to do with village government. The matrilineal groupings play virtually no role in the childhood socialization process for village life, unlike the agnatic groupings. However, the heads of the matrilineages, who, as we have seen, may in some instances be middle-aged, gain valuable experience in property manipulation and in the opportunity to direct others, which may profit them as elders in their villages. Such persons sometimes are or become prominent village leaders. Thus there is an avenue open to acquiring leadership experience for persons who in their patrilineal alignments may not be members of the older village lineages.

The uterine groups do not concern themselves or interfere with village affairs, and neither does the village with the internal or external business of the matrilineal groupings. The uterine groupings are essentially external to the residentially based governmental organization at Afikpo.

AGNATION IN THE VILLAGE-GROUP STRUCTURE

Although the villages which form Afikpo exhibit a high degree of autonomy from one another, there is an integrating organization, the Afikpo elders, who hold certain controls. Also, there are

common village-group properties: a public market, a central
meeting place for the Afikpo elders, and a beach on the Cross
River. And a number of agnatically controlled shrines function
for the benefit of the village-group as a whole. Further, the Afikpo
villagers are grouped into five subgroups and there are agnatic
ties between villages within and across these subgroupings. We
only mention here those aspects of the village-group structure
which are relevant to the analysis of descent.

Ties of patrilineality crisscross the village settlement pattern.
Some of these are due to the common practice of men taking
wives from villages other than their own. This links persons from
major patrilineages in different villages, often neighboring ones,
since marriages tend to be of persons from nearby rather than
distant settlements. But for a man matrimony does not establish a
very detailed link with the wife's agnatic grouping, although for
the female it forms an important patrilineal tie.

Again, some patrilineages in different villages believe themselves to be of common origin from a specific area of Eastern
Nigeria, and are marked by some ritual specializations and a
sense of common identity. In other cases there is a clearly remembered genealogical tie between two major patrilineages, and in
some of these instances they share common remarriage taboos
and farmland, even occasionally secret society title organizations.
We have called these linked major patrilineages by virtue of some
organizational interactivity (see "Fission, Accretion, and Extinction" in chap. ii). And a major patrilineage sometimes carries
out activities with a village where its ancestors once resided. For
example, an agnatic grouping in Amuro still returns to its former
home in another village for secret society activities, though it
otherwise takes part in Amuro village life.

The Afikpo villages are divided into five subgroups, each with
a more or less distinct geographical location and with some
cultural distinctiveness (see Table 1 and Map 4). Each carries
out certain of the general Afikpo feasts at a different time. The
patrilineages within each subgroup are more likely to be connected in terms of a similar home origin outside of Afikpo, or

TABLE 1

THE SUBGROUPS OF AFIKPO *

Subgroup	Population †	Villages
Mkpoghoro	3,662	Mkpoghoro (Ndibe)
Ugwuego	3,020	Ugwuego Elu Amaizu
Itim	6,437	Kpogrikpo Anohia Mgbom Amuro Anohia Nkalo
Ahisu	7,671	Amachara Ukpa Ibi Amamgballa Amachi Ngodo Egeburu Evuma
Ozizza	5,515	Amɔzera Amikpo Amorie Ameta Orra Imama

* See Map 4.

† Population figures based on Nigeria, Census Superintendent (1953–54, Pt. IV, pp. 25–26).

through agnatic ties, than they are to patrilineages external to the subgroup. For example, the two central villages which make up the subgroup of Ugwuego have a number of major patrilineages which claim to be of pre-Igbo stock, and these villages carry out certain ritual activities which are in some ways unique to them. Similarly, the southern subgroup, Itim, contains a considerable number of major patrilineages which derive from nearby Edda Village-Group, and these Itim villages have somewhat different forms of the secret society than most of the rest of Afikpo. Yet a

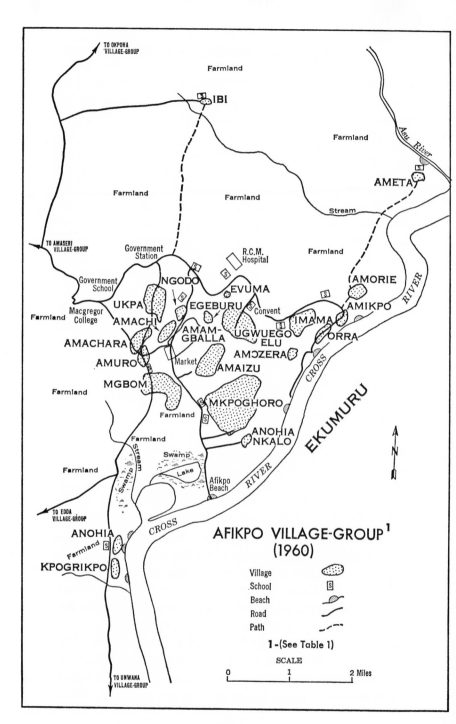

TO OKPOHA
VILLAGE-GROUP

Farmland

IBI

Asu River

Farmland

Farmland

Farmland

Farmland

AMETA

Stream

TO AMASERI
VILLAGE-GROUP

Government
Station

R.C.M.
Hospital

Farmland

Government
School

NGODO

EVUMA

AMORIE

UKPA

EGEBURU

Convent

AMIKPO

Farmland

Macgregor
College

AMACHI

AMAM-
GBALLA

UGWUEGO
ELU

IMAMA

AMACHARA

AMJZERA

ORRA

AMURO

Market

AMAIZU

MGBOM

CROSS

Farmland

MKPOGHORO

EKUMURU

Farmland

Farmland

ANOHIA
NKALO

N

Stream

Swamp

Farmland

Lake

Afikpo
Beach

CROSS RIVER

Farmland

TO EDDA
VILLAGE-GROUP

Swamp

CROSS

ANOHIA

AFIKPO VILLAGE-GROUP[1]
(1960)

Farmland

KPOGRIKPO

Village

School

Beach

Road

Path

1-(See Table 1)

SCALE

0   1   2 Miles

TO UNWANA
VILLAGE-GROUP

Map IV

fair number of these agnatic ties that we have just discussed cut across the Afikpo subgroupings; they are by no means all internal to them.

Agnation, therefore, links the patrilineage groupings in different villages, providing for a network of ties, divisions, and unities, which cut across villages, forming a complex network within which the framework of the village-group organization is found.

The Afikpo elders, who are, in fact, the village elders taken collectively, have a grade organization composed of three subgrades which act separately for some purposes and jointly for others, in a system similar to the village age structure. The junior elders' subgrade of Afikpo, composed of men in their fifties and early sixties, functions as the elders' police arm, investigates disputes for them, and keeps peace in the Afikpo market. It also collects fines for violations of rulings of these elders. The middle subgrade of elders contains the most influential seniors in the village-group. It tries minor cases at the market and until recently controlled this place of business. It sets the bride price and plays an important role in the New Yam Festival and some other rituals. The senior subgrade usually consists of only a few members, who hold important honorary positions in Afikpo and carry out a few rituals crucial for the village-group, but its members are too old and weak to rule.

Each subgrade has its own meeting shed at the Afikpo market; the elders also have a general gathering place nearby where they join together. As a grade they try to maintain traditional custom, to direct its change when necessary, and they act to oppose and to accommodate external governmental agents of change. They are usually involved in trying to resolve a series of endemic intervillage disputes in Afikpo, but without much success. They represent the village-group in its rather limited external relationships with neighboring village-groups. They pass rulings to control the movement of Afikpo to neighboring markets, and for other purposes, but their legislative role is not large. As individuals the elders are asked to take part in settling cases arising out of disputes between persons and between descent groupings. This is a very important function which helps to end divisiveness in the village group.

Within each of these groupings of the village-group elders and among the elders as a whole, decision-making is by consensus, as in the villages. The elders' authority in the village-group is not very great, and there is no highly centralized government in Afikpo. If villages or sections of Afikpo reject the elders' view little can be done to implement them. But these men symbolize the village-group as a whole, and as against other neighboring village-groups.

What is the relationship of their structure of authority to the patrilineal groupings? In general the Afikpo leaders are also the prominent elders in the various villages in the more central parts of Afikpo. Those from the more northern (Ozizza subgroup) and southern villages (Anohia and Kpogrikpo) are much less active, for the distance is too great. Thus there is a tendency for leadership to come from the supposed older major patrilineages of the central villages, especially from those in the larger settlements, and those of early Aro Chuku origin, the *amadi*. However, as in the villages, there is opportunity for others to lead, and the age principle is a pervasive one. But the agnatic influence is clear and it is important in the control of village-group affairs; decision-making tends to be controlled by membership drawn from a limited number of patrilineages. Similarly, the intervillage disputes at Afikpo tend to range men of prominent patrilineages in some villages against similar persons in others, though the disputes are generally phrased in intervillage terms. These disputes are difficult to resolve as the elders lack the right to apply clear-cut sanctions and they divide the elders themselves into camps and make their work difficult to carry out effectively. The elders of the village-group virtually never interfere in the internal affairs of the patrilineal groupings unless they judge as individuals in a special court, or as a group, matters brought to them for litigation.

The agnatic influence in the village-group is also present in terms of the role of certain shrines which are owned and controlled by major patrilineages and yet are for the use and welfare of the village-group as a whole, or in some cases any of its groups or individuals. The major patrilineages involved are of diverse origin and located in various villages, though mainly in the more central Afikpo area. Almost every village has some major patrilineage which has a special role in the village-group. The patrilineages controlling these shrines are not necessarily the ones which provide the bulk of the village and village-group leadership. In some cases they are, in others they are not. This lack of concentration of ritual activities in a single or a few agnatic groupings characterizes Afikpo religion and government. In some cases there is a close and generally positive tie between the leaders of the major patrilineages and the Afikpo elders in carrying out ceremonies for the benefit of the whole of Afikpo. And each major patrilineage having such a shrine, except in the case of those of Aro origins, is essentially autonomous in terms of other like ones. The controlling group selects the shrine priest from among its male members who take part in its rituals.

Perhaps the lineages associated with the yam shrines play the most important role. There are actually two such groups, one for the older and first yam shrine, in Anohia Nkalo village, and the other at Mkpoghoro. There has been, for some years, a dispute over ritual priority between these two which is part of a long-standing general quarrel involving many Afikpo villages which cannot be detailed here. The priests of both, when they are not disputing with one another or with the Afikpo elders, join with the latter in performing rituals and determining the time for the planting and harvesting of yams and for the New Yam Festival, carried out in all the Afikpo villages. These rituals and activities are considered necessary for the welfare of the village-group, the Yam Festival being the most important feast in Afikpo.

The Rain Controller's patrilineage, located in Mgbom village, is through its priest concerned with the regulation of the weather to prevent too much rain which would flood the farms, as well as too little which would inhibit the growth of crops. The middle Afikpo subgrade of elders gives annual presents to the Rain Controller to encourage his work, and individual villages ask him to insure good weather for their important feast days. There is considerable criticism of the priest's actions broached by the Afikpo elders for failure to insure good weather, and the relationship between this descent group and these senior men has been an uneasy one for many years. But each clearly needs the other.

There is one type of major patrilineage, already briefly mentioned in this chapter, which formerly played a very important ritual and judicial role in Afikpo, crosscutting the elders' group and giving Afikpo a measure of centralized authority. This is associated with one of the most important types of shrines, called *ɔtɔsi*. At one time this shrine played a significant role, not only with regard to the patrilineages which possessed it but also in the village and village-group. Of the two hundred or more major patrilineages in Afikpo more than thirty-five, spread throughout almost all of its villages, own this shrine. These major patrilineages were formerly called *amadi* (roughly translated as "freeborn"), in contrast to *ogbeyi*, or nonowners. The shrine originated at Aro Chuku and was brought to Afikpo by Aro when they came to settle there (cf. Anon., n.d.:5–6; Umo, n.d.:81–83). These are not the Aro who are presently at Afikpo as oracle agents, but earlier settlers. Later some non-Aro patrilineages purchased it from the settlers,[4] and also became known as *amadi*. The shrine could be obtained either by a patrilineal grouping or by an individual, and in the latter case his agnatic line also came to share it. The *ɔtɔsi* was usually located in the rear of the patrilineage ancestral rest house of its owners. Its priest, normally an elder, was selected by the major patrilineage elders if the lineage had acquired it as a group, or by the minor patrilineage of a single purchaser.

There was no central shrine for all *amadi* in Afikpo, but there was an *amadi* center for each of the five subgroups of Afikpo, where the first shrine established in that subgroup was located.

---

[4] The price is said to have been about one hundred pounds by today's standards. The seller retained his own shrine, established a new one for the buyer, and taught him the necessary rituals.

This division was for the taking of a certain title, *uhie ci*, for the division of money and goods collected in return for judging certain disputes, and for the members to meet together. Slaves obtained by the *amadi*, who were heavily involved in the slave trade, were chained in the patrilineage rest houses of these five centers until they were sold or moved away, since the *amadi* cooperated with the Aro Chuku slave traders, whose activities in southeastern Nigeria continued until British control brought the trade to an end (S. Ottenberg, 1958).

Owners of the shrine were much feared by non-*amadi*. Only *amadi* had the right to have solid doors on their houses, and they could freely enter the house of non-*amadi* to search them. Until the 1930's they played a role in settling certain types of judicial cases, including theft, revenge for murder, blocking paths, cutting wood on fallow farmland, poisoning and sorcery, and defecation on paths, believed to be a form of evil magic. In all of these except murder, if there was no doubt as to a person's guilt the *amadi* was paid a heavy fine, or failing this, the person was sold into slavery. This was a frequent occurrence, since the fines were large. In the case of a known murderer, the *amadi* seized and held him until the matrilineal clan of the murdered person ransomed him.

If there were doubt as to the guilt of a person, the *amadi* of the village would try the case of wood-cutting, defecation, or road blocking; for the other crimes, their members from the Afikpo subgroup most concerned handled the matter. If the accused was found guilty the punishment was as described above. If he was declared innocent, his accusers paid a heavy fine. If the *amadi* were unable to reach a decision the accused could be made to swear his innocence at an Afikpo shrine. In any case, both accuser and accused paid a fee for having the case tried.

If a landowning group was threatened by another with seizure of its lands it could turn these over, in a form of pledge, to an *amadi* patrilineage, which could protect the land. This formed one of the important sources of agnatic land holdings in Afikpo. Money and goods collected by the *amadi* through fines, judicial fees, and the sale of slaves were divided systematically among their members. If it was a village case the *amadi* of that settlement took the major portion, though those from the Afikpo subgroup where the village was located also shared in the proceeds. If the matter involved a whole subgroup its *amadi* kept the largest share and gave those in other Afikpo subgroupings smaller portions, depending on how many of their members had helped. No matter how the division was made, the senior subgrade of the Afikpo elders were considered honorary *amadi* regardless of their patrilineal affiliations. The *amadi* elders played a significant role in village leadership, and the *amadi* link with the Aro agents was strong. The proscriptions on road-blocking and defecation on paths clearly related to the need for freedom of land movement in trade (S. and P. Ottenberg, 1962:121–28). The *amadi* patrilineages thus held special judicial and police powers. Common ownership of the ɔtɔsi shrine and a like place of origin for some of them united these patrilineages in different villages. They were virtually a separate and distinctive class at Afikpo and were considered so by others: more influential than other agnatic descent groups in village and village-group leadership, wealthier, and more prominent. Nevertheless, there were many important leaders who did not belong to this class, and the authority of the *amadi* was restricted to certain kinds of cases. They lacked special authority in land matters or in the important general rituals in Afikpo. They were not endogamous and their internal authority structure did not differ greatly from that of other patrilineal groupings.

The *amadi* are no longer influential in Afikpo in these ways and today carry out no judicial activities. Their power was destroyed during the 1930's by the British, who, in reorganizing the Afikpo Native Authority system, refused to accept them as a desirable "native institution." The British were aided in this by some non-*amadi* who wanted to see their power ended, and by a few acculturated *amadi* who felt they were too oppressive. Sacrifices are still offered at the ɔtɔsi shrines by their priests, and in the *uhie ci* title ceremony the *amadi* drums are still played.

Owners of this shrine have several times tried to revive their ancient powers and to claim superior authority in Afikpo, but their special influence has largely disappeared. But the *amadi,* often coming from the supposed older patrilineages in the villages, do play an influential role among the Afikpo elders, as we have seen.

There are also a small number of persons of more recent Aro descent living about Afikpo who act as agents of their oracle at Aro Chuku. While they sometimes play significant roles in activities in the descent groups and the villages, they belong to agnatic lineages at Aro Chuku and do not have anything more than minor patrilineage segments at Afikpo. They fall, therefore, largely outside the present discussion. They do play an important role, through their oracle, in settling some land cases.

There are also about half a dozen shrines in Afikpo for swearing oaths of innocence controlled by separate major patrilineages, and located in a number of villages. These are used in trying difficult cases, often where the evidence or the statements of persons are in doubt. An individual in the case is made to swear his lack of guilt and the accuracy of his evidence at one of the shrines. If he is lying it is believed that the shrine will make him ill or kill him within the year, but if he is innocent that no harm will befall him. These shrines are important in settling cases in Afikpo and are in frequent use.[5]

There are also some patrilineages which control special shrines for medical purposes. For example, there are some for eye trouble, at least one for curing madness, and others for the use of specialists in healing broken bones. Males of the major patrilineages involved are the "doctors" and provide medicines as well as invoking the power of the spirit of the shrine when afflicted individuals come for treatment. These are said to be long-term specialities brought by the founders of the lineages concerned when they settled in Afikpo. Another craft of a different kind, blacksmithing, was formerly associated with certain lineages

---

[5] Swearing is also occasionally carried out at the Rain Controller's shrine, a person's patrilineal ancestral shrine, or some other one.

which had shrines to help insure the efficacy of their work, but blacksmithing is today carried out by stranger Igbo who visit Afikpo for periods of time, mainly from the Ezza area. Finally, diviners in Afikpo tend to come from a small number of major patrilineages in the central villages, though in theory any male might "get the call" to do this work. They have a society which regulates the membership and working conditions, largely though not entirely dominated by the members from these few patrilineages, and which receives support from the Afikpo elders in maintaining standards. These specialists play a crucial role in sustaining and molding magico-religious beliefs through their interpretations of particular problems, as we might expect.

It is clear that agnation plays a crucial role in the religious and magical activities of the village-group, and that it is a major basis for the allocation of ritual specialist roles in Afikpo. This, coupled with its importance in the elders' groups and its place in linking together different settlements having a sense of common agnatic ancestry, give it a pervasive though not an overwhelming place in village-group affairs, in conjunction with the principles of age and residence.

In the still larger field beyond Afikpo there are ties with the four neighboring village-groups of Amaseri, Edda, Okpoha, and Unwana, culturally and historically related to Afikpo. Some Afikpo villages and patrilineages, for example, carry out forms of rituals which are similar in style to these others. And the members of one part Okpoma village in Edda Village-Group originally came from Afikpo, and join in certain Mgbom village activities, whence they derive. There is a sense of common patrilineal ties of the Afikpo with these neighboring village-groups which is not extended to non-Igbo ones to the east. But in the few relationships which the Afikpo elders carry out with these four Igbo neighbors agnatic ties play little direct role; it is the relationship of culturally similar groupings to one another through their elders which is the key tie. The link of the *amadi* patrilineages in the past with the more distantly located Aro Chuku Village-Group has already been explored.

THE MATRILINEAL CLANS IN THE VILLAGE-GROUP

The most striking features of the role of the matrilineal clans in the village-group are their lack of regularized relationships with one another and their disconnectedness from other Afikpo organizations. Clans do not meet for any common purpose other than when persons from two or more of them come together at some *rites de passage*, or other ceremony, or to hear a dispute argued involving their members, frequently over land. Even those matriclans which claim a common descent do not carry out any common ritual or activity unless they reunite in the manner already described (see "Fission, Segmentation, and Accretion" in chap. iii). The major ties are not between these uterine groupings as formal entities but are the complex interrelationships between individual members of different matrilineal groupings: essentially the relationships of individuals, rather than of groups with groups. These are discussed in the next chapter.

However, in pre-British times two major crimes, murder and theft, involved members of a matriclan with another, and with other groups in Afikpo. Murder (*ɔco*) called for blood revenge on the part of the dead person's clan. It was defined, in the first instance, as the killing, whether accidental or not, of a member of another matriclan in Afikpo than one's own. Poisoning and sorcery were excluded, being the concern of the specialist patrilineal groups, the *amadi*. If the deceased was of the same matriclan as the killer it was considered unfortunate, and rituals were performed to compensate for the death, but it was not murder. In some cases, as we have seen, this may have led to clan fission (see "Fission, Segmentation, and Accretion" in chap. iii). Similarly, the killing of a slave (*ohu*) or of a member of the special matrilineal clan of low status (*ibɛ osim*) was not murder but killing (*ogbobu*). This is true as well of murder within the nuclear family—of a father by his son, a child by a parent, or a wife by a husband. Though in these family cases the persons involved were generally of different clans, no revenge was involved. It was considered a domestic affair, unfortunate perhaps, but one in which no useful purpose could be served by revenge (which, of course, might involve another death in the same family). The best that could be done was to insure the proper burial of the dead person and the performance of certain rituals.

Murder seems to have occurred mainly through fighting over farm boundaries. In such conflicts within Afikpo, there was usually an attempt to wound and frighten without killing and to avoid fighting a clan member if possible. Disputes between individuals over other matters, such as courtship or theft accusations, also occasionally led to murder. If the assaulter reached his village square and could sweep a section of it in a ritual-like action before the wounded person died, this was interpreted by the Afikpo to mean that no clan revenge was involved since the death was not really due to the fight—a job of work had been done since it occurred. In Afikpo, such cases of "sweeping the village square" were tried by the Afikpo elders at Amuro village to determine if revenge was necessary, and if not what rituals should be performed to "cool" the matter (and the earth spirit, *ale*), and what compensation was to be paid.

If a man was suspected of murder but the Afikpo elders were not sure he was guilty, he would be sent by them to the Aro Chuku oracle where the case would be tried. If guilty, he was returned and killed in blood revenge.

In cases where revenge was indicated the clan of the killer was expected to provide a person for the murdered man's clan to kill, ideally a member of the killer's matrilineage. In fact it could be any adult clan member of either sex and any age, and he or she could be killed by any member of the deceased's clan, not necessarily the dead person's closest matrikinsmen. Clan leaders were frequently involved in the selection of the victim, or in locating a member of the killer's clan to be killed in revenge. Sometimes the members of the murdered man's lineage or clan were immediately able to locate the killer or a matrikinsman and would kill the individual on the spot. At other times members of the special patrilineal groupings, the *amadi*, seized the killer, or he fled to their protection, hiding in one of their shrine houses. The *amadi* would release him after the payment of ransom, either so that he could be killed in blood revenge or so that a substitute of the proper clan could be killed in his place. If he was not ransomed the *amadi* simply took advantage of the situation and sold him away as a slave. At still other times the killer's clan could not agree on whom to give up—the matrilineage of the murderer would often desire that the victim come from another part of the clan, and be perhaps an old woman or a "rascal" person. In this case the dead man's clan would lie in wait for a victim and the members of the killer's clan would hide, a difficult thing to do because of the widespread distribution of clan members. If the killer's clan could agree on a suitable victim, they would arrange for the waylaying of such a person by the other descent group. For example, in one case a man was cutting palm fruit bunches, one of which killed a child playing underneath the tree. The man's clan was asked to produce a victim. The man's mother offered herself to save her son, as she was old and did not want to see the son killed. The man's clan arranged for her to be waylaid and killed at the market place by members of the dead child's clan.

Once revenge had been taken hard feelings might still exist between the clans, but the matter was otherwise settled and no state of feud existed. It seems unlikely, given the dispersed nature of clan membership and the intermixture of clan members in residential units, that the clan feud as an institution could have occurred at Afikpo without the rapid disorganization of the society as it existed. There was also no principle of substituting someone into the killer's clan for the dead man instead of a revenge killing. However there were some cases where property, especially land, was given in place of a revenge killing, but this seems to have developed as a substitute for revenge after British occupation. Today the matter is taken to the police, and no blood revenge or compensation exists at all so far as could be determined. The clans concerned perform sacrifices at their shrines to "cool" the matter, as they also did in former times.

In the past, clan elders sometimes also played a significant role in cases of stealing, particularly of yams, this being considered an especially heinous crime. The thief might be beaten to death on the spot by those who caught him in the act, he might be struck down and then buried in or near the "bad bush" (*ɔtoto ɛja*) of his village, where persons who die unusual deaths are placed, or he might be seized by the *amadi* to be sold out of Afikpo into slavery. If he was killed clan revenge was not involved. If the man's matrilineage and clan were able to act quickly, and if they considered the thief worth ransoming, they could free him by purchasing him from the *amadi* at a high price. Compensation in land was sometimes given by the thief's matrilineage to that of the person whose property was stolen. Such land was permanently transferred and could not be returned. None of these situations normally arise today, the matter going to the police and then the Afikpo Native Authority Court, or the Magistrate's Court. The practice of having compensation for murder in the matrilineal sphere, whatever its historical origins, served to prevent serious frictions breaking out between governmental units at Afikpo, which would be the case if it was centered in the patrilineal groupings (cf. Forde, 1964:112–34).

We see, therefore, that in serious crimes the matrilineal clans were likely to become directly involved with governmental agencies in the village-group, as today they become so with Nigerian agencies which are external to it. But the clans do not form governmental sections or political action groups in Afikpo. It is true that the members, especially elders, of certain larger and wealthier clans play a somewhat more important role in Afikpo affairs than do others. There is some rivalry among the clans to see which have the most members (if any at all) who have taken the highest Afikpo title, *omumɛ*, but this title does not confer a special leadership position in Afikpo. Many of the Afikpo leaders come from these larger and wealthier clans, partly because of their numerical superiority and partly because they provide greater opportunities for experience in directing large groups of persons. Nevertheless, influential leaders do emerge from the smaller groupings. While it is true that larger clans provide better resources in leadership and in money to fight disputes, particularly in defending their lands from encroachment by other clans, there is little feeling that certain clans dominate Afikpo. There is no specific designated clan representation in the elders' groupings at Afikpo, and no feeling that members of all clans should be present before the village-group elders make important decisions, as there is to some extent that all villages should be represented.

Nevertheless, the Afikpo elders are much concerned with matrilineal affairs, especially land cases, which they try in specially arranged courts, matters which are time-consuming and slow of resolution. The elders consider their settlement crucial to the tranquility of the village-group, though cases of this kind are endemic, and the elders themselves, as members of uterine groupings, are heavily and personally involved in them. It is also true that the Afikpo elders forbade clan women to have their own unions or "meetings," and that they set the bride price in Afikpo, which indirectly affects matrilineal groupings. These men also apparently have the right to pass other rulings concerning the clans. But, on the whole, they are not anxious to interfere with clan autonomy, where they themselves play important leadership roles.

Although today the uterine groupings have no important shrines, in contrast to the patrilineal ones, which are for Afikpo as a whole, in former times the shrine associated with the slave matriclan played a ritual role for Afikpo (see "The Slave Matriclan" in chap. iii). Certainly the village-group elders attempted to prevent the cessation of the rituals carried out at the shrine, when slave clan members did not want to carry them out any longer. These elders had, and some still have, the feeling that the rituals were necessary for the welfare of Afikpo.

The neighboring Igbo village-groups of Amaseri, Okpoha, Edda, and Unwana have independently organized clans with the same names as those in Afikpo and recognize a common, if distant, origin. Clan sexual taboos and exogamic regulations are maintained for like-named clans in all five groups. Marriage of women into another of these village-groups than that of her place of birth has always been rare, for this creates a situation where she and her husband and their children have to travel to her village-group to have access to land holdings of her major matrilineage. Similarly men do not frequently move to another village-group, for they remove themselves from close access to their own lands and descent ties. However, in former times a poor person, often one without access to much land within his own matrilineage, could move to live with a rich man of a like-named clan to his own in any of the other village-groups. He could acquire land and assistance in marriage payments from this person and become active in that clan. Today, perhaps because there is greater flexibility of economic opportunity, moves of this kind do not seem as frequent, though enterprising farmers contact like-named clan members, or those of their wives, in neighboring village-groups and arrange for farmland. This seems to be particularly so of the Afikpo, whose land resources are now becoming scarce. Again, there are a few compounds in Edda Village-Group, particularly one section of Ɔkpoma village, whose members or their ancestors originated in Afikpo and who still join with the Afikpo matriclans rather than with those in Edda. This is considered to be a matter of choice and convenience. There is no record that any of these five Igbo village-groups has legislated to the effect that persons living within its borders must belong to its own clan groupings and not to external ones.

The rule of clan revenge was applicable to the neighboring Igbo village-groups of Unwana, Edda, and Okpoha, but not if an Afikpo killed a person from a like-named clan in one of these other village-groups. The killing of a member of any other village-group, whether Igbo or non-Igbo, did not involve revenge, and heads could be "taken" for status purposes. Indeed, many of these groups that the Afikpo fought, as far as to Enugu, had no matrilineal clans at all. Included here was the killing of persons from Amaseri Village-Group, which borders Afikpo. Although this Igbo group has like-named clans it was in a state of constant warfare with Afikpo, mainly over village land boundaries; thus Afikpo could "take a head" there without clan revenge.

Unwana Village-Group has a closer historical tie with Afikpo than the other three village-groups. As a result of this, and because of Unwana's small size, its clans have usually been anxious to maintain close relations with like-named ones in Afikpo. There have been times when during a serious land case involving Afikpo or an Unwana clan that its counterpart has helped to fight the case. In addition there have been sporadic attempts by the Afikpo and Unwana members of some of the young men's unions of like-named clans to join together. These have usually failed, partly because the distance between the two village-groups makes regular contact difficult.

Though the Afikpo are aware of a common history and interest with like-named clans in these neighboring Igbo groups, no such feeling exists with regard to their non-Igbo neighbors, the Agbo, Yakö, Ekumuru, and Erei (Enna). Here there is suspicion and hostility, and awareness that these non-Igbo groups also possess matrilineal organization but little knowledge of their nature and no sense of common uterine ties.

The Afikpo clans, like the clans of the other four neighboring Igbo groups, have a strong sense of identification with the people of Aro Chuku. While other Afikpo groups, such as the patrilineages and villages, have contacts with the Aro, these contacts are also characteristic of the matrilineal groupings. Many sections of matrilineal land are protected against seizure by shrines to *Ibini ɔkpabe*, the Aro oracle; the oracle may be consulted in the case of infertility of crops, or of clan members; its advice is sought in clan mergers, and in settling clan land disputes. There is little ethnographic information available concerning the Aro (see Forde and Jones, 1950; Easterfield and Uku, n.d.; Anon., n.d.; S. Ottenberg, 1958). The Aro at Afikpo were reluctant to talk, as many were acting as agents of their oracle, now an illegal activity. It appears however, that the Aro lack corporate matrilineal groupings, and that the association of the Afikpo clans is with the oracle and its agents, not with matrilineal organizations at Aro Chuku.

The role of Aro agents at Afikpo with regard to the matriclan is similar to that in the major patrilineages. They are informal advisers to the clan elders and priest on matters which may concern the oracle, and they encourage these clan leaders to hire them and to make use of the oracle. Because of their prestige their advice is seriously considered, but they are not a formal part of the clan administration and are not normally clan members themselves.

DESCENT AND THE LARGER SPHERE

The main theme running through this chapter is the intimate manner in which the patrilineal groupings are joined together to form the larger residential structure and Afikpo government in contrast to the isolation, and to some extent the hostility, of matriclans to one another, coupled with their lack of a distinct interconnection to the larger structures of Afikpo. More than with the neighboring Yakö, the fact that the patrilineal groupings have a residential feature relates closely to their governmental roles, in contrast to the uterine groupings. Yet the links of matrilineality, in the dispersed residential nature of the uterine groupings, helps reduce an isolation of the members of villages from other villages that might occur in a more purely patrilineal condition, even though here there are certainly agnatic ties between persons in different villages as well. But the very condition of matrilineality, which ties together persons of different villages, gives the uterine groupings little place in government.

And over and over again at both the level of the village and the village-group there is another theme. This is that the older and specialized patrilineages have favored positions in the governmental structure, operating in contrast to the principle of selection for leadership and authority on the basis of age and personal qualities. For the uterine groupings this is not the case. And the control of many of the major shrines in Afikpo by agnatic groupings gives them a crucial ritual role in contrast to that for the matrilineal organizations.

Some aspects of the governmental position of the matriclans have disappeared, of course, following British control in the area, especially clan revenge and the special role, ritual and otherwise, that the slave matriclan played at Afikpo. On the converse side, there has also been a reduction, as the position of the patrilineal *amadi* groupings is no longer of great significance. The two descent lines have, and still play, largely complementary rather than antagonistic or conflicting roles in the larger arena of Afikpo.

V. DOUBLE DESCENT
AND THE INDIVIDUAL

U P to this point in the analysis we have examined double descent in terms of formal structures. We have been concerned with the organization of the unilineal groupings, and their internal functions and activities. And we have viewed their external relationships with like descent groups and with the residentially based organizations. In this analysis the individual has not loomed very large.

The Afikpo, as it is probably evident, do not usually view descent in terms of seeing these structures as wholes. They provide data for the anthropologist to analyze which enable him to construct a model. But while they are familiar with the details of their own ethnography they do not perceive it and act toward it in quite this manner. In fact, it is not easy to say how they view double descent. Doubtless they do not even view it as a totality. But from the way in which they talk about it and act it out, the following suggestions can be made:

1. An Afikpo sees the relationships of descent as a series of ties to other individuals for specific purposes, with an acute awareness of what descent groups the individuals belong to and how these groups are linked to him and his descent groupings.

2. In some cases he does not think and act in terms of major and minor patrilineage, matrilineage, and matriclan, but in terms of descent lines, often no more than three or four generations in depth, and in terms of persons in authority to him or over whom he has authority in these lines. It is his own immediate lines which are most important to him, at times, and not his groups of descent as a whole.

3. He sees his field of activity with other persons in descent relationships not as one with highly rigid behavioral requirements in which he cannot select, but as a situation where he has considerable alternatives for action, and where he weighs his various descent ties against one another in terms of his needs and acts toward persons accordingly. In short, he lives in a field of varied and multiple ties where he has choice.

4. In double descent the individual plays a large number of roles in terms of complex sets of ties with many persons. To an outsider he may, at times, seem to play contradictory roles, but he does not usually view them as such, with a few notable exceptions.

This, however, is not a study in Afikpo perception. The field research, being of a routine anthropological nature, did not employ the kinds of skills necessary for such an analysis. But we can profitably distinguish this interpersonal level of analysis from the more formal study of the groups as entities. We can also show the links between an approach in terms of individual relationships and one stressing group structure, a point to be discussed in the final chapter.

But let us be perfectly clear. There are all sorts of kin relationships (using "kin" in its broadest sense) between persons other than descent, but we are primarily concerned here with those between individuals that involve at least the descent group of one of them. Thus at Afikpo there are domestic relationships that do not directly involve descent (P. Ottenberg, 1958; 1959; 1963). We are not treating the whole system of kin ties, only unilineal descent. We are concerned with ties between individuals in which: (1) the descent groups to which they belong put them in a special position in relationship to one another over property, rituals, or some other concern of at least one descent group; (2) an individual has a special relationship to persons in a descent group to which he himself does not belong, but is linked through marriage or through having a parent who is a member.

If neither one of these conditions is met we are not concerned here in the analysis, except to provide background information.

The matter is not simple since various types of relationships go on between persons and it is difficult to ferret out their exact nature. For example, at Afikpo a brother and a sister belong to the same patrilineal and matrilineal groupings, have the same parents, and some of their relationships may express one tie or the other. And there may be still other bonds between them that are not of either but simply express domestic ties. Or a boy and his father are linked because of membership in the same patrilineal grouping, because the father has obligations to his wife's matrilineal groupings in the name of the son who is also a member, because the son has rights in his father's matrilineage, and because there are also ties of a purely domestic kind between father and son. Schneider (1962) has shown quite clearly the danger, which he attributes to those who tend to view kinship mainly from the point of view of descent, in assuming that certain ties are necessarily of descent rather than of domestic relationships simply because the persons involved belong to the same unilineal descent group and it looks as if the ties should be descent links. For example, on Yap certain behavior of sister's children with their mother's brother are not necessarily matrilineal even though matrilineal descent exists; the same is so with a person and his father's sister on the patrilineal side where agnatic descent is also found. In our analysis we hope to make these distinctions clear and to eliminate as much as possible those relationships that seem to be purely domestic and not of descent, for, after all, the focus of the study is on unilineality.

However, in studying the network of role relationships associated with the descent structure, we start with their operation within the domestic groupings. In no other area in Afikpo are the links of individuals to individuals representing many descent groupings so closely meshed. We then go to ties that include but go beyond these groupings in considering burial rites, inheritance and succession, the establishment of shrines by individuals, and the control and use of farmland. These comprise the major areas in which the web of descent occur. Though others exist, such as in reincarnation, they suffice to show the pattern of role relationships in which persons are involved.

THE DOMESTIC GROUPINGS

The most desired form of family in Afikpo is polygynous in nature, perhaps with three or four wives, and with numerous children. Here we usually find a situation in which the husband and his children belong to the same patrilineal grouping, but his wives to different ones from him and often from one another. These women are also of different matrilineal affiliation from him, and again, often from one another, and his children belong to his wives' uterine groupings and not his own. This is the key pattern of the family at Afikpo in terms of descent. It is established by matriclan exogamy, the considerable tendency of males to marry outside of their own patrilineal groupings, and the habit of men marrying females of diverse agnatic and uterine background. The kinds of organization, interests, and functions of the descent groupings, as we have described them, work themselves out in the framework of the domestic groupings. Let us look at some of the details.

In the polygynous family each wife and her children generally comprise a separate unit, *ulo,* roughly translated as "house." They live in their own dwelling and form a matricentric group of which the husband is not a member. The husband, who lives alone, is responsible for the welfare of his wives and children, but the immediate needs of the younger children are met by the wives. The first wife has little authority over the others, each having a relatively independent, and supposedly equal, relationship with the husband.[1] The wives generally are from different matrilineal clans in Afikpo, or at least different matrilineages of a clan. Marriage to a wife's sister is not favored for a man except on the grounds that the two women will get along well, since it gives the husband access neither to more matrilineal farmlands nor new social contacts. Thus wives frequently come from different matrilineal backgrounds as well as from different villages and compounds, and thus they come from different patrilineal groupings as well. They are strangers to one another. These differences in origin are reinforced by the fact that wives often live among other persons in different parts of the husband's compound, as he is able to obtain houses for them. The husband usually does not attempt to bring them together; he may in fact fear that this will only lead to quarreling and accusations of poisoning and sorcery among them.

As soon after marriage as possible, especially when she is bearing a child, a man obtains a house for a wife. Some husbands give a bride a small sum of money to start trading, in which most women engage. Though this practice is becoming more common today, men often feel that a wife should produce enough from her farming activities to start trading on her own. While the husband provides clothing, wives must secure much of the food for themselves and their children. Exceptions are yams, which the man grows, and palm oil, for which he often collects the fruits. In practice, many husbands give their wives a little money now and then for food, as well as soap, cosmetics, kerosene, and other items. Therefore, not only is there a sense of independence of each wife from the other, but also of each from the husband.

A husband must see that each wife has sufficient farmland for her own and her children's needs. He may obtain this from his major and minor patrilineages and from his father's matriline-

[1] The first wife, however, teaches new wives joining the family the daily routine, and they sometimes live with her until they get their own houses. The junior wives must fetch water for the first wife as well as performing certain other duties for her. See P. Ottenberg (1958, chap. ix).

age, though the source of much of his land is from his own matrilineage. As an affinal relative of a wife's matrilineage he also gets land from this group for her and her children. Of the land thus obtained, he farms some jointly with his wives, gives some to them to farm alone, and cultivates the rest himself or shares it with male relatives and friends. A wife usually has only a vague idea of who actually controls the land she is using or where it was obtained. Her main concern is that she has plots adequate for her needs and that they are not smaller than those of her cowives.

Except for the planting and harvesting of yams, cowives rarely work together, nor are they expected to. However, some do get along well, and one may care for the other's infant when she is away, or they may help each other in cooking or other ways. But the basic pattern is that each "house" is a separate unit, the wives going their separate ways, seeking help in domestic matters from female friends in the compound, not from cowives.

A husband helps his wife with the cost of taking titles, performing age set ceremonies, offering sacrifices, consulting diviners and herbalists, and supports her when she is involved in a dispute with persons outside the family. After she has borne a child she stays at home and cares for it for a period of several months or more. At this time she is dependent upon her husband and he is expected to treat her with special care. A woman is not supposed to have sexual intercourse during the period of lactation, about two years, though this customary rule is frequently violated.

The principle of the husband's equal treatment of wives pervades all family relationships. By so doing symbolically he is treating their respective uterine groupings with equality. Not only farmland but money, cloth, and other items must be given out in roughly equal amounts. The husband must allow them equal sexual access to him and not publicly distinguish between them as to personal qualities, number of children, or in other ways. The relationships of wives to him are of individuals, not of women acting as a group. If the latter were so, they would merge socially and lose their various uterine identities.[2]

Children in Afikpo represent wealth and are a source of pride and prestige, and are believed necessary so that men may carry out certain ceremonial obligations. They are loved and well treated by their parents and other adults, and success or failure in marriage is sometimes dependent on whether any children are born of the union. The desire for children is linked with the wish to perpetuate and enlarge the descent groups, and with the pattern of prestige and achievement.

The eldest son of each "house," as he matures, acquires authority in this family unit, especially as matrilineal ties become more vital to him and his full siblings. As an adult, he is partly responsible for seeing that matrilineal land is provided for his full brothers as they grow up and for his sisters after they are married. If his father is dead he is in charge of funeral ceremonies for his mother, though her eldest daughter and other relatives play important roles. When the eldest son is still a boy, he holds little authority over his brothers or sisters and is not particularly concerned with matrilineal matters. Likewise other sons of the house show this lack of concern. But as adults, sons of different mothers develop separate interests which divide them around their respective matrilineal groupings.

Yet paradoxically, for other interests of a patrilineal sort they are drawn closer together. At the age of five or six a son leaves his mother's house and lives, until marriage, in one of the boys' houses (*ulote*) in the compound, though he may sometimes sleep in his father's home. At the *ulote* the youths sleep, study if they are students, make mats to sell at the market, and play games; they are still fed by their mothers. A boy usually lives in such a house near his father, if the latter is alive. If not, he may occupy one near the head of the extended family and become a kind of

---

[2] It is interesting to observe that in patrilineal Igbo societies there is usually greater status differentiation between the wives of a man than at Afikpo; they are more cooperative and they are not treated so individually by the husband.

servant to him, carrying messages, helping carry tools to the
farms and yams from them, and so on, tasks he would have done
for his father if he were alive. The boy learns much about
farming and matters affecting men in general, and makes useful
social contacts with relatives and friends of his father and the
head of his extended family. Sons of a man are thus drawn
together, by their maleness, around their father and the head of
the extended family, regardless of their differing maternal ties.

The eldest daughter of the "house" supervises her younger
sisters and brothers who have not yet moved away from the
mother's home. She is subject to her mother's authority, and the
amount of influence she actually has varies among families. She
may send the younger children on errands, have them fetch water
or help with preparation of food and farming. If a first-born child
in the house is a girl, she may even hold a position of influence
over younger brothers in matrilineal matters affecting the family
after her marriage. For females of the house the major ties are
with the mother until they marry. Sisters of different mothers are
not brought together around a common father figure as are their
brothers.

When daughters marry they often move to different parts of
the village or to different villages, and lose most of their contacts
with one another. They return home for informal visits, as well as
for funerals, the taking of titles, and other ceremonies, and
occasionally to perform a sacrifice to insure fertility, but their
patrilineal ties after marriage are secondary. Their ties with their
brothers and mother remain strong and fruitful, with their father
very much less so.

Though most men have two or more wives at some point in
their lives, monogamous families are common. Here the tensions
which enliven relationships among cowives are lacking, and the
wife gauges her husband's treatment of her in terms of how her
friends and relations are treated by their husbands. Here the
question of the nature of the relationships of half-siblings does
not arise, but the pattern of behavior which she establishes with
her husband will be a standard by which any later wife of the

husband can measure her own behavior. The basic links of descent are the same as in the polygynous family.

When patrilineal relatives, friends, and age mates feel a man is old enough to marry, or wealthy enough to take an additional wife, they and his father, if he is still alive, bring pressure on him by offering to arrange a match and sometimes by helping to pay the bride price if he or his father is unable to do so. If a man refuses to marry over a long period of time, he will be accused of being miserly and of not helping the patrilineage increase its wealth in children. Marriage is considered a major and minor patrilineage function. No formal action is taken against him, but his position in his patrilineage may be affected since, unless he has an unusually good reason, he will be considered odd and will lose prestige. Most men, however, actively seek wives, though sometimes holding off until their investments in farming, trading, or some other enterprise begin to pay off.

If it is a first marriage, the father will often pay the bride price and other ceremonial costs, and may arrange for the marriage. Otherwise the man does it himself. The marriage proceedings bring father and son and their patrilineal relatives into contact with the girl's patrikinsmen, but there is little contact between them afterward except through courtesy visits, or when there is trouble with the marriage. The key tie of marriage is that of the husband with his wife's matrikinsmen, mainly over farmland of her group and with regard to their children. When Afikpo men consider an "advantageous" marriage, they often like to marry a girl from a large and influential major patrilineage, but they may be more directly concerned with the wealth and landholdings of her matrikinsmen.

Marriage brings a woman into contact with her husband's patrilineal groupings, but she is not incorporated into them. She develops much fewer direct, significant ties with his matrilineal relations, although she may farm his matrilineal land. The primary tie of marriage for the husband is with his wife's matrikinsmen, for the wife, with her husband's patrilineal groups. In each case the other descent group plays a less significant role.

When a marriage is being arranged, the parents of the prospective bridegroom go to the girl's parents, or sometimes send a friend or compound relative, to state that the bridegroom is prepared to pay the bride wealth of five pounds.[3] The bridewealth ceremony itself is normally held in the compound where the girl's legal father dwells, whether she lives there or not. Neither the girl nor her groom is normally present, and women do not usually take part in this ceremony. The bridegroom chooses a man of his compound, frequently a member of his minor patrilineage who is a good speaker, to see that the food and drink are provided for the ceremony and to pay the five pounds. The bridegroom also provides the food, and either he or his father contributes the bride wealth. This representative is accompanied by other compound elders, particularly members of his minor patrilineage and his father and brothers, all of whom act as witnesses. No representatives of his clan or matrilineage need to be present, though one or two may attend. The girl's father chooses a good speaker, normally one of his patrikinsmen, to receive the food and the bride wealth. Her patrilineal relatives, including her father and brothers and other men of the compound, are present at the event. Several men from her matrilineage witness the ceremony. It is considered more important that representatives of the girl's matrilineage be present than those of the future husband, since the children of the marriage belong to the former grouping. However, this ritual, the legally binding part of the marriage rite, is primarily the concern of patrilineal groupings.

Examination of what happens to the bride price after it is received reveals that matrilineal factors are also operative. The girl's father receives three pounds, her mother the remaining two. He usually gives several shillings of his share to the members of his compound, clearly a gift to members of a residential grouping. He also gives a few shillings to the elders of his minor

[3] This is the "official" price, set by the Afikpo elders. The actual payments are usually higher, although the principle of division of the bride wealth is the same.

patrilineage. He spends or keeps the rest as he wishes. The girl's mother sees that the male elders of her husband's compound receive a few shillings, and sometimes her matrilineage elders as well. She keeps the rest and is expected to buy her daughter's household equipment with it. Both parents give small sums to friends or other patrilineal or matrilineal relatives as gifts to express their pleasure. There is no notion that this bride price money should be reserved to marry off a son; the money can be used as the parents determine.

If the girl's father is dead, a representative of his matrilineage receives the three pounds and gives shares as the father would. The remainder is divided among the men of the matrilineage. The stepfather, if there is one, may be given a share by the matrilineage, but their members are not obliged to do so, and whether this is actually done depends on how friendly their relationship is. If the mother is dead, a close female relative of her matrilineage, often a sister, receives the money and passes out shares as the mother would, the matrilineal relatives sharing the remainder. Usually they give the stepmother a substantial portion, regardless of whether or not she is matrilineally related to them, in recognition of the time and effort involved in rearing the child. This disposition of the bride wealth in the case of the death of one or both parents follows the normal Afikpo pattern of matrilineal inheritance of movable property. Thus, while ceremonial marriage obligations are primarily patrilineal, legal rights to the bride wealth have a matrilineal aspect. The marriage ritual symbolizes the breaking of the girl's ties with her agnatic groupings and the establishment of a new form of relationship with her husband's patrilineal groupings. But the matter of the bride wealth symbolizes the property and legal rights which her uterine groups retain in connection with her.

The preferred form of marriage in Afikpo is for a man to marry a daughter of his father's sister, that is, marriage into his father's matrilineage. The reasons for this have mainly to do with land controls. A man has the right to use the land of his father's matrilineage, as a "son" of the lineage, but he cannot normally pass this right to his own sons, for they are considered to be too distantly related.[4] However, a man sometimes has strong interests in land of his father's matrilineage to which he wishes his sons to have access. This is possible if he marries a woman of this lineage, since his children by this wife will have legal rights to the land. Children of his other wives, if of different lineages or clans, have courtesy rights. The man thus farms the land not only as a "son" of the lineage, but also as the husband of a member, and he holds the land in trust for his sons by this wife. Though no detailed figures are available, this form of marriage is common, occurring in about one out of eight marriages.

A man who marries in this manner is not necessarily more "patrilineally minded" than others, and he may take an active interest in his own matrilineal groupings. He may view this form of marriage as a channel through which he can maintain control over land he is already farming, through persons whom he already knows. There are benefits to marrying outside a father's matrilineage, of course, as in cases where the wife is from an influential matrilineage grouping or one which has a great deal of land. Marriage into his father's matrilineage does not give him access to new land resources, though he may be able to somewhat increase his holdings. If a man does not marry in the preferred manner he will have to deal with matrilineal relatives of his wives, who may be strangers and whom he may not trust. Again, a man's father's matrilineage may favor the preferred form of marriage since the girl marries someone whom the matrilineage already knows and who is already active and interested in the land of the group. If such a marriage is repeated in alternate generations it means, in effect, that matrilineal land is passing in the agnatic line. This does not, however, mean that the land passes under the control of patrilineal groupings.

In divorce the wife must leave the compound, and we have already seen that a rule of patrilineal remarriage exogamy exists and have discussed its implications. There is no formal rule that

[4] Females, however, do not seem to have access to their father's matrilineal land to any extent.

she cannot remarry another member of his matriclan; there is no implication here that she possibly has caused the man's death to marry a matrikinsman of his as in the equivalent case in patrilineal affairs. However, if a woman divorces her husband she will not usually remarry into his clan. If she attempted to do so the former husband could complain to the clan elders who would pressure the intended husband to desist. Such a marriage is believed to produce hostile feelings among clan members.

If she does not remarry there is usually no refund of the bride price. If she does find another to marry it is a matter of negotiations between him and the husband, the amount of repayment of this and of other things, such as the cost of courtship presents, varying with the presence or absence of children and the reasons for the breakup of the marriage. In this patrilineal relatives of both men take part.

Divorce and remarriage are common; both husbands and wives are often skeptical about the permanence of marriage. It is a common belief among men that there is something incomprehensible about women, that no matter what a man does to please his wife she is likely to leave him. Since men are free to remarry among many women living outside their compound they often look for new wives among the married as well as the single, while women are on the lookout for new husbands if a marriage is unsatisfactory.

But there are also structural reasons. The wife cannot be fully incorporated into her husband's patrilineal groupings without breaking her matrilineal ties, her links with her brothers and matrilineage head. Nor does her husband wish for this, as these ties are a major source of farmland for him and his children. And the presence of these matrilineal descent ties divides wives from one another, and distinguishes nonuterine siblings. The hostility and competitiveness of a man's cowives (P. Ottenberg, 1958, chap. vi) mirrors the suspicion and hostility that sometimes occur among matrilineal groupings, especially in land cases, as we shall see. This divisiveness is probably much greater than if there were only patrilineal groupings in Afikpo. So there is a sense of social distance in the wife's ties to the husband's agnatic groupings and to her cowives. It is perhaps this which the men are really complaining about. The rule of remarriage exogamy in the major patrilineage further states this principle: the wife is not to develop strong ties with any other potential mate of her husband's major patrilineage. There is to be no substitute husband while he is alive, or if he dies, who is of his agnatic groupings. The rule says in effect: if marriage is fragile as a result of the matrilineal interests, the patrilineal grouping of the husband prevents the possibility of this causing internal dissention by prohibiting women from remarrying within it. Since women often marry men many years their senior, the possibility that he will die and she remarry elsewhere does not add to the development of close ties to his living groups.

Thus the polygynous and monogamous families are under constant tension to maintain themselves in terms of the multiple and divergent interests of the descent ties of their members. Outwardly the authority of the husband in relation to his wives seems strong, as is that of his agnatic male relatives, but he is faced with the ever-present threat of her departure, and his wives play him off against one another in attempting to gain favors and a special position while he tries to treat each equally to avoid criticism, though he often has his favorites.

In the extended family we see the growing unity and dominance of patrilineal aspects of domestic life. This larger domestic grouping, generally composed of full brothers, agnatic half-brothers, and their wives and children as its core, is another stage in the development of the polygynous family, after the sons of the husband's wives have grown up and are themselves married and begetting children. Its matrilineal associations are even more diversified than in the smaller domestic groupings, and the patrilineal tie represents a two- or three-generation agnatic line within the minor patrilineage. The father, if living, is its head, though he also belongs to another extended family which includes his own brothers and their families. The extended family may also include uterine half-siblings who came when their mother married into it, foster children who are matrilineally related to family members, and distant patrilineal relatives of male members, as well as widows of members, and even in some cases a father's brother's widow. It also may include divorced or separated sisters who are living in the compound temporarily. If the father is dead, his eldest son is its head.

In actuality, some persons are not closely bound to this grouping. A man may have only one son who lives to manhood, or only one who remains at home after he reaches adulthood. In such cases the son and his family will usually be attached as a junior unit to the extended family of his father and his father's brothers. If none of the father's family are living, the son may seek support from other close patrilineal relatives in his minor patrilineage; there is almost always some senior patrilineal relative with whom he may align himself.

As the eldest son of the extended family grows to manhood his father, who heads the group, permits him greater authority in family matters.[5] If the father does not think this son is capable, he may try to pass the family leadership to the next eldest. This also happens if the eldest son does not live at home, though as a father grows older this son will often return to take over. Occasionally a particularly aggressive younger son will usurp the eldest brother's position, but this is rare unless the latter is incapable of leadership.

The head of the extended family sees that its members are physically protected, and he may call on other lineage members to help him in this. In pre-British times family men and women sometimes went to the farms together under his protection, though this pattern has broken down with peace. He is concerned that all members receive farmland from their various descent and kin groups, and he may support their demands for land if he feels that it is being withheld from them.

When a younger brother or a son is away, the head sees that the wives have enough land for their needs, and for this purpose

---

[5] The eldest son is the first of a man's sons to be born, regardless of the order of marriage of the man's wives.

he will help arrange for farmland for them from their matrilineages and from his own sources. He will supply them with market money if necessary, and check periodically to make sure that everything is going well. If they or their children are in trouble or ill, he will consult a diviner and pay the necessary fees for this and the ensuing sacrifice. He will also pay assessments imposed on a younger brother or son who is away from home, dues for absence from certain ceremonies which he later collects from him.

For the younger brothers, married or unmarried, the head is advisor and guide. Disputes between husbands and wives will be brought to him if they have not already come to the attention of the young men's grade in the compound. In the latter case he will take part in the settlement.

He aids younger male members in trade or other enterprises by advancing them money; he helps them to find jobs, go to school, buy yams for planting, take titles, and discharge ceremonial obligations. He also helps them arrange for housing and, if a brother dies, is responsible for bringing up his children unless the mother remarries and takes them with her. In the latter case, or when a wife divorces a member of the extended family and remarries elsewhere, it is one of the duties of this head to keep in contact with her children, or, if their father is alive, to see that he does so. The head may endeavor to induce the sons to return, for example, by offering to help them secure good farmland or arranging advantageous marriages for them.

The head of an extended family often helps his younger brothers obtain wives, especially in first marriages.[6] He takes a strong hand in settling a younger brother's divorce case, generally backing the brother. Similarly, he helps to arrange marriages of his younger sisters and settle their marital problems. He contributes to ceremonies of his married and unmarried sisters, to sacrifices made on their behalf, and other rites.

[6] He may arrange for a marriage with a daughter of one of his close friends. In this case the bride wealth is often waived by the friend, to the advantage of the husband.

He is also responsible for the welfare of widows attached to the family. A widow may be older than the head, and must in any case be treated with respect. He sees that she has housing, farmland, and sufficient funds for herself and her children, and must treat any other person who has joined the extended family grouping in a similar matter.

In turn, he expects respect and cooperation at all times from the younger men and their families and from other members. They are supposed to help when he performs ceremonies or takes titles. This is particularly true of some funeral ceremonies and titles open only to the eldest brother of a family. If he does not have sufficient funds, his younger brothers and agnatic half-brothers usually give him the necessary support.[7]

Age is the major criterion which distinguishes behavior among males in the extended family. That brothers may have different mothers is not so important, and in the extended family every effort is made to prevent such distinctions being drawn; to do so is considered very bad form as is also the case with a father and all of his sons. The head of the extended family must be careful to treat all full brothers and agnatic half-brothers equally, and especially must not favor the former over the latter. This would be looked on with disfavor by the elders of the minor patrilineage to which they all belong. The unity of the patrilineal tie against the diversity of matrilineal affiliation is strongly emphasized in the extended family.

Thus, the extended family is organized around a line of patrilineally related males. Authority follows the same pattern as in the smaller families: moral authority is dominant; legal and ritual controls are less important. Considerable responsibility for welfare rests with the family head, and how he performs his duties is

[7] A younger brother may provide the major share of the cost of a title. Many people may be aware of this, but the older brother still performs the ceremony and is said to have taken the title. In such a case the younger sibling will receive the largest shares of title benefits from his eldest brother as they accrue to him.

very important to the successful functioning of the group. Organization of the extended family represents a condition between the strong agnatic emphasis of the minor patrilineage, and the smaller domestic groupings, which are more cut up by divisive matrilineal affiliations.

SHRINES

There are important individual shrines at Afikpo which are believed to bring welfare and good health (S. Ottenberg, 1969). These include *Nkamalo*, for the welfare of men, formerly used in headhunting and warfare; *ɛgɛro*, for the welfare of young girls; *ci*, for married women; *Ibini ɔkpabe*, the shrine established by individuals who have been to Aro Chuku to consult the oracle; and *adudɔ*, the individual matrilineal ancestral shrine for women, which has been discussed (see "Other Lineage Activities" in chap. iii). These are established by individuals in a variety of ways. But there are also very important shrines in which the matrilineal and patrilineal descent ties of the establisher are intermixed in ritual fashion at the time they are set up, indicating specific concerns of the descent groups. These include the ancestral shrine, *Mma obu*, and the yam shrine, *Njɔku*. The first has already been discussed (see "The Ancestral Aspect" in chap. ii), and we only mention here that in the ritual of placing the pot in the patrilineal ancestral shrine for a dead man, the presence of his matrilineal relatives symbolizes the links of the deceased to both of his descent groupings by birth, and also of his eldest son, who directs the ritual, to his father's uterine relatives, from whom he still receives land to farm and to whom he should show courteous and deferential behavior.

Njɔku, which virtually every adult male owns and which is for the fertility of the yam crop and for welfare, is located in the compound, usually near its entrance, and is in the form of a pot. Those of a major patrilineage are often grouped in one shrine, the pots nearest each other representing men of a single agnatic line. A man establishes his when a diviner advises him that the

Njɔku spirit is calling him, as a result of poor crops or illness. He purchases a special pot from an old woman potter who has passed the menopause, and a small wooden plate obtained at the Afikpo market. Procedures differ, but in one case a man went with the plate and a fowl to the oldest living male member of his matrilineage who had this shrine. This relative took a stone and some sand from his own *Njɔku* pot and put it on the plate, and in return was given a small sum of money as a thank-offering, and asked to come to establisher's compound later in the day. When the man's father is alive and has a shrine, he repeats the same procedure with him, but in this case he was dead, and the establisher approached a close matrilineal elder.

In the evening the two elders came and, joined by a male elder of the man's own minor patrilineage, brought the pot to the shrine and put into it, with the help of these three elders, special sacrificial materials which this particular shrine spirit is said to like. The stones were then put into the pot and sand placed in the mouth of a chicken. The man from the establisher's father's matrilineage killed the chicken, dropping the sand from its mouth and letting the blood fall into the pot, and placing some of its feathers in it. Then the other two elders each placed blood and feathers from the same chicken in the pot. The establisher roasted the chicken, providing a special soup without greens (*asarara*) and yam fufu. All returned to the shrine, where the elders of his father's patrilineage dipped the fufu in the soup and placed it in the shrine pot, adding pieces of chicken heart, liver, and intestines. This was repeated by the other two elders.

Here they were joined by other elders of these three descent groups, and all returned to the cooking place to feast. The establisher gave the three representative elders yams, and one shilling —said to be the price of buying the shrine—to the two matrilineal representatives. All then returned to the shrine. The establisher kneeled over it, extending his palms upward, and those who accompanied him rubbed sand from the pot into his palms in the same ritual order as above. This formally transferred the shrine to the man, though he later offered a special sacrifice to it to complete the ceremony.[8]

Two reasons are given by the Afikpo for the fact that representatives of these three descent groups join in the ceremony. The first is so that the man may inherit good farming skill from all these lines, the second because he obtains farmland from these three groups. Since these are descent groups which also aid a man in other matters, taking the yam shrine is symbolic of a male's relationship to three of his most important lineage groupings. It is symbolic of the generally cooperative links of descent lines through a single individual.

When a man dies, his *Njɔku* is usually maintained by a son, often the eldest, who sacrifices at it and other unattended pots in his section of the shrine when he does his own. Sometimes, if the deceased was prominent and his sons neglect the pot, the Afikpo say that his close matrilineal elders will take it, putting it in the shrine of their eldest member. This is because a neglected spirit is believed to affect the welfare and farming fortunes of the deceased's matrilineal relatives. No such case was observed while at Afikpo, however.

Men from both unilineal descent lines of a man play a part in establishing *egwu Nsi*, the shrine for those who lose money at trading or who tend to become lost in the bush or farms, and *ɔrθrθ ɛko*, which is for general prosperity. We have also seen how a man visits the matriclan shrine (*Nja*) and feasting groups of his father and each of his wives, as well as his own (see "Internal Clan Activities" in chap. iii), on the annual ritual day for this shrine, again linking him to various uterine ties. A woman's religious activities link her closely to her matrilineal relatives, but she is also tied by marriage to some of the compound and patrilineal shrines of her husband. For a man, his matrilineal and patrilineal religious associations are all significant, symbolically

---

[8] In addition to the shrine in the compound, some men like to have another *Njɔku* pot in their personal section of the village yam barn, where yams are normally stored until needed, to protect them from rotting and theft. This pot is established at a later date in much the same manner.

reiterating his ties of descent and the concern of these relatives belonging to these descent groupings with his welfare.

DEATH AND INHERITANCE

In the funeral there is a further symbolic statement of descent ties, though here the whole matter is overshadowed by a strong concern over the inheritance of the deceased's property. Here, also, we see that serious frictions can arise which involve a person's descent links. This has been analyzed elsewhere in detail (S. Ottenberg, 1965).

When a mature male dies his eldest son, or the eldest son then living at home, is responsible for burial and the funeral ceremony. He is strongly supported in this by his patrilineal relatives, particularly those of his minor patrilineage. He must call the male matrilineal relatives of the deceased to the burial and let them see the body and examine the dead man's house (for movable wealth). He also gives them money, usually five shillings, which ritually represents the wealth of the deceased in the house, and informs them of any money or trade goods which he possessed. The son, through his patrikinsmen, feasts these matrilineal relatives and gives them presents of cloth, rods, and yams, some of which will be used in the burial, the rest divided among them. The eldest son of each wife of the dead man helps out in this as a representative of each of the deceased's "houses."

The matrilineal members who attend the burial are generally of the deceased's matrilineage, especially his lineage head, and subhead if there is one. The extent to which clan members are called and come to the burial depends upon whether the deceased was old, prominent, or wealthy; if he was any or all of these, clan members in his area of residence and prominent clan elders from elsewhere in Afikpo will come.

The matrikinsmen who attend, particularly prominent matrilineage members, bring certain goods which they give to the eldest son as an indication that they are ready to bury the man if the sons are not. These are politely returned by the eldest son with the comment (through his representatives—the two descent groups feast separately) that of course he and the patrilineage are prepared to bury the man. If the patrilineage did not bury him the matrilineal relatives would do so, and thus have claim to land, yams, and other property which the man owned or controlled which would not normally pass to them. No such case of matrikinsmen burying a man was noted during my time at Afikpo, but in several pending land cases matrilineal groups claimed that land a man had originally obtained many generations ago belonged to them because their matrilineal ancestors had buried him. The matrikinsmen who come to the burial characteristically grumble over the quantity and quality of wine and food given them by the eldest son, and demand more and better fare. Sometime this is given; sometimes money is given instead, the representative of the son saying, for example, "Here are your extra yams, here is another pot of wine," while giving sums of money to the matrikinsmen. This is expected behavior; it would not really be a proper funeral otherwise. It is part of a broader feasting pattern at Afikpo, but here it implies that the sons of the deceased are capable of burying him in proper style.

The members of both descent groups at the burial are not really unfriendly, and Afikpo say that they must both cooperate in order for the burial to be properly done. There exists, however, an underlying air of hostility and sense of competition over property.

The burial is followed by a series of related rituals, which generally continue to express the relative positions of the descent groups. The first is the "goat funeral" (*olili madθ*: bury-person), in which each "house" of the deceased gives a goat, food, and drink to the dead man's matrikinsmen, mainly his male matrilineal relatives. This is an obligatory ceremony, in which the eldest son of each house plays the leading role. The goat of the deceased's eldest son is killed, the breast given to the matrilineage head. The other goats usually are sold and the money divided by the lineage members in terms of seniority of age. This ceremony is followed by the ritual of placing a shrine pot for the deceased in his ancestral house, and a representative of deceased's matrilineage, frequently the lineage head or someone he designates, is present as a witness (see "The Ancestral Aspect" in chap. ii). It is important that the "goat funeral" and this ceremony be done. Otherwise, it is believed the spirit of the dead man may be angry and haunt the living, including matrilineal relatives.

At any later time the deceased's eldest son may perform the "cow funeral" (*eka-ehi-uhie:* leg-cow-drum), giving his father's matrikinsmen a cow,[9] and a horse as well if he is rich. Sons of the other "houses" of the deceased do not do this, but simply help the eldest son. The ceremony, sometimes done as many as thirty years after the father's death, is optional, and is a prestige ritual to honor the father and display the son's wealth. It is similar to the "goat funeral" and is important enough that most of the senior males of the dead man's matriclan will attend, receiving shares of the uncooked meat by seniority of age, though the matrilineage head again receives a special, large share. In both the "goat" and the "cow" funerals the deceased's patrilineal relatives help with the ceremony and are feasted by the deceased's sons, receiving small shares of meat. In both rituals, the matrilineal elders present perform a sacrifice, using part of the head of the dead animal, to announce to the ancestor that the ritual has been properly performed and he should be pleased. In both ceremonies the matrikinsmen complain over the quality of the food and drink (and even of size of the goat or cow) as in the actual burial, and receive financial compensation. They view these small monies as their right as inheritors of the man's movable property.

The deceased's personal effects, boxes, guns, cloth, and yams —whether in the house, the village yam barn, or still in the ground—are divided soon after burial among the man's houses by the deceased's matrilineage head or someone as his representative. This is done in the order in which the houses are ranked in Afikpo, the house of the eldest son first, then among the rest the house of the next eldest son, the house of the next eldest son, and

---

[9] The small variety living in Southern Nigeria, called *muturu*.

so on. Houses with only female children or none at all get virtually nothing, but the number of children in each house is irrelevant. The house of the eldest son gets the most, and this person usually receives the prize possessions, a gun, a machete, and so forth. It is important, of course, that the divider carry out this procedure without creating friction between the houses or favoring one over another.

A man's home passes to his eldest son, remaining within the patrilineage (see pp. 82–84). His trade goods are sold, usually by the eldest son or another patrilineal member, and the money handed over to the matrilineage head along with any money he may have had. If the sum is small, the male matrilineage members divide it among themselves by seniority of age. If it is considerable, the clan elders come and receive shares, again by age. It is this money which Afikpo consider the most important aspect of inheritance. In turn, the clan, particularly the matrilineage and its head, is responsible for any debts of the deceased, and this sum is deducted from the total before division.

But the inheritance of movable property often gives rise to dissension and dispute between agnatic and uterine groupings. There are two basic aspects involved, one traditional, the other relating to culture change. In the former, records indicate that in the past a son, perhaps the eldest, sometimes wanted to keep his father's movable wealth for himself. This may have been because he was opportunistic, because he was at odds with his father's matrilineage, because he felt that the father's matrilineage would not press the issue, or because of a patrilineal bias derived from personal experience or contact with patrilineal Igbo groups west of Afikpo. It must be remembered that some Afikpo originally came from that area. The possibility of success was enhanced by the fact that men were secretive about wealth, and money was often kept hidden, conditions which still exist today. If a son knew of money belonging to his father, and brothers of other matrilineal relatives of the father did not, he could declare that there was none. If the money could not be found the matrilineage, supported by its clan, could claim that it existed, but they would be pressed for proof. Even if it were found, the son could claim that the father had given it to him before he died. However, this claim was usually not validated, since the elders who tried the case would generally favor matrilineal inheritance, and the son would have trouble producing witnesses, particularly someone from his father's matrilineage.[10]

A son's attempts to claim his father's wealth led to ill feelings between him and his father's matrilineage, since a "son" was expected to show the same respect for it as for his father. The matrilineage might retaliate by removing the son from its land, as will be described below, and by refusing to have anything else to do with him, so that the price the son paid for his action might be high.

This type of inheritance situation was not particularly common in the past, partly, one suspects, because there was little movable wealth in money or trade goods. That which existed was mainly in the hands of Aro traders, who remained outside the Afikpo system, marrying Aro wives and following Aro custom. For the ordinary Afikpo there was not very much wealth of this kind.

The developing economic situation [11] has brought increased wealth to the Afikpo through (1) increased opportunity to grow cash crops such as yams, cassava products, and rice; (2) the expansion of fishing, for Afikpo now move freely up and down the Cross River as far as Calabar in the south and Cameroun in the northeast; (3) the growth of trading opportunities; and (4) the increasing number of Afikpo who hold salaried positions either in the area or elsewhere. As a result of increased individual wealth considerable economic differentials have developed. Two features have grown out of this.[12] First, matrilineal relatives of a deceased person, particularly the clan elders, show a greater interest in the individual's wealth and have become quite rapa-

[10] The elders would argue that if the father had really intended to give the money to this son, he would have called in one of his matrilineal relatives to witness the transaction.

[11] See P. Ottenberg (1959); S. and P. Ottenberg (1962); S. Ottenberg (1968), for analyses of some of its aspects.

[12] Goody (1956: 108–11) is quite helpful here.

cious and bold in attempting to acquire it. They consider that it is their right, of course, by custom.

Second, attempts to pass such inheritable wealth from father to son have increased greatly. A man who has wealth is not anxious to see it distributed to his matrikinsmen, some of whom, especially nonmatrilineage persons, he considers distant uterine relatives. These persons live in different areas of Afikpo and may have little contact with him, and he may have been involved in land conflicts with them. Persons of means may be working away from Afikpo, and may have little interest in the matrilineal descent groupings, are not dependent upon them for land, and are more concerned with their immediate family. We have seen, for example, how an Afikpo who goes abroad may lose contact with his uterine kin (see pp. 140–41).

Two other factors reinforce father-son inheritance of movable wealth. First, a number of men who are educated in the European sense or who have had contact with European culture, with patrilineal Igbo, or with other patrilineal peoples in Nigeria have come to believe that father-son inheritance is best and that the matrilineal system is not so desirable. Some of them have not really rejected their matrilineal groups—they may be quite active in them—but they conceive of the paternal line as of greater importance than in the past. Some attempt to obtain their father's inheritance, and if they are themselves fathers try to will their movable property to their sons.[13]

Second, the court system now tends to favor father-son inheritance. The Afikpo Native Authority Court, which tries many of these cases,[14] is composed of elders who regard the traditional mode of inheritance as correct and make their decisions in these terms. However, appeal to the district officer, or from the Native Authority Court to the Magistrate's Court, is possible in some

---

[13] Little knowledge exists in Afikpo as to the proper procedure for making wills, so that they are often not accepted by the Nigerian courts.

[14] Including many which are first tried in the traditional manner by the Afikpo elders but the results of which do not satisfy one or more of the litigants.

cases. While this latter court supposedly follows native law and custom so long as it is not opposed to Nigerian law, many Afikpo believe, with reason, that it favors father-son inheritance more than does the Native Court. The same is said to be true of the district officer. Those who follow father-son inheritance attempt to reach the Magistrate's Court or the district officer, while those who follow traditional inheritance try to keep their cases in the Native Court or outside of the modern courts altogether.

Patrilineal relatives of a son claiming his father's money sometimes support him in court and give him advice, even if they do not believe in father-son inheritance. They do so because patrilineal ties are close, because increased prosperity of one patrilineal member increases the prosperity of all, and because a patrilineage is expected to aid its members in almost any dispute. Thus the forces of a man's father's matrilineal relatives sometimes are allied against those of his patrilineal relatives, though if the case is successful, the money passes from father to son and does not become property of the patrilineal grouping.

There is no formal meeting to divide a deceased man's land. His sons and wives farm it until the season is over, when it reverts to the owners. His children usually continue to use land he allocated to them through his patrilineage and matrilineage and they may receive his share as well, but this depends upon the corporate groups controlling the land. Land of the deceased's father's matrilineage that he was farming reverts to them, for land of this kind cannot be used by his sons. Land of his wives' matrilineages continues to be used by them and their children for whom it is intended in any event. There is no strict inheritance of land as of other properties, and this is usually true of groves as well.

The subject of the succession of roles has been discussed in detail elsewhere (S. Ottenberg, 1965). Only a few comments will be made in terms of the roles of father, political leader, and priest. No single person properly succeeds to the father's role. The deceased's eldest brother takes nominal control if the children are small, the eldest son has considerable actual control when he is mature, and the eldest son of each "house" guides the affairs of that group. Wives of childbearing age frequently leave and remarry, taking the small children with them. While the eldest son is said eventually to carry the responsibilities of his father, they are thus actually divided.

An influential leader's position in Afikpo is not inherited by his eldest or another son; there is no simple line of agnatic inheritance of authority. The son will be greatly respected, more so than the sons of other persons, but he must show his own capabilities as a leader when he attains a suitable age. The form of property inheritance just discussed means he does not inherit much of his father's wealth and property to give him power. Further, leadership does not fall to the dead man's sisters' eldest son, who receives only a small part of the deceased's movable wealth, and frequently lives in a different compound and village than his mother's brother. There is one exception. If the deceased was the matrilineage head and the eldest male child of his sisters is the next oldest matrilineage male, he will normally succeed to that headship.

In the case of the succession of priests, they are associated with shrines controlled by either patrilineal (the great majority) or matrilineal descent groupings, or by compounds, wards, or villages. The priest is almost invariably from the controlling grouping, and, of course, so is his successor, but the latter can be any senior or responsible man of the group that the diviner consulted chooses, not necessarily the male in direct line of succession. This is true of the priests of both the matriclan shrine, *Nja,* and the patrilineal ancestral shrine, *Mma obu,* and for many other shrines as well. Similarly, while diviners tend to fall into certain patrilineal lines, as do carvers and palm-wine tappers, there is no strict line of inheritance of skills; sons may decide not to take up the work, while outsiders are not prohibited from doing so.

The succession of most male roles in Afikpo is thus not usually automatic in terms of specific descent positions. This fits well into the general pattern of ritual and secular leadership.

In the funeral for an adult woman her eldest son performs the burial and her matrilineal relatives come, though the feasting and ritual are not as elaborate. Her goods and wealth are divided among her children, generally without dispute, usually by the eldest daughter if she is mature, or by the matrilineage head. Most of the goods go to the eldest daughter, who also is responsible for establishing the ancestral shrine *adudɔ*, as described elsewhere. This daughter also performs another ritual for the females of the matrilineage, which if omitted is said to cause the pots of the lineage women to break on being fired. Both the eldest daughter and eldest sister, or other sisters living nearby, cooperate in helping out with the children, but no single person succeeds to the maternal role. The death of a woman is thus more a concern of females of the domestic grouping and of her matrilineage than her clan, and the role of her husband's patrilineage is not as significant as in the case of males.

FARMLAND

Farmland matters at Afikpo are complex. They represent one of the major areas of patrilineal-matrilineal relationships, as well as those between matrilineal groupings, and they often involve tension and conflict. We have already indicated how all but about 15 per cent of farmland is matrilineally controlled, and how farm holdings of descent groups are small, dispersed, farmed in rotation, and involve descent groupings in relationships with villages and their administrators. Beyond these points land questions involve individuals in enterprising manipulations of and aggressive behavior toward other persons and groups. It is one of the most exciting sectors of activity for the Afikpo, a topic of much discussion and argument, and one in which individual initiative and the weighing of alternative choices looms large.

In order properly to discuss land questions we must retrace our steps and examine the origin of the farmland holdings at Afikpo. Afikpo say that in former times there was plenty of virgin land to clear and whether it went patrilineally or matrilineally depended upon the wishes of the clearer if he did so alone. If he had help it depended on whether it was his matrilineal or patrilineal relatives who assisted him. If matrilineal relatives, it went that way, and the reverse was also true. Afikpo also state that in some cases both types of relations helped out and the land was divided, some to go one way, some the other. Of course, the issue was clouded if full brothers helped a man to establish new farmland since they belonged to both of his descent groupings, and it seemed to have been a matter of choice for the individuals involved. When land cases are brought to the elders or the Native Authority Court for judgment, these matters are crucial in determining ownership, though in truth the evidence is often conflicting and not at all clear.

In fact what is likely to have been the case is that at an earlier time when Afikpo was matrilineal, all of the land cleared (and this was often land nearest the villages as the population was smaller then) was matrilineally controlled. When patrilineal Igbo came to live at Afikpo they married local women, thereby acquiring access to these land holdings through spouses. They also cleared new land, further from the village, which became patrilineal or matrilineal land, depending on whether they retained their own custom or adopted the local one. There is a tendency for patrilineal land holdings to be further from the village than matrilineal land. In addition a considerable amount of the present patrilineal holdings do not really belong to agnatic groupings. It has been received in the past on pledge from a matrilineage and is in theory redeemable. Today there is no more virgin land and patrilineages increase their holdings only through this system of pledging, while giving other holdings up through redemption. The reverse is true for matrilineal groupings. They can redeem land pledged to patrilineages. In addition there is considerable transfer of matrilineal land from one lineage to another within a clan, and at other times across clans. There is thus considerable shifting of land holdings at Afikpo. Let us look at the various practices in some detail for they bring forth some of the crucial relationships of individuals to individuals as well as between descent groupings.

Matrilineage land, as we have seen, is spread about, and some of it may be too distant for its members to farm. Perhaps they live in the central area of Afikpo and the land is far out in the Ozizza to the north. Whether land is far away or not depends upon the marriage patterns of the women of the matrilineage. The matrilineage head may then arrange for a fellow clansman of another matrilineage of the matriclan living nearer the land to take charge of it. The matrilineage may lose track of the land through time, and thus it passes into this man's control and into another matrilineage. The matrilineage would of course prefer to prevent this if possible. One device is to arrange for one of its females to marry into a village near the land. She and her children then fall heir to it. But it is not always possible to arrange such a marriage; there may be no female of marriageable age, or matrilineage girls may not wish to marry into that area, so that the alternative procedure described above may be adopted.

Again, when a matrilineage is dying out, when it has no child-bearing females and will become extinct, its land may be transferred to other matrilineages within the clan, through arrangements for the marriage of females of the clan into the areas where the land is located. Eventually the land passes to their children and matrilineages. In this and the proceeding case there is little wish to let the land fall into the hands of persons outside of the clan, and every effort is made to prevent opportunistic entrepreneurs of this kind from seizing it. The principle is that if it is impossible to keep land within one's own matrilineage, it is most important to keep it within the matriclan if this can be arranged. There is one form of agreed interclan land transfer, however, and this is in reparation for a murder or a theft (see "The Matrilineal Clan in the Village-Group" in chap. iv). This is an old procedure which is rarely employed today.

Another device in land transfer involves the direct seizure of matrilineage land. Sometimes, because the land is far away from those who control it, or because of sudden deaths of those who have knowledge of it, when a single member of the matrilineage who dominates the land suddenly dies, or when those who know the true ownership of the land are away, someone outside of the matrilineage or even the clan may simply appropriate the land. It could be a friend, a son, a nonuterine brother, or an age mate to the person or persons who last used or controlled the land, someone who may have farmed part of it and who knows its boundaries and its vulnerability to seizure.

It is the task of the matrilineage head, supported by the matriclan elders, to prevent such seizures, but he may not know the full history of the land, particularly if it is not near his village and he does not farm it himself. He will certainly make a case over the land if he can, but it is sometimes lost if its origin and history cannot be proven while the man who seized it presents a convincing story. For example, the appropriator might claim that the land belonged to his matriclan because it was originally cleared by one of its members and then given to a nonuterine brother belonging to the clan of the matrilineage from which it is being taken. The seizer states that he is simply claiming it back for his own matriclan, the rightful owners. If he is influential and able to get his clan to support him, he may win the case even if his arguments are shaky, and the land may pass to his matrilineage. It might also pass to another lineage within the same clan by this procedure.

These cases may seem crude or unjustifiable, but they are endemic in Afikpo, difficult to settle, and the cause of a great deal of friction, particularly between members of different matriclans. Interclan cases are the most troublesome to resolve because there are few checks on the financial and political pressures which become involved. Those occurring within a clan may also be difficult to settle, but the matriclan elders act as a centralizing agency to force a settlement. Such strong authority is lacking in interclan cases, since the elders of Afikpo are able to suggest solutions but have difficulty in enforcing them. There are men in Afikpo with a practical eye for such land as may possibly be had in this manner; any holdings not firmly controlled, the history of which is vague, may be subject to this type of seizure.

Another major technique by which a matrilineage acquires land is through redeeming land once pledged away by a matrilineage or an individual within the matriclan. Normally, only a matrilineage from the clan of its original owner may redeem it, but this need not be the one that originally owned it; it may no longer exist. The intricacies of pledging and redeeming would occupy a whole volume. For example, the procedures involved differ if the land has a shrine to the Aro oracle, *Ibini ɔkpabe,* on it or not.

Matrilineage land is generally pledged to a patrilineal grouping or sometimes a ward (more rarely to an individual). This is one of the major ways that patrilineal and residential groupings gain control over land, and if knowledge of the land becomes lost to all but its receivers it is never returned. Land is so pledged when a matrilineage or matriclan has a dispute, usually a big land case, and needs support in the form of wealth and leadership assistance in order to win. Pledging is usually to a group with whom some of the matrilineage members live. In practice then, the group receiving the land is supporting the uterine group in its dispute, a technique used by matrilineages to gain aid in land matters. Other pledgings occur when a lineage member is in debt to a patrilineage. In this case the creditors seize a piece of the matrilineage land of the debtor (the whole section, not just the portion farmed by the debtor) as payment. His matrilineage must then pay his debts and be reimbursed by him, thus redeeming the land. If they lack funds, or he is a troublemaker, they may let the land go to be redeemed at some later date. Similarly, a matrilineage member who is in desperate need of money, or who has been at odds with his matrilineage and wants to "punish" it, can pledge its land, usually in secret. If it is land that other matrilineage members have not been using or are uninterested in, the group may not hear of the pledging for a long time, but once it is discovered they will eventually want to redeem it. They can then punish him with fines or throw him off other sections of matrilineage land which he is farming. Such a man may pledge the land secretly to an individual rather than to a patrilineal group or a ward. The receiver then keeps it entirely for himself if he wishes, unless it is redeemed, and in a sense it becomes his personal property. Such land usually passes matrilineally to his descendants in time, and thus may in effect become transferred from one matrilineage to another.

It is rare for a matrilineage to pledge land to another matrilineage within the clan or to a matrilineage outside of it. Little is gained in the first instance, since a matrilineage will have the financial support and leadership of the whole clan in a dispute with outsiders without transferring land to another segment of it, and no matrilineage would be interested in securing land from another matrilineage of the same clan in debt payment or as a secret transfer. These actions would only cause friction within the matriclan and the clan elders would not allow it, having other ways of handling debts and other difficulties of their members. In the case of pledging land to a matrilineage of another matriclan, the Afikpo see matriclans as essentially in competition with one another over land; interclan land transfers occur largely through land seizures and subsequent litigation. Residential and patrilineal groupings, on the other hand, are seen as relatively uninvolved in land conflicts (though in fact they sometimes are), and as supporters of matrilineage members who live with them. It is for these reasons that pledging seems to take the direction that it does.

The Afikpo say that while patrilineal groups receive some land on pledge from matrilineal ones, their own patrilineage land should not be pledged, and it rarely is, being considered communal property. Very occasionally, an individual at odds with his major patrilineage may pledge some of its land to his matrilineal relatives. The patrilineage usually quickly collects funds to redeem it through its *ukɛ ɛkpɛ* organization. The pledger then faces ostracism and heavy fines from the patrilineage elders. The close contacts of patrikinsmen usually prevent such pledging; unless a person plans to leave his agnatic group he cannot long exist in the compound without the cooperation of his kinsmen.

There is no time limit on redeeming land; there can be, and frequently are, many generations between pledging and redemption. If land is redeemed soon after pledging, the redemption and pledging prices are usually the same. If a long interval elapses, the redemption price is higher, as land values have risen. Those who hold the land on pledge set the price, though the redeemers may bargain with them over it. Unless pledging and redemption are done in secret, both sides bring several elders to act as witnesses. The person or persons who pay the redemption price, as those who pay the pledging costs, as a rule have greatest control over the land.

A husband redeeming land in the name of a wife who belongs to the proper matrilineage, and this is common, may actually control the land and even try to seize it if they are divorced or if she dies, though the matrilineage of the wife will naturally try to prevent this. If the line of the original matrilineage has been lost, any matriclan members have the right to redeem the land. What sometimes occurs is that a man hears that land of a patrilineage or residential grouping is pledged from a matrilineage of his matriclan. Such information is difficult to come by, as the holding group is always quite secretive about its source of land for fear of redemption. The person or persons involved redeem the land at an agreed price. If a descendant or member of the matrilineage that originally pledged the land hears of it he can ask for it to be transferred to him. By matriclan ruling this must be done, the man paying the redeemer the full redemption price, or agreeing to split the land between them for a lower fee. Frequently there is no member of the original matrilineage alive. If there are such persons they may not know of the redemption, or know that the land was originally theirs, for the redeemer does not broadcast the matter, and they may never get it back.

Once a matrilineage has acquired land by any of the techniques discussed above, who controls it? In theory, the land becomes property of the lineage, open to all its members. This is generally the case with land originally cleared from virgin ground that has not since changed hands. But in the other cases of land acquisition, the sort of controls that exist depends upon the manner in which the land has been acquired. Generally, if the land is obtained or seized by a single individual he has several choices. He may try to hold it in secret and keep it entirely to himself. This is most likely when an individual redeems land "on the quiet." Such land is not individually owned, however, as it will pass to uterine descendants at his death. If he is unable or unwilling to keep it secret, he may still keep tight control over the land division for farming, usually giving shares only to a few matrikinsmen. He will probably give portions to his wives and his patrilineal relatives to use (but not to control) rather than matrilineage members, for they are less likely to "open up" the land than are matrikinsmen. In this situation, his matrilineage head has little say over the land; it is controlled by the man who acquired it. This is particularly the case in the use of seized and redeemed land, but in all cases the acquirer of the land justifies what would otherwise be considered greediness because he took the initiative in obtaining and paying for it, and is thus entitled to it. Matrilineage heads themselves may take this attitude if, alone or with a few matrikinsmen, they have obtained land by one of these means, and refuse to open such land to the general use of the matrilineage.

Tightly controlled matrilineage land may become more open by a variety of means. Its owner may throw it open to all matrilineage mates to use if he is no longer interested in it. Tightly controlled land may, through time, become more open as it passes to the descendants of the single controller. Or, if a person had considerable help from other persons in gaining the land and cannot keep them from it, the land becomes fairly open, though the acquirer will still control it. Again, if the matrilineage redeems land as a group, as sometimes happens, the land most certainly is never tightly controlled but is open to all of its members and stays under the head's control.

In cases of seizure and of redemption it may sometimes be that a man's father, nonuterine brother, friend, or other nonclansman has helped him. As a result even though they are not members of the redeemer's lineage, they receive rights to farm, but these rights are not passed on to their relatives.

In all these cases women may be involved as well as men,

though not as commonly. Females can obtain land directly on pledge, or with the assistance of their husbands, and they may pledge matrilineal land to others. A woman is generally unable to seize land, but there are many cases when wealthy female traders or farmers have redeemed land by themselves and kept it for their children's use. Some women also rent land. That matrilineal land rights normally pass through females is obvious, but their controls over land exist only as they take the initiative to secure it for their personal use and that of their children.

In fact a changing feature of land affairs is the increasing role of women in it. In precolonial times and the early part of this century, women were much more dependent on their husbands, brothers, and other male relatives for land; since few men were away from home, women rarely had the opportunity to play a leadership role in land matters such as that played by Nnachi Enwo's elder sister (see "Fission, Segmentation, and Accretion" in chap. iii). Today, we sometimes find them obtaining land themselves rather than relying on husbands and brothers to do this for them, and they farm further from home and are more independent in acquiring land. All of this is related to the coming of peace in Afikpo, and to the greater economic independence that women exhibit today, matters which have been discussed elsewhere (P. Ottenberg, 1958; 1959).

Money or other movable wealth have become more common in Afikpo to both sexes, and they are more valuable as a result of the lack of virgin portions, the development of cash crops, and the presence of a good-sized body of administrators, teachers, and others who buy foods at Afikpo. It seems likely that conflicts among matrilineal groupings and between patrilineal and matrilineal groupings over farmland have increased.

Land disputes are encouraged by the opportunistic tendency of some Afikpo to seize land when those who control it are poor and uninfluential. A patrilineal grouping using land on pledge from a matrilineage may suddenly claim that it was always theirs if they feel they can successfully push it through the courts. A matrilineage may claim that land belonging to a patrilineal group was originally theirs and offer to redeem it if they feel that the patrilineal grouping is weak or unable to defend its claim or title to the land. Such cases did occur in former times, but seem to be more prevalent now.

There are some who favor the increasing development of father-son land inheritance, often the same individuals who favor this procedure for movable wealth. We have already seen how paternal cross-cousin marriage facilitates this in a traditionally acceptable way. As in the case of inheritance of money, an attempt is made to bring such a father-son claim to the court that is believed to favor the position taken. If a person needs support in such a case, his most likely nonmatrilineal sources will be his patrikinsmen. If they aid him they may receive shares to farm if he wins the land, but it will remain under his control. It does not become common patrilineal land. In the past, such land eventually became more open, in terms of the role played by others in its acquisition and the wishes of the controller.

What will happen in the future to land obtained in these ways today is uncertain. But it is sure that in many of these cases, involving either money or land obtained by a son from his father at the expense of his father's matrilineal relatives, the intent is that the property pass to the son or sons and not to the major or minor patrilineage as a whole. This is not a shift from matrilineality to patrilineality, but rather from matrilineality to a greater emphasis on the father-son tie within the domestic group. If it were a true shift to partrilineality, we would expect that the properties acquired by an individual would become corporately owned by the man's patrilineal groupings.

At the same time, in some other cases of land inheritance, patrilineal groupings are active in permanently establishing control over matrilineal land, while in the past they acted more as holding companies, receiving such land on pledge. These cases we can only interpret as a true shift in emphasis from matrilineality to patrilineality, toward the greater corporate character of patrilineal groupings at the expense of matrilineal ones. Thus two tendencies exist side by side, a greater emphasis on father-son property ties and the importance of the domestic group, and some shift from matrilineality to patrilineality in land matters. While both have occurred, the first is the more common and striking change.

The question of land conflicts is confounded by the difficulties involved in their resolution. They take a long time to settle, sometimes many years, they may go to a special elders' court, the Native Authority Court, and the Magistrate's Court, and some even reach higher courts in Nigeria. They are expensive to resolve in terms of fees and bribes, and sometimes the cost is very high in terms of the value of the land. However, once dispute commences over land the parties involved are reluctant to pull out despite the expense factor; a matter of principle seems to become involved. While many originally start as disputes between individuals, they invariably involve descent groups. The general procedure is for each side in the case to call in elders for fees, who judge the case. This is the special Afikpo elders' court. These men can come from anywhere in Afikpo and frequently, but not always, are unconnected with the descent groups involved in the dispute. In any case each side tries to get prominent and influential elders to act as judges, and hopefully those who will favor their point of view. They examine the land, obtain its history, and judge the present source of conflict. They may come to a final decision themselves, but in difficult cases, where the evidence is obscure or conflicting, or where they cannot agree, they resort to the Aro oracle, to oath swearing, and sometimes to both. Even when they arrive at a decision they have no power to enforce it. Those involved may still squabble over the land, and one or both sides may take it to a regular court hoping for a different decision. A great deal of time of the Afikpo elders is occupied during the period between the harvesting of yams and the planting of the new crop, from about September to February, in judging cases, and also in taking part in them as disputants and witnesses. This is the major source of conflict between male individuals and between descent groupings in Afikpo.

One is struck with how personal matrilineal land affairs are compared to patrilineal land controls. The latter type of land is simply divided into relatively small shares, and is thought of as part of the property rights of those who live together. It is not subject to manipulation or secrecy by the users of the land. Matrilineal land, on the other hand, has an element of personal control about it. Individuals attempt to dominate it at the expense of fellow matrikinsmen. Duplicity is common. Access to even small sections of land given during the division for farming is access to knowledge of the boundaries and perhaps the history of the land, and this knowledge may give an individual some opportunity in the future to seize or otherwise gain control of it though he has no rights to do so. There is a sense of power and of excitement concerning the control and use of matrilineal land, the bulk of all farmland. There is room for the opportunistic and the daring to operate. Rewards to the skillful manipulators of land are high, albeit at the expense of matrikinsmen as well as others. Those who have plenty of land find others obligated to them: it is the others who must come and ask for the use of land when it is divided for farming. Those who have access only to small shares of their matrilineage's land do not go without, but they must get land from other matrilineages, those of their wives, fathers, and agnatic brothers, or from other sources. They find themselves under obligation to others, for they are the beggers after land. In a society that emphasizes individual achievement of wealth and status, and individual goals, such persons are clearly the losers, even though in terms of survival, of obtaining necessary food, they may not be badly off. Actual starvation conditions are rare today. While a major reason for increasing one's holdings is to enlarge his potential food supply and to acquire a surplus for sale, an equally important factor is that large holdings permit the individual to let others use the land, and thus become obligated to him. As we have seen, land holdings, as a form of wealth, are a secondary feature of leadership in the agnatic and uterine descent groupings. The man who controls much land can give out shares to many persons, who will then be reluctant to oppose him when political issues or disagreements arise, often over other land holdings.

If matrilineages and matriclans were residential units in which clansmen and lineage mates lived side by side, it is likely that the pressures to maintain residential unity would be strong enough to reduce some of the intra-uterine land controversy in Afikpo. The dispersed residential pattern for matrikinsmen permits frictions to continue, since the amount of cooperation necessary within the lineage and clan is limited and members do not have to maintain daily face-to-face contacts. The clan elders themselves find it difficult to settle internal land disputes. Some of them know little or nothing of the particular matrilineage land involved, and they must rely on evidence, sometimes contradictory, from a few lineage members. The clan's ultimate means of dealing with a land speculator, throwing him out, is considered dangerous, something which is likely to upset the clan spirit, *Nja*. Such a person could be ostracized, but this means that his matrikinsmen would have to withdraw from land that he lets them use. Even the matriclan and matrilineage rules make decisive action difficult. As we have seen, any clansman can redeem land pledged by a matrilineage member in the past; the redeemer does not have to be of the same matrilineage as the pledger, and is not bound to tell the proper original owners that he has redeemed the land. There is no real punishment meted out to a man of the clan who obtains land in secret and fails to share it with matrilineage mates. The structure of matrilineal organization and its rules of behavior are related to the pattern of flexibility in land matters.

There are other situations in which a man has the opportunity to view alternatives and to make decisions to better himself through the use of land. One of these is the answer to the question of to whom does he give portions of land to farm that he receives in the yearly division of holdings for farming through matrilineal and patrilineal groupings. In theory he can use any or all of this land himself or give it to anyone he wishes to use. In practice he must see that it is used or he may lose his rights to a share in the division in the future. And he is certainly under strong pressure to provide land to his wives and growing children from their matrikinsmen. But he does not even have to let a wife have land he has received for use through the division of holdings from her matrilineage, as long as she has sufficient holdings for her needs somewhere. Some of the land given her is for cassava, which she farms alone, but other sections are land on which the man farms yams, among which she grows vegetables.

Beyond this the man gives part of his shares, if he does not wish to farm them himself, to friends, brothers, and others. He may use these gifts to gain influence and prestige, even though the holdings are small, or to repay someone for a like act. Thus he can employ his shares of land to enhance his position.

There is also a procedure by which a man may give his children land in connection with some special occasion or event which differs from the usual form of land division for farming. These occasions include: when a son succeeds in a special test of strength by building four hundred yam heaps in a day, by killing his first enemy in warfare (now done in the form a ritual where the son kills a bird), by the ritual of running and walking in secret society costume to Edda Village-Group and back to Afikpo, or by performing certain special and extra initiation rituals in the village secret society. There is also a ritual in which a son presents his father with forty good-sized yams, the sign of the son's maturity as a farmer, and the father may give him land as a sign of thanks. When a man takes the highest Afikpo title, *omumε*, he may give land to each of his daughters who dance at the ceremony. A man may, on the other hand, give nothing at all, depending on his feelings in the matter. The gift is usually announced at the ceremony with which it is associated, and where there are numerous witnesses to the event. In addition, if a man is especially fond of his sons he may, when he is dying, give them land in the presence of both patrilineal and matrilineal witnesses, though such cases are relatively rare.

In these instances the farmland or grove concerned is matrilineal land that the father has close control over, that he has obtained on pledge or has redeemed largely by himself. The sons have the right to use such land until the original holders reclaim it, so that while they may use it for many farming seasons they lack permanent controls over it. Thus a man may use gifts of land to enhance his prestige, and to show his love and generosity.

Another type of situation where a man makes decisions on the basis of alternatives in land arises if we view his own sources of land collectively. While a man gets much of his holdings from his own matrilineage, he also is entitled to small shares from his father's matrilineage, and from those of his nonuterine brothers. He also receives some from his wives' matrilineages in their names and for their children or those as yet unborn. He is eligible for land from his agnatic groupings, and from his ward if it has any. He does not rely on any single source; most of his land shares are not large, and the amount that he gets from any one source varies year by year as the land is rotated for farming. But there is considerable variation in the extent to which men actually ask for and obtain and use land from these sources. Some will use only a few descent and kinship connections, but others will seek to develop close and intensive ties with particular relatives in order to increase the possibilities of obtaining larger holdings. This may involve visiting such persons and giving them presents beyond what would normally be expected when they perform certain rituals and attain titles. The channels a man develops and the extent to which he develops them depend upon his initiative.

THE INDIVIDUAL IN CONFLICT SITUATIONS

What becomes of a person whose matrilineal and patrilineal groupings are engaged in a dispute? If he sides actively with his matrilineal group he may find himself fined, ostracized, and denied land by his patrilineal relatives; if he favors his patrilineal group, his matrilineage may deny him farmland and refuse to aid him in ceremonial and other activities. Yet each side will want his support. His position obviously calls for diplomacy, and he will frequently withdraw or try to reconcile the disputing parties. There have been cases, however, in which a man boldly favored one side and attempted to evade the consequent social pressures from the others.

A similar situation occurs when there is a dispute between a man's patrilineal grouping and his father's matrilineage or matriclan. His patrikinsmen will expect him to favor them and will exert social pressure if he does not. His father's matrilineal group will not expect him to aid them actively as he is not a member of their group, but they will not want him to take sides against them. If he tries to oppose them they may say to him, "We are your father. You are hitting us hard. Remember that a son is not higher than his father." A man, at any rate, would certainly not oppose his father's matrilineage if his father were alive. A similar situation exists in a dispute between two clans, when a man belongs to one and the other is that of his father or one of his wives. In each case he must carefully weigh the consequences of any action, and usually plays a cautious and reserved role.

If a man is in constant conflict with his dead father's matrilineage, the group's elders may simply refuse him land. He may accept this, or he may call in selected Afikpo elders to judge the case. The matrilineage will want him evicted from the farmland he is using as its "son" on the grounds of noncooperation. He may claim that the group is at fault, and retaliate by threatening to "give the matrilineage his father's house." This means that he vacates the house or asks whoever is living there to do so, the point being that the house will eventually collapse, and rain will fall on the dead father's grave under the floor, causing the matrilineage great shame. This threat is rarely carried out because it would also upset the man's patrilineage and also probably because it is difficult and inconvenient for persons to move.

When a man is in constant conflict with his dead father's matrilineage, an attempt at a final resolution will be made. This consists of an agreement by both parties to quit matrilineal land they are using that belongs to the other.[15] At this settlement, a representative of the matrilineage describes the portion of the man's land his father's matrilineal relatives are using to the elders selected as judges by both sides, and the man states which part of his father's matrilineal land he is farming. The elders then decree that all such land should be vacated by the parties concerned. The ownership of the land is not under discussion here, merely the usufruct. This terminates formal relations between the man and his father's matrilineage, and in theory prevents future conflicts between them. This type of settlement can occur only if a man's father is dead. If he is alive he would never permit his matrilineage to eject his son from the land, and the son would not go against his father by removing him from his land. These would be considered very bad even to attempt to do, since the father-son bonds are supposed to be very strong. Following the settlement a ritual feast is sometimes shared by the disputants.[16]

A similar situation may arise between two sons of the same father by different mothers. Each normally extends to the other farming rights in his matrilineal land. If it is clear that they are likely always to be unfriendly, one of them, or the male elders of their major patrilineage, may initiate the settlement, which is done in the manner just described. It is more difficult to end the ill feeling in this case, as the brothers live in the same compound and other events of daily existence may still aggravate matters.

While individuals are placed in difficult positions because of conflicts between descent groups with which they are affiliated, more often the contributions of these groupings are positive and

[15] Not only is a man likely to be using his father's matrilineal land but his father's matrilineal relatives, particularly his father's brothers, may share in his lands.

[16] An indication of the closeness of a son to his father's uterine groupings is that if the priest of the matriclan shrine dies, his eldest son at home, who frequently helps him prepare the sacrificial materials and is familiar with the shrine rituals, takes charge of the shrine, offering sacrifices until a new priest is selected. It is indicative of the trustful relations that Afikpo believe should exist between the son and his father's matrikinsmen.

help support the person in his daily activities. A man carries on a variety of relationships with his own patrilineal and matrilineal groupings, with his father's matrilineage and clan, with his wife's matrilineal groupings, as well as with his village organizations. A woman has important relations with her own matrilineal groupings, and with her husband's patrilineal and residential organizations. For a man or woman there is not just one source of land, one source of political and social support, one major source of ceremonial help, but a whole series of groups whose reciprocal duties and obligations in relation to him or her are delineated by custom.

The variety of organizations with which a person has contact, on the other hand, gives him the opportunity to show initiative. His success or failure depends largely on his ability to deal shrewdly with them, on their relative strengths, and on his own personality. It is a rich field and one that allows for considerable enterprise.

For a man to obtain the aid of members of a grouping to which he belongs in order to gain advantages from outside groupings, particularly in the case of land seizure, is considered proper. Groups which support him often share in his success. Inheritance and land disputes are important areas for individual and group enterprise. The Afikpo place great emphasis on property, particularly land and money, and the extent to which they measure their relationships with groups and individuals in these terms is striking. Many of their ceremonies are expressions of wealth or property controls. For example, the portion of a title ceremony of greatest interest to the Afikpo public is that in which the title taker's matrilineal relatives and his "houses" each present him with money gifts. Here the strength or weakness, wealth or poverty, of a man's relationship groups become public, and the extent of the title taker's ties to these groups is often expressed in the degree of financial interest they manifest. It is not that ties of affection are lacking, that kinship or social relationships are unimportant, but that they are so often expressed in terms of property and wealth.

VI. TWO VIEWS OF DOUBLE DESCENT

T HE ethnographic information on Afikpo double descent requires final interpretation. In an overview there may be a tendency to see this form of descent as a *system*, to write of the double descent *system* of the Afikpo Igbo. While there is pattern and organization to it, and it differs in numerous ways from the arrangement of corporate matrilineal and patrilineal groupings in other societies, it may be a reification to call it a system at all. In the first place, following Schneider's caution (1962:1–2), it is only part of a larger network of kin ties which also include some relationships of affinity and filiation that are relatively free of descent ramifications, albeit double descent plays a dominating role in this larger sphere. A second reason for avoiding the term *system* is that it implies a level of order and division of functions and activities which are more clear-cut and precise than are found in Afikpo double descent, where there is some overlapping of interests and behavior between the two unilineal lines.

With these cautions in mind we will first comment on the view of descent from the vantage point of the individual and his network of roles, conflicting and supportive, and then from the view of the descent groupings as entities, with their internal organization, functions, and activities, and their external relationships. In so doing discussion of the interrelationships of the two viewpoints is inevitable, for while they are separate they are not isolated from each other.

ROLES AND THE INDIVIDUAL

In reviewing the character of individual relationships, both as a network of interpersonal ties and from the orientation of persons in specific roles, we will comment on some of the points raised by Schneider in his exceedingly helpful statement of the "logic" of matrilineal descent (1961).[1] Also of use are his comparisons of matrilineality with patrilineal features, though the latter are not fully developed, and he only briefly mentions double descent.

Every individual in Afikpo is linked through membership by birth with two descent categories, that of his father's patrilineal groupings and the uterine ones of his mother. In addition his or her birth by a particular pair of parents gives the person a potential link but not membership with the father's matrilineal groupings and the mother's patrilineal ones, whether in fact these are important in actuality or not. Further, marriage provides the potentiality of ties between a person and his or her spouse's matrilineal and patrilineal groupings of birth. Again, the prevalence of polygyny makes for possible relationships between a person and the matrilineal groupings of half-siblings. Other possible descent relationships exist, as between a person and his stepfather's patrilineal and matrilineal categories, but those mentioned form the framework from which there is selection, as determined by the society's norms, with special emphases, activities, and behaviors associated with each tie. The two most fundamental features are that the intensity and nature of the ties vary according to the sex of the individual concerned and also in terms of age.

In the case of a female, as a child her ties with her mother are

[1] See also Richards' (1934; 1950) pioneer work in the study of matrilineality.

very strong. She lives in her mother's world with her uterine sisters, and she has contact with other matrilineal females. Her mother's brother or other male matrilineage members have a general interest in her which is, in part, an outgrowth of an interest in the welfare of her mother, but they do not have a great deal of direct contact with her and no authority over her. In terms of these features it is not clear that, at this stage, her matrilineal ties are fully developed, for these can also be seen to a large extent as domestic relationships. She has established strong ties with female matrilineal relatives that will last her throughout her life, but it is not evident that they are purely matrilineal ties; they are probably best seen as mixed.

As a child she and her father have a somewhat distant relationship. She sees him in the compound, she may do errands for him, there is affection between them, but she lives in her mother's house and is extremely close to her. Her ties to him and his agnatic grouping are important for her support and survival in such crucial matters as clothing, housing, some food, and in rituals. While there is a domestic element to these ties she is seen as fully a member of the major and minor patrilineages of her father, and these groupings have obligations to her and she to them.

Her ties, as a child, to her father's matrilineal and her mother's patrilineal groupings are unimportant.

When she reaches adulthood and marries crucial changes occur. Her links with her father's matrilineal and her mother's patrilineal relatives remain as weak as ever. On marrying, she becomes independent of her father's help, afterwards seeing little of him and of her major and minor patrilineage relatives, and she depends upon her husband and his patrilineal relations for support, housing, and in the regulation of her behavior. However, she can always renew her own patrilineal ties in the event of the failure of her marriage, by returning home to live. Marriage histories indicate that this is likely to be a temporary arrangement and that she soon remarries or returns to her husband.

There is almost an equal exchange of distant attachments to a male figure. She develops some ties with her husband's matriclan, mainly over the use of its land, but on the whole these are not too important and her main links here are through her husband and his patrilineal relatives. Her matrilineal ties remain strong, but they change in character. Her mother and sisters still play important advisory roles, particularly in domestic and ritual matters. However, they are supplemented by the role her brother plays, especially her eldest brother, or in the absence of mature brothers, of a mother's brother, often the eldest. Also the head of her matrilineage, if he is not one of these, may play an advisory role. It is through the agency of such persons that she and her husband gain access to the considerable land of her matrilineage, and it is her brother or other person who is her advisor for many matters concerning her relationship to her husband.

Thus the key figures in a woman's life are first, as a child, her mother and to a lesser degree her father, and then, as an adult, her husband and her brother or mother's brother. Her sisters and mother still play a role, but her father hardly any. She may, of course, also have strong ties with friends and others, but those outlined above are the most significant in terms of support and legal rights. Her view of the world is basically matrilineal, first through her mother, then her brother or mother's brother and in terms of her own children. She is always something of a stranger in her own patrilineal groupings and in those of her marriage.

The pattern differs for the male. As a child, he has strong ties with both parents. Those with his mother are the most important in the first few years of life; they are a reflection of domestic rather than unilineal descent ties. After the age of five or six it is his father who begins to play a more significant role. As a growing child he has little to do in a direct way with his own matrilineal relatives, though they mark his presence and await his adulthood. It is his father and his patrilineal relatives that play the supporting role during this period of growth. They see that the important *rites de passage*, such as circumcision and initiation to the secret society, are carried out. Matrilineal relatives come to many of these as representatives, as we have seen, but do not hold the responsibility for carrying them out. Agnatic kin also help him to arrange for his first marriage. If his father is not in a position to direct these matters it is his patrikinsmen, not his matrikinsmen, who act in his place. In many cases, there are strong bonds of affection between a boy and his father.

The adult male plays an increasing role in his agnatic groupings as he ages, taking part in its ritual activities and first in its police and then its leadership functions. His everyday life has a strong agnatic cast.

But his heavily patrilineal ties are counterbalanced upon reaching adulthood by very important matrilineal links, especially with three groupings. First, he begins to use farmland of his own matrilineage, and to associate with his matrilineal relatives in common activities. His full brothers, whom he has viewed largely as playmates with common agnatic and uterine ties, now take on another image. They become set off from nonuterine brothers, in terms of an interest in matrilineal land and other uterine matters. The adult male comes to know and to rely on his mother's brother and his matrilineal leaders for land and in other property matters, persons with whom he had little contact as a child. Second, through his father's introductions he also comes to know his father's matrikinsmen, and to make use of their land, as a "son" of the matrilineage and matriclan. Third, he develops ties with his wives' matrilineal relatives, mainly concerning land and his children. Characteristically his links with his wives' patrilineages are weak, being mainly a matter of courtesy relations following marriage, though they are important during the period of courtship and the marriage arrangements.

Thus, while females retain what is largely a matrilineal orientation throughout life, males live in childhood first with a strong maternal tie, then in essentially a patrilineal world, and as adults move more equally into the sphere of double descent. They take on a double orientation; double descent is more fully expressed in direct action through males than females. As a result, men and women experience the double descent system in quite different ways, have different orientations toward it, receive different rewards from it, and view different points of the descent structure as supportive or troublesome.

Despite the common experience of all young children with their mother, there is thus an early separation of the interests and activities of the sexes in terms of the descent groupings. There is even a strong air of distinctiveness in the way that the sexes carry out some activities together, for example farming. The male is firmly anchored in an agnatic residential unit which forms a governmental block, the major patrilineage. A woman leaves her own agnatic group at marriage, usually in her teens. But she is never fully incorporated into her husband's patrilineal groupings; frequently she remarries at least once into another like situation, and she is pulled strongly toward matrilineal interests associated with her children. She never has a firm residential base anywhere, never a real incorporation into residential groups either by birth or marriage. It is no wonder then that her position in society is distinctive from that of males, and that she has little status in relation to them. Her adult life is essentially determined by the authority of her husband and his patrilineal groupings, and by her brother and other male uterine relatives.

Key factors here are that women bear children and yet it is the males who hold authority in the society. Further, there is matri-clan exogamy and not much in-group marriage in the major patrilineage (Schneider, 1961:5). From these much of what occurs in double unilineal descent at Afikpo can be "explained." In the patrilineal case the line of authority and of descent both run through the man; in the matrilineal the authority is in male hands but the descent line is through females. While men are involved in authority over females there is a difference in the ones that they are concerned with in the two types of descent groups. In the patrilineal case it is primarily with in-marrying spouses, in the matrilineal with women of their own descent group. In the matrilineal situation men are involved in the control over their own males and the spouses of their females, while in the patrilineal they are concerned again with control over their own men and with the male uterine relatives of their wives.

A wife's matrilineal relatives at Afikpo are very interested that she have children to perpetuate the uterine descent line. It does not really matter, as Schneider correctly states (1961:14), who the male is, as long as she has them, and some male provides for her welfare and that of her offspring. Her male uterine relatives are not by any means as concerned as the husband is with the preservation of her marriage. This takes second place over the need to fulfill her childbearing capabilities and to care for her children. And, in fact, we see at Afikpo that lack of children is a major reason a woman leaves her husband, obtains a divorce and remarries, and for a practice which sometimes occurs of a barren wife living with another man than her husband until she conceives, when she returns to him.

Her brothers, or at least the eldest one, are therefore interested in her sexual activities, mainly in the sense that she has sexual relations, and they are likewise concerned for her general welfare. It fits into the picture at Afikpo that a man who is angry at a wife can punish her by denying her sexual relations with him. He can use this device to force a reconciliation, or at least an attempted settlement of the differences between them, for this brings her uterine relatives to the scene, first perhaps her mother and sisters, then males. And a wife can also use her husband's sexual denial as a major ground for divorce, which is accepted at Afikpo.

From the patrilineal point of view a man's daughter's marriage provides him with little in the way of financial resources. The bride wealth payment is small. Her children are not important to the continuation of his patrilineal line, except in the few cases where she marries within the major patrilineage. Thus, although he may retain affectionate feelings for her he has little interest in her after she marries. It is his wives, who come from other descent groupings on both sides than himself, who are his interest. He is very much concerned with a wife's behavior, with sexual rights over her, and with the manner in which she treats the children, especially his sons. And from his point of view, unlike the matrilineal case, it is important that she not leave him. If she does he loses her as a potential childbearer for his agnatic line, and if she takes children with her it is not at all clear whether those who are males will ever return to live with him and to rejoin his patrilineal groupings as adults—the choice is theirs. Her departure and remarriage is a threat to his agnatic descent line. He wants her to feel comfortable and relaxed in the compound; yet because of her matrilineal ties, especially to her brothers, there is never any possibility of full incorporation into his agnatic groupings. She will always necessarily have external interests over which he has no or little control. Her patrilineal interests of birth are given up in marriage but her matrilineal ones cannot be. This is unlike a patrilineal society where full incorporation following marriage is possible, though external factors sometimes prevent this. This does not mean that at Afikpo there is little or no affection between husbands and wives. They are expected to have such feelings, and in some cases these run strong, while in others they are absent.

As a result, as in purely matrilineal societies, there is often an uneasy relationship between the husband and whatever male uterine relative of hers is in direct authority over her—let us say her eldest brother. In theory each male wants the same things for her, that she have children and that she and her children be treated well and that they prosper, and that, in view of her considerable responsibility in feeding the children, she be given sufficient land to farm. In practice her husband is often suspicious of her brother's authority over her, of the fact that she may feel the husband is treating other wives better than her, a common wifely complaint. The rule that a husband should treat his wives equally is functional in this regard, though in fact it is often violated. And a wife's brother can interfere in a man's relationship with his wife with just such a complaint. The husband may also worry that her brother will advise her to leave him if he feels that the marriage is a doubtful one. The brother may be suspicious of the husband's lack of interest in his wife. As

Schneider points out (1961:13), the brother's incestuous wishes toward his sister may be important in determining his relationship toward her husband.

Thus there is a delicate tie between the wife's matrikinsman in authority over her and her husband, counterbalancing forces in her life. Her husband is reluctant to have her male matrikinsman interfere in his domestic life, yet he wants access to farmland of her matrilineage, not only for her but also for his own use. The two must cooperate with regard to the same women though there is sometimes suspicion between them. It takes a certain amount of skill on the part of all three persons to handle this situation without conflict.

What makes the relationship between the two men even more crucial than in a society that only has matrilineal descent is that in the latter instance the marriage contributes only to the husband's domestic groupings, but at Afikpo it also contributes to his agnatic line and organizations; it makes their existence possible. We would expect, therefore, that the level of authority of the husband vis-à-vis the wife and her brother would be greater in this form of society than in a purely matrilineal one, as well as the degree of tension between the two men. This seems to be true at Afikpo. Neither man is dominant over the other. While the husband exerts immediate daily controls over his wife, backed up by the authority of his major and minor patrilineage, he is deferential towards her uterine authority figure; it is the husband who comes to ask for land, and who pays the courtesy visits to this man. But if the husband's role is not weak, neither is that of the brother. In most cases there is a formal rather than a friendly relationship between the two men, and this is what we might well expect.

It is likely that part of the motivation of a man to marry his father's sister's daughter lies here. In such a marriage the girl does not belong to the husband's major patrilineage, of course, but her mother does, and there is in some way a reason to think that the husband, because of this patrilineal link, may be able to hold extra authority over her. More importantly, she belongs to her husband's father's matrilineage, with which he has a relationship, albeit one of deference with respect to its males. These two features place some claim upon her by the husband that other wives do not show. A not too dissimilar situation also occurs when a girl marries within her own major patrilineage. In this uncommon form of marriage she has two roles in relation to her husband, as wife and as a female member of his agnatic grouping, so that she is more clearly bound to him than if she is from the outside. Whether this is why there is no strict rule of patrilineal exogamy at Afikpo, at least with regard to a woman's first marriage, is not clear. But it is evident that both in the case of paternal cross-cousin and patrilineal in-group marriage that there are tendencies for the husband to acquire a stronger measure of control over his wives than otherwise. It seems that while the woman's brother would prefer her to marry in a manner that would avoid this situation, he has little control over whom she marries. And in the paternal cross-cousin situation he may know the husband-to-be and feel confident that they can get along.

There is also a strict rule of patrilineal remarriage exogamy. From the agnatic point of view this prevents disharmony among the males of the compound by preventing accusations among them of wife-stealing and poisoning the husband if he has died, though it would seem that, on other grounds, they would favor such a remarriage in order to retain the wife and children in their patrilineal groupings. But from the matrilineal orientation the existence of such a procedure, for example, the levirate, would imply the close incorporation of the women into a major and minor patrilineage, which groups would have clear authority over her; this would contradict her brother's authority and undermine it. From his viewpoint, he is primarily interested that she have a husband, not that she develops a host of ties with male authorities in her husband's patrilineage. His minimal role in the marriage preparations and the ceremony itself are indicative of this, as well as in any bride price settlement if she remarries. He refrains from entering into a relationship with her husband's patrilineage as much as possible. To do so would imply that it has authority over her. The bride price payment itself legally allocates the children to the husband's patrilineal line. It is not necessary for there to be an allocation to the wife's matrilineal line for this is automatic.

If wives are not well incorporated into their husbands' agnatic groupings, what of husbands in terms of the matrilineal groupings of their wives? The question has been well discussed by Schneider (1961:16–20) in the matrilineal context. He has outlined the reasons why it is impossible for matrilineal groupings to incorporate such men and still to retain their identity, and this is true at Afikpo. They remain at the edge of the matrilineal organization, probing its land resources but having no ultimate authority over its land, often with a formal rather than a relaxed tie with its male members. For men in these matrilineal groupings who deal with such male outsiders, over whom they have few controls other than to threaten to pressure their sisters to withdraw as wives, the task is to see that the strangers sire children and treat the wives well. The matrilineal males have no way to force the husbands to do so.

It is evident that the practice of men marrying wives from different matrilineages not only has advantages for husbands in greater potential land resources, but also for matrilineal groupings. If a man were to marry three or four persons from a single matrilineage it would increase his potential authority in relationships to its members, possibly to the point of conflict. This would certainly be so if many members of major or minor patrilineage married women from a single matrilineage, an unlikely event. The male agnates would threaten the authority of the matrilineage males in terms of land and inheritance, and matrilineal groupings might in fact cease to exist. The matrilineage, in turn, would have little to gain by this arrangement, in land or other rewards. It is true that paternal cross-cousin marriage is favored and that this tends to establish a tie between a patrilineal line and two matrilineages. But the tie seems often to be of different matrilineages with separate lines in a major patrilineage, so that no large-scale relationship develops. Also here because considerations of father-son-grandson authority are involved—the deferential behavior of man toward his father's matrilineage reflecting his relationship to his father—the possibility of a patrilineal take-over are minimized.

There are close ties between patrilineal and matrilineal groupings in the case of land pledging and redemption, and in the support that patrilineal groupings sometimes give matrilineal ones in disputes, as we have seen. But these are not as much through a man's sisters by marriage, to her husband's agnates, as they are through his own patrikinsmen linked to his uterine relations.

Social interaction for the adult male is linked around the problem of controlling his own wives vis-à-vis their matrilineal ties while trying to insure that his own sisters and sisters' daughters are well-married and well-treated by their husbands. The kind of role an adult male plays in regard to women may make him act in ways that seem contradictory. He is trying to retain his authority over his wives at the same time he is trying to keep his control over his sisters or their daughters with reference to their husbands. He may be angry at a wife's brother for interfering in his domestic life while at the same time he is in the opposite role: he is upset at a husband married to one of his sisters for not acting well towards her. These are not conflicting roles for him, rather they reflect the nature of his relationships to these two types of women.

Two other important relationships at Afikpo are those of a person to his father and to his mother's brother. In patrilineal societies the role of the father is usually dominant, in terms of descent, legal matters, and rituals. The mother's brother lacks authority but may have an affectional and supportive role unencumbered by questions of control. In matrilineal societies there exists a different division of these roles. The father's side is concerned with affectional, and sometimes, ritual needs, and the mother's brother with legal and property rights, through other arrangements exist.[2] What is the pattern in a double descent society, such as Afikpo, where both the father and the mother's brother, each in his respective descent group, are the most immediate male figures of the senior generation?

Again, we must distinguish between the sexes. As we have seen, a female child has little to do with her mother's brother. Her father is legally in control and has the responsibility of support, but the child's ties of affection are mainly with the mother. In adulthood the paternal tie largely disappears and her brother, especially an elder brother, develops into her advisor and supporter. Her mother's eldest brother or another mother's brother if the eldest lives at a distance, may or may not play this role depending on whether her brothers are alive, dead, young or mature, and whether she can gain land directly through the lineage head, but there is no clear-cut priority for a mother's brother.

A male child's father plays the dominating role, as an authority figure though there are also affective feelings involved. His mother's brothers have little to do with him, do not take part in his training, and are secondary figures at his *rites de passage*. When the child matures, the relationships he develops with his mother's brothers, especially the eldest, rarely seem to be ties of affection, but are bonds of common interest in property and other matrilineal matters. It is the responsibility of his mother's senior brother to "show him the land" of the matrilineage, whether this man actually controls it or not, and to see that he receives shares when it is divided for farming. His father may help by bringing him to the mother's brother, but here he plays only a supportive role. Because much matrilineal land is not under the control of the mother's brother (unless he is also the matrilineage head), but of the head and other matrilineage members, the mother's brother's position vis-à-vis his sister's son is not strong. Further, the pattern of land use is such that a man has many other sources

    [2] See Schneider (1961); Fortes (1950); Richards (1950). The discussion here can be contrasted to Goody's analysis (1959) of the LoDagaba and LoWiili.

of land outside of his matrilineage. He is not fully dependent upon his mother's brothers; the extent to which he relies on them varies in terms of what other sources of land exist for him. A man may be as concerned about the role of his wife's brother in land matters as he is with his mother's brothers. As an adult, there are virtually no rituals, titles, or ceremonies that a man cannot perform without his mother's brothers' aid, though the support of one or more of these is often expected and desired. Tensions may develop between Ego and a mother's brother over internal land matters, the withholding of land from Ego that the mother's brother acquires himself, and as a part of the segmentation process in the matrilineage. Again this occurs if Ego tries to pass his matrilineal land to his children on a permanent basis. These tensions also rise between the man and other matrilineal relatives for like reasons; they are not exclusively focused on the mother's brother.

A man's role as he matures frequently changes in relation to his father, a situation similar to that in many African societies, if not elsewhere. He begins to strike out on his own and may wish greater control over family affairs. His ties of affection with his *pater* often wane. He finds he is forbidden publicly to speak at variance to his father's public pronouncements, that he cannot take titles his father does not hold until the latter has died, and that it is difficult to gain recognition while his father is alive as he is still considered a "small boy" regardless of his age. He also finds that he may not care for his father's advice in domestic matters. There is not always growing tension between father and son, but it is common enough to be discussed and commented on. The son is held in check by his patrilineal residential groupings, for its members will not permit him to "go beyond his father," while the father is alive,[3] nor will his father's uterine relatives, if they can prevent it. Of course, his father still aids him in family rituals and sacrifices and serves as guide and advisor. Thus the ordinary father-son conflicts over authority which exist in many

---

[3] He is in a similar situation with regard to older brothers.

patrilineal societies occur here, but the son cannot play off his mother's brother against his father to his advantage as he might in a matrilineal society, and his patrilineal relatives apply pressure to keep him under control.

The pattern which has developed at Afikpo fits neither the purely matrilineal or the purely patrilineal situation found in other societies. The mother's brother's role is not so clear-cut or authoritarian at Afikpo for either sex as it is in some matrilineal societies. There is no complementary or neat division between the types of relationships of a man with his father and mother's brothers. Both have legal and property controls over him, and both are involved in some of his ritual and ceremonial activities. In the case of females there is greater distinctiveness, however. And for men there are *both* legal and affectual ties with the father in the context of the agnatic groups.

Let us now look at the relationship of persons to their mothers. In a patrilineal system, or perhaps in any system, we would expect that a son, under his mother's authority as a child, would have a measure of authority over her when he is an adult, especially if his father is dead. At Afikpo he does in terms of assisting her, though it would be hard to say he controls her, and often men of her husband's minor patrilineage also help. But his matrilineal tie through her adds another dimension to his relationship with her that he would not otherwise have. In the case of a female the presence of a matrilineal system as a formal organization pegs her relationship as always being inferior to that of her mother in authority—these are the respective roles that they play within the matrilineage. In a sense it keeps her infantilized symbolically, for her mother is always a senior relative in the matrilineage in regard to her. This would be less likely to be so in a purely patrilineal system.

Some comment should also be made concerning the relationship of a person to his father's brothers, especially the eldest one. In patrilineal societies this person is generally strong and supportive, one who can act as a father-substitute and advisor, and this is so at Afikpo. In addition, this bond is reinforced by the special relationship of a son to his father's matrilineage. His father's brothers are in authority over him in this regard, and this continues, in a matrilineal sense, after the father's death. For a female it is a different matter. As a child she has little to do with her father's male siblings unless her father dies and her mother chooses to remain as a widow in the compound, when one or more of them help to fill his role. But she has no ties of great importance to her father's matrilineage and her marriage virtually ends all links with it and her father's brother.

Schneider suggests (1961:4) that the characteristic features of exogamic matrilineal systems which should exist in a logical sense are not seriously altered in double descent. His point is well taken for Afikpo, where matrilineality fits his scheme surprisingly well. There are, however, three major areas of actual variation in this specific case. First, the presence of agnatic factors is related to a stronger and more stable residential pattern for males. There is a tendency in African matrilineal societies for settlement patterns to be shifting, and for conflicts among matrilineally related males to be related to this. This seems particularly so in South Central Africa (Colson and Gluckman, 1951). Or else the pattern is, as in the Ashanti (Fortes, 1950), one where marriage residence for males is highly variable, though settlements seem stable. In Afikpo, as in the case of the Yakö (Forde, 1964, chaps. v, vi), villages are relatively permanent, and patrilocal residence is the almost universal rule. The presence of patrilineal groupings seems to provide for stable residence, where matrilineality frequently leads to residence variation and movement. In Afikpo the conflicts that occur among uterine relatives over land, especially within the matrilineage, do not lead to the disruption of settlements, and contests over the leadership of matrilineages likewise do not affect the basic governmental structure. Of course for women there is great physical mobility through marriage and remarriage and the social instability is focused on them, but this is not reflected in unstable or shifting residential groupings.

Second, we have discussed how the presence of agnatic groupings strengthens the role of the husband in relation to his wife's brother or other uterine authority. No more need be added here. Third, the ties of a man to his mother's brother are weaker in Afikpo than we might expect in a matrilineal society because of the strong role of the patrilineal groupings. This role includes the emotional link between father and son, at least when the latter is young, and the socialization and *rites de passage* of the child in the patrilineal setting. The mother's-brother tie is also weak because there is an important counterbalancing tie of a man to his father's matrilineage, and because of the lack of a single well-defined system of authority over matrilineal land controls, which diffuses a man's ties with several senior male matrikinsmen.

On the other hand pure patrilineality is modified by matrilineal conditions. There are limits to the degree to which the wife can be incorporated into the agnatic groupings, and marriage stability is not high.[4] The authority of a husband over a wife and children is limited by matrilineal considerations. The wife brings economic resources to the marriage which do not come under the direct control of her husband. The resources of the patrilineal groupings are limited.

Nevertheless, one is struck by how in so many areas the principles that we associate with matrilineal life are able to exist side by side without contradiction or strong antagonism with patrilineality, and how, in many cases, such as in an interest in children, and in the health and welfare of the nuclear family, the goals of one type of descent group are similar to those of the other, though not necessarily for the same reasons. It is an additive situation, an intricately wrought series of ties between groups and among individuals. It is mainly in the area of the treatment of wives, and in disputes over land and inheritance, that frictions break out. These have to do with wealth, for in Afikpo children are this in a way, as well as land, money, and goods, and they are areas where the prestige and status of a person are important, as well as his or her survival and that of their descent groups. That

---

[4] Other factors than this also affect the divorce rate.

there should be friction and the breakdown of cooperation across matrilineal and patrilineal ties and groups in these sectors is no surprise, particularly when we consider that matrilineality was probably the first to develop at Afikpo, so that patrilineality, coming in later, must have competed with it in these areas. Today, however, while it is possible to locate sections of Afikpo which are of later origin, and probably were patrilineal in origin, and other sections which were early and once heavily matrilineal, all areas of the village-group seem to follow much the same pattern without essential variation.

If these two forms of descent are largely additive, what is missing that we would likely find in unilineal societies? It is the kinship ties of bilateral relationship external to the descent system. It is not, however, that domestic groupings are absent, far from it, nor that nonunilineal descent ties of kinship by birth, or ties with persons through marriage, or through the marriages of their siblings and of their parents, are unimportant. But the most striking feature of the domestic roles is that relationships between individuals in their domestic units are potentially or actually relationships between single persons and descent groups, or between descent groups. For example, a son's tie to his father is not often simply a father-son tie. It takes place within the context of patrilineal groupings to which they both belong, and also involves the ties of the son to the father's matrilineage, and of the father to the son's matrilineal relatives. If father and son quarrel, it is not simply a family affair, but may involve the agnatic kin and the matrilineal groupings of the father as well. Again, when a man quarrels with an agnatic half-brother, the matrikinsmen of both brothers as well as the patrilineal groupings to which they both belong may eventually become involved. A similar situation occurs with a married couple; a quarrel brings his patrikinsmen and her matrikinsmen to bear on the point of the dispute.

There are some, but there do not seem to be very many bilateral relations *per se* in Afikpo, since almost all family ties potentially (and frequently do) involve the descent groups of their members. Mother-child and cowife relationships are two areas where descent ties may be unimportant for a good deal of behavior. But in a sense, family members are almost always acting as representatives of their descent groups in the daily activities in the domestic groupings. It is true that the relative importance of certain unilineal groups in terms of the family may vary greatly. The wife's patrilineage is less important, as a rule, than her matrilineage. Yet domestic links continually involves descent ties in complex ways. This is so not only in the case of such negative features as family quarrels but in terms of positive elements such as avenues to obtain land, financial aid, and political and ritual support. Individuals exploit their domestic ties in order to derive positive gains from the web of descent groups of which they are a part. Thus Afikpo view bilateral ties in a different light from societies in which only domestic groupings systems are found, or in societies characterized by a single line of descent. Many family roles in Afikpo are heavily involved with descent ties. Bilateral ties exist in every society, but the evidence from Afikpo suggests that the degree of autonomy of domestic groupings is least in double descent societies, greater in single unilineal societies, and greatest in societies where unilineal descent is completely absent.

We also note that when an individual operates through ties of descent, by birth or otherwise, he sometimes functions only in terms of two or three generations of a descent line. His concern for the whole descent group may be important but secondary, and may only come into play if certain matters arise. For example, in the case of a wife he is sometimes less concerned with her whole matrilineage than he is with her, her brother, her (and his) children of the marriage, and perhaps her mother's brother and the matrilineage head. In his own agnatic ties his main concern at times may be his father and full brothers, and his children. The larger descent group is there, potentially and frequently involved, but it is the smaller line within which he may have certain contacts in his daily life.

The implication of the various channels of fruitful relationships and of action is that individuals will take advantage of these and manipulate them for their own needs. There is a great deal of weight on individual achievement and enterprise in social relationships, and it is not surprising that achievement qualities as well as ascribed ones are stressed in many spheres. For example, the ability to speak well, one of the primary criteria of leadership among elders in the matriclan and major patrilineage, and the historical knowledge required of a good leader, are often skills based upon the past experience of one who has thrown himself wholeheartedly into relationships with these descent groupings, and with associated matters concerning land controls and the adjudication of property disputes, and who through his contacts and actions has gained support and a following as well as experience. There are varied sources of land a man may draw upon and he develops these in terms of his own skills, his own conception of his relationships in and to these descent organizations, and the quantity and quality of land available to him through these different groupings. And he can use his land resources to cement friendship and alliance. Similarly, if a man is involved in a court case, he may invoke his descent group ties for support. He may not be on good terms with all these groups at one time, but the multiplicity of descent groups means that neither is he dependent on a single group or even two for land, political support, or other matters, as he might be in a society with single unilineal descent.

As Leach has suggested (1962:133), it seems particularly with a person's ties of filiation and affinity that he has alternative avenues of action. For a man of Afikpo this is mainly with his father's and his wives' matrilineal groupings, and to a lesser extent those of his half-siblings of the same father but different mothers. For a woman, a lesser case, it is mainly the varied support of her husband's patrikinsmen that allows for flexibility. There are, in addition, significant variations in the extent to which a person uses his own descent groupings by birth to his own advantage, and these kinds of situations are also important as well as ties of affinity and filiation. For example, we have seen the interplay of persons within a matrilineage at Afikpo when land matters involving the group are concerned.

We do not argue that for the Afikpo a high achievement motivation is a result of the presence of double descent. The Igbo in general are strong achievers (LeVine, 1966; S. Ottenberg, 1959), an orientation that has played a crucial role in the political problems of their country in recent years. The Afikpo share this general Igbo pattern. Rather, the point of view expressed here is that double descent has not seriously inhibited achievement, but rather gives it its particular form within the traditional aspects of the society. While it is true that the Afikpo area has not modernized or developed as rapidly as other Igbo regions, for example, the Onitsha, Owerri, and Aba areas, the difference seems largely a matter of the length and intensity of European contact —the development of roads, railroads, and certain economic enterprises in these other groupings through external sources. The Afikpo area has been more isolated than these other regions. Although the fact that much of Igbo country is patrilineal might suggest a link between agnation and achievement, the argument of the influence of history and economic development is more forceful. Further evidence, perhaps, is that among the Eastern Igbo groups, where double descent is common, the Afikpo are one of the most "progressive" and Westernized. This is undoubtedly due to the presence of the Government Station there, which in turn is related to the growth of the area as an educational center.

Rather the Afikpo double descent organization contains important areas where individuals can make choices to enhance their status. In a society with either purely matrilineal or patrilineal descent there may be a similar range of alternatives open to the individual, or greater or less possibilities, but in any case these operate to a larger extent through other agencies than descent, for example, through bilateral family ties. Choices also exist at Afikpo in the bilateral sector and again in the political sphere through the village and village-group organizations. Achievement at Afikpo is clearly not restricted to the sector of descent. Nevertheless many of the alternative choices are made *through* rather than *external* to the descent groupings. This is necessarily so as a result of the pervasiveness of descent, despite the presence of other forms of organization. We agree with Leach (1962) that double descent is not necessarily rigid, despite the presence of so many formal descent groupings that are concerned with everyday life.

Rosemary Harris' study of Mbembe society (1965a, esp. pp. 34–35) suggests that achievement activities do not necessarily have to be stressed within double descent *if* other avenues are open. Here unilineal kin appear particularly unsupportive and ties of filiation unexploited. It is through ties between persons who are in association groupings and with age mates that support can be achieved. While these two elements are also important, at Afikpo the unilineal groupings are more fully developed and offer much more positive assistance to persons associated with them as members, through filiation and by marriage. Mbembe society therefore fits a model of a more rigid double descent organization in terms of variation in behavior than Afikpo, suggesting that there may be considerable range in this type of descent in terms of flexibility. Whether Afikpo is an exception in terms of its particular pattern, or at the end of a range, remains to be seen, but it seems unlikely that either would be so. Harris' work also indicates the importance of viewing descent within the framework of the larger society rather than as a distinct and isolated system.

It would be unfair to give the impression that all is a matter of alternatives at Afikpo. Far from it. In many situations the individual has little or no choice. A man must play a role in the patrilineal activities of his compound according to his age. If he has sons he must see that they are put through the *rites de passage*. He is under pressure to take titles in his major patrilineage according to his wealth. He is under obligation to treat his father's and wife's matrikinsmen with respect, and to play at least some role in his matrilineage, though he may be involved in land acquisition activities which set him off from some of his matrilineal relatives. There are areas where there is little freedom of action. It is with regard to productive property and political and status considerations that these alternatives operate rather freely, that he may exploit his roles in reference to the descent group.

One is struck by the number of different roles that a person has in terms of his descent groups. There are those associated with his major and minor patrilineages, matrilineage and matriclan, those of his father's matrilineal groupings, his agnatic half-brothers' uterine organizations, and his wives' descent groupings. In each case he can carry out specific relationships with descent group members in different fashion, for example, in his own matrilineal ones with his mother, mother's brothers, his sisters, the matrilineage head, and the matriclan elders and priest. The extent of multiple roles at Afikpo may seem surprising at first, and this phenomenon occurs outside of descent as well. But we have to consider that the population density is over four hundred persons per square mile, and that although the traditional technology is not complex or highly specialized, the population factor has something to do with the presence of many roles. Certainly it would be hard to conceive of double descent, as it operates at Afikpo, existing in its present form with a light population base. It may be that Durkheim's equation (1933:256–82) of organic solidarity with role differentiation and increased population density is a useful idea here, however misleading is the basis of his theory of solidarity. The large number of roles is, of course, related to the presence of a fair degree of alternatives to action. We would argue that double descent would be difficult to maintain under conditions of light population. Not only is the Afikpo population high, but that of the LoWiili is some 330 persons per square mile (Goody, 1956:27), and the population density of the Yakö is also considerable (Forde, 1964:4).

THE DESCENT GROUPS CONTRASTED

We now turn to the comparison of the descent groups as organized entities. The characteristic pattern is one of a certain distinctiveness of activities and functions with some important overlapping, and a surprisingly over-all uniformity in administrative organization and leadership practices.

It is common, when discussing double descent, to differentiate between matrilineal and patrilineal activities and to examine to what extent they complement each other and overlap (see, e.g., Forde, 1939b; 1950a). This seemingly innocent matter is fraught with problems: what really is meant by double descent, and to what extent is there balance or polarity of interests and activities between the two descent lines (see Goody, 1961; Leach, 1962)? There is no need for us to enter these controversies, which in the Afikpo case involve some quite spurious questions. What is useful, in bringing together the threads of double descent, is simply to contrast the activities of the two types of descent groupings.

Let us first look at matrilineality. Major preoccupations of the matrilineal groupings are with farmland rights and over the inheritance of money and goods. The ownership, use, and protection of farmland are the main concerns of matrilineage heads and the elders of the matriclans. Many of the rituals of the uterine groups are associated with land, and in these the clan shrine, *Nja*, may play a role, and also the Aro oracle, *Ibini ɔkpabe*.

The fertility of members, especially females, is important, and rituals and sacrifices are carried out to ensure this. The women of the clan, as a group, take initiative and act in this regard, as well as males.

On the other hand, the ritual aspects of matrilineality seem much more restricted than those of patrilineality. Matrilineal groupings are concerned ceremonially with the fertility of their females, and that of the land. When they play a role in some of the *rites de passage* of their members, they more often act as witnesses than direct the ceremonies. It is true that the slave matriclan formerly played an important ritual role for all of Afikpo, but the uterine groupings lack the numerous shrines and the associated rituals of patrilineality for internal affairs, social control, and for Afikpo as a whole.

The *Nja* spirit of the matriclan shrine is, on the whole, positive and supportive. However, the ancestral shrine spirits of the major patrilineage, its closest equivalent, as well as supernaturals of other patrilineal shrines, have an element of unpredictability and idiosyncracy about them. Sometimes they are destructive and negative, and at other times they act positively.[5] More attention seems to be paid to the ancestral spirits than to *Nja*. The positive aspect of the matriclan shrines mirrors the strong emotional tie between males and their mothers; the mixture of positive and negative actions attributed to the spirits of the ancestral and other patrilineal shrines reflects something of the relationship of a man to his father—positive and supporting, yet as the son reaches adult life containing some conflicts and hostilities.

With the exception of the now-outlawed blood revenge, matrilineal groupings play a lesser role in government than the agnatic groupings, though individual clan members may be active in the Afikpo government. Matrilineality is not the basis of the major governmental units or the judicial system, for residence seems to be necessary for these in Afikpo, and the uterine groups lack a genuine residential base; even the matriclan shrine and meeting place are moved in time. It is not that the matrilineal groups lack structure and leadership, but rather these are limited to the matriclan and matrilineage itself, and are not administratively linked to other governmental forms, as are those of the patrilineal groupings. The uterine administrative organization stands in relative isolation from the Afikpo government, though it plays an important role in regulating and supporting its members. It is true that the presence of matrilineal groupings brings persons into contact with others who live in different compounds and villages, supplying an underlying unity to the village-group, but the lack of cooperation among different matriclans is evident. Unlike other African double descent societies discussed by R. Harris (1962b:88–89), the main unity of Afikpo in organization and ritual behavior is provided by the village and village-group age grade structure, and at a lower level of organization, by the cooperation of coresident patrilineages in the village.

[5] Contrast with the Yakö. See Forde (1964:262–83).

Conflicts between matriclans or their members are not, as a rule, adjudicated by themselves. This is especially true in land cases, where outside agencies, the Afikpo elders, or supernatural devices such as swearing innocence at a shrine or consulting the Aro oracle are typically employed. It is in the settling of serious disputes involving matrilineal groups in which the Afikpo elders' court is brought into play that these uterine organizations seem most directly concerned with Afikpo government. But even here the elders' decision does not have to be accepted, and the courts are amorphous, changing in personnel from case to case.

Only in former times, in cases of blood revenge, did matriclans come close to playing a jural role with reference to one another. Even here outsiders often played mediating roles. R. Harris' point (1962b:89–93) that in African double descent societies the attribution of the blood feud for murder to the dispersed matrilineal groupings rather than to the residential patrilineal ones prevents enmity between the main residential groupings of the society, which would be highly disruptive, makes sense for Afikpo in the days of blood revenge. It certainly seems to have helped prevent conflict between compounds and villages over murders. The role played by the centralizing governmental agencies of the *amadi* patrilineages and the village-group elders in resolving matriclan tensions over murder, or suspected murder, helped prevent these from reaching a state of perpetual intermatriclan feuding that would have been very disruptive of all social life in Afikpo, both patrilineal and matrilineal.

Turning now to the patrilineal groupings, the most striking feature is their residential basis, and the fact that the family groupings live within the agnatic sphere of control. The agnatic groups are characterized by a cheerful openness in membership, a willingness to incorporate almost anyone regardless of whether or not they already possess agnatic ties in Afikpo, unlike the case of matrilineal groupings, where land matters make for a tendency toward restrictiveness. These patrilineal organizations are also the seat of many important rituals in Afikpo from birth to death, and patrilineal members play major roles in many of these.

The everyday interplay of patrilineal groupings within the domestic arena as against the less frequent contacts of members of these families with the matrilineal lines is another important characteristic. The patrilineal groupings have a major role in the social control of the families in the compound, preventing fighting or arguments, trying disputes, and maintaining codes of sexual and moral behavior. Any matrilineal grouping is interested in its members' behavior, but matrikinsmen come to the domestic scene as outsiders with limited rights of control. It is within the broader context of the patrilineal groupings that the child is socialized and grows to adulthood.

The role of patrilineality in governmental matters has already been stressed. The major patrilineage forms an organization of elders and young men that mirrors the ward, village, and village-group authority system. These large agnatic lineages also form the governmental building blocks of the ward and village; it is the cooperation of neighboring agnatic lines that makes these effective residential organizations.

However, there are some curious features to the governmental situation at Afikpo. If it were consistently matrilineal throughout it would seem to subvert the residential structure and its administration. On the other hand, if at Afikpo the governmental controls were greatly centralized in patrilineal hands there would be a tendency to extend this control to farmland, which is largely matrilineal, and to dominate the uterine groupings. We have seen how villages already have some measure of control and interest in the matrilineal land in their farming areas. Two interrelated features seem to prevent further encroachment by a government with an essentially patrilineal bias. First, there is the heavy emphasis on consensus among the elders in decision-making. This allows matrilineal interests to be defended in governmental organizations by persons who feel that they are being threatened. Since authority is weak in the village and village-group, and matrilineal interests largely external, the elders are not in a position to threaten these groupings, something which might occur if leadership were more centralized about single men fulfilling specific leadership roles on the basis of patrilineal descent.

Second, while agnatic groupings play a role in the governmental system, there is no direct succession of secular leadership roles in the village and village-group which might lead to stronger patrilineal control over matrilineal activities through lines of designated heads or chiefs. In the past history of Afikpo the *amadi* patrilineages played a stronger leadership role, but even here it is interesting to note that they rarely interfered with internal matrilineal matters, and, in fact, were supportive in matriclan revenge and in establishing shrines to protect matrilineal land.

Thus we find the interesting feature in Afikpo that productive property and wealth pass matrilineally while governmental controls have a patrilineal aspect. This is not so contradictory, though logically we might expect them both to go with the same unilineal line, for the patrilineal aspects are not a strong threat to the property interests of groupings. Rather they are generally supportive, and the elders as members of both types of descent groups, and as leaders, maintain this balance of interest except where modern-day changes have forced their hands.

In contrast to the matrilineal case, the corporate ownership of productive property in the patrilineages is not too important; land, and tree and water holdings are relatively minor and not a subject of conflict within the group. Similarly, while some personal effects are inherited within the patrilineal grouping, these are not considered very significant by Afikpo, or generally the subject of litigation. But there are two "productive" aspects of patrilineality that are important: shrines and wives. The patrilineal shrines are productive in the sense that proper rituals performed at them are believed to lead to fertility of persons and crops, to bring forth health and wealth, and thus to increase the size of the groups. Wives are not property in the usual sense, but the patrilineal controls over them, albeit without incorporating them, and with the expectation that they will produce children, indicate that the agnatic groupings consider that they possess corporate responsibility over them.

And this productivity aspect is quite generalized, for the birth of children aids the uterine as well as the agnatic side, and the growth of crops may be on matrilineal land, for the concern is that members of the patrilineal group grow good crops everywhere. In contrast matrilineal farming rituals seem more restrictive.

Thus the activities of matrilineal and patrilineal groupings are distinct in character from one another in many spheres. In some areas, however, this is not so. Both are concerned with land, though to varying degrees. This is one of the major areas of overlap and is related to the history of Afikpo and to a host of special ties between the two types of descent groups involving pledging, redemption, and seizure. Both groupings have important shrines, although different in character, which are concerned with ritual actions associated with human and crop fertility and the general health and welfare of their members. Some activities that may at first seem to overlap are, in fact, a bit discrete. Both types of descent groups are interested in the fertility of females— as expressed through sacrifices and other rituals—but matrilineal groups are interested in the child-producing capacities of their own females while the patrilineages are mainly concerned with those of their male members' spouses. Again, both types of descent groups have sexual controls over persons, but the patrilineal ones have to do with controls over adolescent children, over adult male members and their in-marrying spouses, while the matrilineal ones are concerned with matriclan sexual taboos.

On the whole, the activities of each type of descent group complement each other. Although conflicts do break out, there is normally a cooperative and supportive relationship between the two types and their members, who weave a complex web of ties in a wide range of matters, from establishing individual shrines to land affairs. One line of descent does not have consistent authority over the other. The two exist as cooperating equals with defined rights over individuals and over property in specific situations, neither dominating the other in over-all perspective. Conflicts arise between them, mainly over land, and these can be considered political in that they are over the most fundamental productive resources in Afikpo, but they are not conflicts in which one type of descent grouping is simply trying to gain a dominant position over the other.

Another manner of contrasting the two types of descent groupings is to examine their structures. If we compare the organization of the larger matrilineal and patrilineal groupings, the matriclan and major patrilineage, striking similarities exist, despite the fact that these groups frequently have different functions and carry out different activities. In contrast, the smaller lineage organizations show forms of leadership quite different from the larger ones and from one another.

In the matriclan and the major patrilineage a fundamental style of authority exists. Both groups have like qualities of primary and secondary criteria of leadership roles. In both, selection of elders depends on the same factor of age group membership. The methods of choosing the *Nja* priest of the matriclan and the *Mma obu* ancestral shrine priest of the major patrilineage are similar, and the leadership relationship of priest to elders of the descent group is alike. In both groups these priests, like most Afikpo ritual leaders, act as intermediaries between the supernatural and human worlds, and in neither case are they highly authoritarian. In each there is a like relationship of elders and priest to diviners, and to the Aro oracle and its agents.

In each case there is the lack of formal representation of the segments of the descent organization in the elders' meeting of the group as a whole, nor is there an effective ranking of these segments in the larger group. Decisions in both types of groups are arrived at solely by consensus of elders and priest. There are outstanding personalities but no real chiefs. In both types of descent groups leadership is not strictly inherited; it does not characteristically follow descent lines, but hops here and there.

The kinds of control which the elders and the priest exercise over rituals and property are essentially the same in each case.

The leaders punish members by fines, ostracism, and expulsion, and can tax all members. They act as moral guardians of the rules and customs of the descent group. In both the younger men have little real authority in the descent line, the women virtually none. In the major patrilineage, however, young men play a greater role than in the matriclan. They act for the elders in maintaining peaceful face-to-face relations in the compound, and they direct communal labor. While the general features of elders' leadership in both types of descent groups are the same, that found in the major patrilineage is closer to those of residential groupings, especially the village, in regard to relationships between the elders and the young men. The agnatic grouping is more involved in daily matters of social control than the matriclan. Further, the major patrilineage elders meet more frequently than matriclan elders, having more to discuss, and are on a more informal basis than the latter, who reside in different parts of Afikpo. Again, because of geographic distance matriclan elders from the more distant villages usually play a smaller role than those from the more central areas, while in the major patrilineage all elders usually are active.

There are thus important general features that the matriclan and the major patrilineages share in common: both are judicial agencies that try cases involving their members; both play a general supportive role for their members and help direct rituals of their group; and both are concerned with their property holdings when a dispute arises over them, but otherwise generally leave this to specific segments of the group or to individual members. Both are large protective administrative structures which share features similar to village and village-group organization.

Each type of descent grouping formerly had 2 distinct ranks, the matriclans into a single slave clan and over 30 other unranked clans, the major patrilineages into about 35 *amadi*, the most influential lineages in Afikpo, and about 165 ordinary lineages. And both in the case of the ordinary clans and the non-*amadi* patrilineages there were differences in size, influence, and prestige, and for the agnatic groupings differences in degree of political power. The rankings by descent groupings formed the basis of a three-tier class system at Afikpo: *amadi*, ordinary citizen, and *osu* slave, with variation for ordinary citizens according to the prestige of descent groupings to which they belonged and the status that they themselves acquired as individuals. Since *amadi* were apparently never also *osu* the system was clearcut, if we add the personal slaves, *ohu*, who did not form descent groupings, to the *osu* category. Upward mobility through marriage was possible, since *osu* could "marry" or cohabit with freeborn, but only in the case of a male slave and a female nonslave, hardly a popular form of marriage, would the children of the marriage advance in status. In contrast, a freeborn male could not advance by marrying an *amadi*; the reverse had to be so for the children to belong to the high status group. In neither case, of course, did marriage itself change a person's ranking. The point is significant, though, that the traditional class system throughout Afikpo was basically derived from the ranking of descent groupings, not surprising since these groupings were variously associated with controls over productive resources, wealth, and political power.

The segments of the large descent groupings, the matrilineages and the minor patrilineages, both share some characteristics which differentiate them from the larger organizations. Theirs is a different structure of authority, having a single male leader, the eldest of the group, who as head has influence and makes decisions himself. Consensus is not necessary, particularly in the uterine group. No priest or religious official is found; the head consults diviners for advice on ritual matters. The head may represent his segment to the larger descent group, but if he is not an elder he takes no real part in their deliberations. The structure of authority in these segments, both patrilineal and matrilineal, follows that of the domestic groupings, where a single male also dominates the leadership.

Leadership differences in the two types of segments of the larger descent groups are related to residence and land controls.

The head of the matrilineage may be autocratic, secretive about land matters, hostile to some matrilineage members, and relatively unconcerned over the daily face-to-face behavior of members, particularly males. The minor patrilineage head is often a more gentle leader, more open, more willing to accept counsel of other senior men of his segment, and concerned over the daily behavior of the group's members. The problem of property controls in the dispersed uterine lineage, under the strain of potential segmentation, makes for a different type of leadership than in the minor patrilineage, where the task of the leader is to maintain daily harmony and to help guide the performance of necessary rituals.

With regard to relationships between the matrilineage and matriclan, and the minor patrilineage and major patrilineage, in each case the descent segments are separate for some activities and join together in their larger descent group for others. The sense of opposition to one another as segments is weak compared to their sense of unity in the larger descent group, in contrast, say, to the Nuer (Evans-Pritchard, 1940). Further, there are only two organized levels in each descent group, not three or more. The minor patrilineages are rarely hostile toward each other, though their members live close together. They have a friendly, cooperative attitude and are not highly distinguishable as segments. The matrilineal lineages are less in opposition than in isolation from one another within the larger matriclan, each going its own way, often unconcerned with the existence of some of the other matrilineages of the clan. Where we find a situation fairly similar to that of the Nuer is in the residential groupings; wards of a village unite in opposition to other Afikpo villages, and the villages unite against the outside world. It is in these residential organizations that much that is governmental occurs. The descent groups, narrow in genealogical depth, with only two significant levels of organization, each level having a distinctive form of leadership, do not exhibit this characteristic sense of opposition at one level, as against their unity in the larger whole. The closest to this pattern is in the case of disputes, mainly over

land, between two matrilineages of a matriclan. But these altercations do not usually interfere with other clan activities, the pattern is not generalized, and other matrilineages of the clan are
not usually involved.

The lack of genealogical depth and of the accompanying differentiation of unilineal segments at several different levels seems
characteristic of double unilineal descent systems, as both Goody
(1957:90) and R. Harris (1962b:86–88) point out. This is also
so at Afikpo, although not because "an extensive calculation of
specific genealogical ties in both lines would be highly complicated" (Goody, 1957:90), since the Afikpo are most capable
of structural complexities. Nor does it seem that the genealogical
shallowness at Afikpo exists because agnatic ties lessen the
solidarity of the matrilineal group and uterine ties of the patrilineal ones, as R. Harris suggests for the Mbembe (1962b:86–
88). Rather it relates to (1) the locus of leadership roles in
Afikpo government being at the village and village-group levels,
and in age grade and judicial matters external to the descent
groupings, and (2) the system of patrilineal inheritance of male
prestige but matrilineal wealth inheritance. The first means that
the governmental organization, while it has a basis in the agnatic
descent groupings, is also external to it, and that the processes of
governmental role recruitment and differentiation partly occur
outside of the descent groupings. The second precludes the development of a single line of leaders over many generations
either matrilineal or patrilineal. The argument here, then, is that
both factors make it impossible to use generational differences or
genealogical distinctions along a long descent line as focal points
in the differentiation of governmental units and of leadership.

In terms of the role of politics and administration within the
descent groups, differences exist between the agnatic and uterine
lines. The major patrilineage is heavily administrative in its
internal organization. Internal political conflicts over property,
the control of lineage leadership, and other essentially political
matters, are minimal. Those internal disputes that arise in the
compound, and there are many, involve individuals and occasion-

ally family groupings rather than minor lineages or other large sections of the major patrilineage and do not divide the descent group into camps. Further, the general tone of the external relations of the agnatic groupings with the ward and the village, of which they are segments, is administrative rather than political. They do become involved in land conflicts with matrilineal groupings, and they have friendly and cooperative interrelationships with them, and these positive and negative ties are largely political. But the major focus of the patrilineal groupings is administrative.

In contrast, the internal activities of the matriclan are heavy with conflicts over land, and the administrative aspects of matriclan government, while crucial to its maintenance, are not as fully elaborated nor as controlling as in the case of the major patrilineage. External relationships are highly political; the matriclans and matrilineages live in a world of conflict with like matrilineal groupings and with patrilineages, largely over land holdings. The external administrative functions of the matrilineal groupings arise mainly insofar as they are involved in the agnatic and residential aspects of the social life of their members. Thus, while the larger matrilineal and patrilineal groupings have similar forms of leadership, the relative weight of the administrative and political aspects in the internal and external affairs of each differs considerably, and relates to the specific activities with which each is concerned.

What is suggested here is that in the larger descent groupings of both uterine and agnatic types the internal structure, the pattern of leadership, is quite similar and derived partly from the age organizations of village and village-group. This is so despite the fact that matriclan and major patrilineage carry out different activities and have different functions, regardless of whether they act in a political or an administrative manner. A broad general type of organization exists at Afikpo. This is also true for the minor patrilineage and the matrilineage, but here the nature of organization and authority is closer to that found in the domestic groupings. The growing child, especially the male, learns two basic patterns of authority in the compound: consensus relations in general patrilineal activities and the authority of single individuals in his domestic groupings, especially that of father and older brothers. These patterns are extended, with modifications, to his matrilineal groupings when he matures; thus new authority patterns do not have to be learned when he becomes involved in descent affairs as a young man.

CHANGE

Both the activities and the organization of the matrilineal and the patrilineal descent groups have been altering as a result of Western contact and the increase in population. As always at Afikpo, the matter is not simple; there are shifts in various directions.

There has been a decline in the use of force associated with authority in the descent organization, on strength as a basis of prestige and leadership. There has been a breakdown of the slave organization, both of *ohu* slaves and the matriclan slave group, and in the power of the patrilineal *amadi*, as a result of British nonrecognition of them and Afikpo opposition to their influence. The significance of head-hunting and warfare rituals, mainly patrilineally organized, has also declined, though wrestling activities and rituals still play a role in patrilineal life. Wealth, particularly as expressed in title-society membership, has replaced strength as a secondary element in leadership. The lessening physical conflict in Afikpo is related to a disappearance of matriclan fission and the rejoining of related matrilineal groupings. Today the matriclans are probably larger in size and more effectively organized than ever before. Similarly, the lack of patrilineal fission today has led to larger-sized major patrilineages, despite the movement of persons to work and live elsewhere in Nigeria.

A result of British, and now Nigerian, rule has thus been to emphasize a more egalitarian, less force-based view of leadership in and between descent groups. Decisions involving these groups are made through group consensus arrived at in a leisurely manner, by supernatural techniques, or through the modern courts, rather than through the seizure of persons and properties by force. Automatic killing of thieves has been stopped, and the role of the *amadi* in punishing certain crimes has been abolished. Today the control of force rests outside the descent groups in the Nigerian government, and the governmental role of the patrilineal groupings is decreasing.

The class structure has also altered. The three-level system of *amadi*, ordinary person, and *osu* has largely disappeared. In its place a more Western class form is emerging, emphasizing wealth (in other areas than titles and land), education, political power in the new governmental organizations, and skilled training. This is not tied to the descent structure but based on individual achievement of persons apparently relatively independent of their descent status. The descent basis of class organization is rapidly disappearing.

Other changes in the descent groups as a result of the increase in wealth in Afikpo and the development of Western economic patterns need only be summarized here. The economic changes have played on the father-son tie which exists in the patrilineal context, traditionally expressed in paternal cross-cousin marriage, and in the role of a son in his father's matrilineage. The increase in wealth and the tendency of wage earners, traders, and persons who work away from Afikpo to develop independent families have strengthened this tie. Fathers are reluctant to let their wealth pass to a group of matrilineal relatives when their children's needs in terms of education, other training, and social and political advancement in the new Nigeria seem so evident. Families that have been away from home for a long period of time may not feel that their matrikinsmen are important.

On the other hand matrilineal relatives have become increasingly forceful in demanding their rights to inheritable wealth, since the amount of the inheritance in money and trade goods has increased so markedly. Not only movable wealth in Afikpo but land holdings are involved. Population growth has led to a situation where land, now quite scarce and rising in value for use in growing cash crops, is more a source of contention than previously. Increasingly attempts are made to gain access to land through "seizure" of land holdings, and there is the growing practice of renting land to strangers for cash crops. Attempts of fathers to gain land for sons are becoming more frequent. Conflicts between matrikinsmen over control of land, related to matrilineage segmentation, are accentuated by the land situation.

Growing economic opportunities affect the descent group in other ways. One expression is the development of unions as loan associations in both the major patrilineages and the matriclans. The presence of a full-scale money economy at Afikpo is directly related to a change in rituals, particularly patrilineal ones, which formerly involved large displays of wealth in the form of food and other goods, often with considerable waste, now partly replaced by gifts of money. The Afikpo prefer this; the recipients feel that shillings and pennies are more usable than yam fufu and palm wine, which must be consumed within a short period and may be difficult to exchange for other goods. Many ceremonies now take on a strong financial aspect; there is less emphasis on joint feasting and less sense of camaraderie than previously.

Increased wealth is related to private house-building, mainly outside the compounds, rather than by communal labor in the traditional manner within the patrilineal residential area. Such houses are often rented out or turned into bars or hotels, and by 1960 they were beginning to replace titles as a source of prestige and as a secondary quality of leadership at Afikpo, particularly for nontraditional leaders. Beyond this, the pattern of house-building is leading to a semi-urban condition; many of these houses, which are now filling in the areas between the central Afikpo villages, are occupied by strangers who take no part, or educated or acculturated Afikpo who take little interest, in the activities of the patrilineal and matrilineal groupings. Thus the traditional residential pattern, so intimately associated with patrilineality, is in an early stage of disintegration.

Another set of factors which makes for change in the unilineal descent groups is the general orientation of British culture, as expressed at Afikpo, toward patrilineality and the father-son tie. This is evident in decisions of the courts and in Nigerian government matters, where there is either simple ignorance of the existence of matrilineality at Afikpo, or a reluctance to accept traditional Afikpo views of the uterine role in land and inheritance. Some of the British administrators at Afikpo had never worked in an area where matrilineality existed—there are few such regions in the country—and such persons seemed to have difficulty in understanding it. For example, the major Intelligence Report on Afikpo (Waddington, 1931) followed a model prepared largely by C. K. Meek on the basis of his own field work in patrilineal Igbo areas (Meek, 1937; Nigeria, 1933; Perham, 1937:206–54; Gwam, 1961). The report says virtually nothing about matrilineal groups and the system of matrilineal land tenure and inheritance; only in the subsequent correspondence attached to it is there evidence that later officials were aware of these. The transfer of the administration at Afikpo into African hands within the past ten years has not changed this pattern; the administrators have been trained in the British approach, and most of them come from Igbo areas or other parts of the country where patrilineality is the normal rule of descent. The result of administration policy and court action has thus been to favor father-son ties and patrilineality at the expense of matrilineality.

Women have been less affected in descent by the changes than have the men (P. Ottenberg, 1959), despite considerable freedom and economic opportunities for them. The fact that women's unions form largely to gather money for traditional sacrifices, while men join unions to obtain business loans, is a case in point. Afikpo women have been less exposed to European education and other acculturative influences than men, and since they do not control or dominate the affairs of the descent groupings, they are less involved with changes in them brought about by European contacts. It is the authority structure of the males, the concepts of property controls of men, the rituals led and dominated by them, that are most receptive to change. The more limited activities of women in these groups, concerned mainly with the birth of children and their care while young, are less directly involved.

However, there has been increasing autonomy for women as a result of the coming of peace, for they are not so dependent upon men for physical protection, and there are increased opportunities for trade open to them. Today they seem to have a somewhat greater voice in matriclan affairs than they apparently had before, albeit a conservative one. Now there are some "independent" women, sometimes divorced or separated from their husbands, who rely on their own resources in farming and trading to a large degree, rather than totally on those of their two crucial male links, husbands and brothers. As a result the triadic husband–wife–wife's-brother relationship that is so characteristic of Afikpo and which is based on a relatively passive role of the women is altering for some females.

All these basic factors of modern-day change at Afikpo have been important in affecting the nature of the Afikpo descent groupings. In some cases descent through one line has been strengthened at the expense of the other; in others, the reverse is true. The only consistent pattern is not a strong shift from matrilineal to patrilineal ties or the reverse, but one of lineal descent to bilaterality centering around the father-son relationship and the increasing importance of family ties. There is no reason to believe that this will not continue.

In a long-range view, double descent has been sensitive to changing conditions, adjusting its balance of interests and activities between the uterine and agnatic groups as external forces have impinged on it. The governmental administrative structure at Afikpo associated with descent has undergone fundamental changes, and today is adjusting to modern conditions, perhaps eventually to disappear. The Afikpo elders, however, view the descent organization as a relatively stable and conservative element, though they recognize that it has changed. In the short-range view of a man's lifetime, this is certainly justified. However, from the anthropologist's view the multiplicity of descent with its alternate channels of support and action for the individ-

ual, and its balance of activities between patrilineal and matrilineal groupings, makes for a high degree of adjustability.

The question of whether this form of descent is inherently
unstable was raised in the first chapter. This is difficult to discuss
for Afikpo, as it is for other such societies. For one thing we have
no accepted criteria of stability. The relative rarity of true double
descent and the fact that some cases reflect a movement for
matrilineality to a patrilineal condition, as does the Afikpo case,
suggest that it may be unstable. However, from the experience of
this anthropologist, working in intimate contact with the society,
and with six and a half years between the first and second field
experiences, it seems a perfectly viable and on-going system of
human relationships. Certainly this form of descent does not
seem fragile on a short-term basis. In terms of internal structural
contradictions, the split between patrilineal governmental controls and matrilineal land ownership is the major sensitive area.
It is impossible to estimate the degree to which this contradiction
would eventually push the society more toward the patrilineal
side, given the lack of outside influences.

Two points need some discussion. First, the degree of balance
in terms of matrilineal and patrilineal activities and functions
logically suggests that any time there is modification at any one
point there will be ramifications elsewhere. For example, the
procedure of dispersing movable wealth in inheritance matrilineally is predicated on the principle that there is not too much
wealth to inherit. Once this increases, as it now has at Afikpo as a
result of economic changes, there are likely to be conflicts between sons of the deceased and the dead man's matrikinsmen,
with whom the sons have ties which are not close, over inheritance, and pressures must arise to modify the traditional system.
This is especially so in view of the extensive agnatic bonds at
Afikpo between father and son. There is therefore sensitivity
in this area and in others as well. But this does not mean that it is
necessarily easily destroyed any more than unilineal descent in
another society.

Second, there are other double descent societies with a clearer distinction of activities on the matrilineal and patrilineal sides, for example, the Yakö (Forde, 1964) and the LoWiili (Goody, 1956), than at Afikpo. This suggests that in double descent a point of some stability is reached when this condition has occurred, and there is no conflict between matrilineal and patrilineal groupings for the control of like activities. In Afikpo either this point has been reached and passed or it was being approached at the time of European contact. Its history suggests that it has not been attained and only would be when land controls became patrilineal as in the other two cases. This is suggested by the difficulties inherent in a society in which productive resources are mainly matrilineally controlled but the uterine groups are external to the political system, and in which both types of descent have land interests. Therefore, it is likely that Afikpo was moving toward a more stable form of double descent at the time of Western penetration, but had not reached it, nor will it ever now.

FINAL COMMENTS

The study of double descent at Afikpo has been divided into two views, that of group structure and individual relationships. To look at the formal structure in terms of its general organization, activities, and functions is extremely important. Within this orientation it is easy to move to the matter of the interrelationships of the descent organizations with like ones, such as interclan ties, and then to their relationships with other types of descent groups, such as patrilineal-matrilineal group contacts. Then one looks at descent groups in terms of organizations external to them, for example the village and village-group. This totality provides a reasonably systematic procedure for handling the larger elements of double descent and offers a consistent viewpoint.

But it is not in itself sufficient. The view of structure from the outside is one thing; the view from the orientation of individuals operating within the structure is another. In the second we see individuals, often acting as "representatives" of their descent groupings, whether consciously or not, interacting with other individuals who likewise stand for their descent groupings. We see that the domestic groupings are strongly dominated by descent considerations, probably more so than in any other form of society. While from the view of formal structure the life-way of an individual seems cut-and-dried, laid out as a series of actions, some of which he performs as a member of uterine groups and others through his agnatic associations, from the second point of view all is not regulated; he makes some choices in terms of his particular interests and the strengths of his goals. This is not to say that these alternatives do not exist in either matrilineal or patrilineal societies. There may be like or even greater possibilities of choice, as is clear from even a cursory examination of the material on other Igbo groups which are patrilineal. In other cases, however, many of the alternatives occur *outside* the descent system. While there are also external choices at Afikpo, for example, in the realm of village life, double descent itself allows for manipulation and individual enterprise, most especially in the case of males.

The point is an important one because there has been a tendency to see double descent systems more from the first than the second orientation (Goody, 1961; Forde, 1964), though there have been other studies dealing with the second aspect as well (Forde, 1941; Goody, 1959). Both views are significant, related, and needed in a balanced presentation: neither alone is sufficient. The link between the two is the affiliation of individuals to descent groups with predetermined structures and activities. A person is born into a matrilineal clan which has a certain organization, and he is under obligation to take part in it and to carry out specific activities. There are some areas of precious little freedom and choice. There are other areas of descent where he has greater freedom to act. The extent to which he is close to and has contact with his father's matrilineage, for example, or the degree to which he cooperates with other members of his matrilineage or carries on his own may involve matters of selection. In these areas he does make choices. And he has alternatives as to what extent he makes use of and manipulates his total field of descent ties to gain his own ends, to what degree he takes advantage of all his ties. The over-all view then is of a series of descent structures which play a major role in the life of the individual, which are themselves sensitive to changes from internal and external pressures, where the individual has areas of freedom of choice as well as sectors where he is committed to clearly defined methods of behaving. Double descent certainly is complex, but it would be inaccurate to see it as rigid.

GLOSSARY

adudɔ.	The shrine of a female ancestral spirit.
ahɔ.	The third day of the four-day Afikpo week, on which two small markets meet.
aja ale ɛzi.	See *ɔma ɛzi.*
ale.	(1) The ground or earth; (2) the spirit of the ground.
amadi.	Descendants of the original settlers from Aro Chuku at Afikpo, and also descendants of persons who became associated with these settlers. Traditionally the *amadi* were influential in Afikpo affairs.
asarara.	A form of sauce, unusual in that it is made without greens.
awata.	The rental of farmland, usually for use in cash cropping.
cukwu na ɛlu.	One of the several terms for the Afikpo High God.
ebo.	Farmland near the village and outside the six-block farming area.
egbeja.	A special form of consultation with a diviner, carried out by Afikpo before farming, to discover what ritual steps should be taken to ensure good crops.
eka ehi uhie.	An elaborate feast and ritual, the so-called "cow

266

funeral" to honor a male or female parent. Often
performed many years after the death.

ɛgɛro. A general welfare shrine for unmarried girls.

ɛgbo. A shrine located above the compound entrance
which guards against evil entering this residential
area.

ɛgɛlɛ. An iron gong, about nine inches long, hit with a
stick.

ɛgwu Nsi. (1) A shrine established by a man who has had
bad luck or misfortune; (2) the spirit of the
shrine.

ɛkɛ. The first day of the four-day Igbo week, on which
the main Afikpo market meets.

ɛkikɛ. A form of protective charm or shrine.

ɛzɛ. A chief, or, more properly at Afikpo, any prominent leader.

ɛzi. A compound, usually the home of a major patrilineage.

fufu. Mashed yam or cassava.

gari. Cassava meal.

ibɛ. Side or part; used as the first part of the name of
a specific matrilineal clan.

ibɛ osim. The slave matrilineal clan, that is, the matriclan of
persons who are *osu*.

iko okoci. The major dry season feast at Afikpo.

ikwu. Matrilineal relative.

ikwu ɛra. See ɔnu θzom.

itθ Nri Mma. An annual ritual at the time of the dry season to
renew the sexual regulations governing husbands
and wives.

imo ɛkwu. A ritual performed by a newly married woman
which binds her to the rules of her busband's compound and major patrilineage.

Ibini ɔkpabe. (1) A famous Igbo oracle located at Aro Chuku;
(2) a form of shrine at Afikpo associated with this
oracle; (3) the spirit of this shrine.

mɛmɛ. A general term for title.

Mma. (1) Ancestral spirit; (2) a pot used in various
Afikpo shrines.

Mma obu.	The ancestral rest house and shrine of a major patrilineage.
muturu.	Dwarf cattle found in Igbo country. They are resistant to sleeping sickness brought on by the tsetse fly.
Ndε.	People.
Ndε iciε.	Elders.
Ndε Mma.	Ancestral spirits.
Ngwo.	A major patrilineage shrine associated with wrestling and warfare.
Nkwɔ.	The fourth day of the four-day Igbo week, on which the Ozizza market meets at Afikpo.
Nja.	The major shrine of the matrilineal clan.
Njɔku.	(1) a shrine owned by an individual male associated with yam fertility; (2) the spirit of this shrine.
Nkamalo.	(1) A shrine owned by an individual male and associated with his general welfare; (2) the spirit of the shrine.
Nri Nsi omɔmɔ.	A fertility feast associated with the major patrilineage fertility shrine, *Nsi omɔmɔ.*
Nsi omɔmɔ.	A major patrilineage shrine concerned with fertility.
ogbeyi.	Freeborn; a person who is not a slave.
ogbobu.	Killing.
ogirisi.	(1) A tree whose leaves are used in announcing decisions made by the Afikpo leaders; (2) the leaves of this tree.
ohu.	An ordinary slave (see *osu*).
okpo Ntu.	An organization of unmarried girls in the compound who maintain the latrines and garbage dump.
olili madθ.	A funeral ceremony carried out for a deceased parent some time after the actual burial rites. Popularly called the "goat funeral."
omumε.	The popular name of the highest Afikpo title.
omumε ale.	See *ɔgwugwa ale.*
onyε ɔrθ ale.	One who "spoils the ground" by angering its spirit through some misconduct.

osohɔ.	The area immediately to the rear of the homes in a compound.
osu.	A slave who traces his status matrilineally, in contrast to the ordinary slave, *ohu,* where this is not done.
owa.	The personal spirit of a male.
ɔbase ɔha.	A major patrilineage shrine associated with wrestling and warfare.
ɔco.	Murder.
ɔgo.	A general term for a relative by marriage, or one who is connected by birth but does not belong to the patrilineal or matrilineal groupings of a person.
ɔgwugwa ale.	A ritual to pacify the spirit of the ground, angered when an uncircumcised boy has sexual intercourse. Also called *omumɛ ale.*
ɔhoha ɛkwu ukwɔ.	A sacrifice carried out at the farmland to the spirit of the ground.
ɔhoho.	A pot-firing field located at the rear of certain compounds. Used exclusively by women.
ɔma ɛzi.	An important shrine of the major patrilineage. Also called *aja ale ɛzi.*
ɔnu era.	See *ɔnu θzom.*
ɔnu θzom.	The matrilineage. Also called *ɔnu era* and *ikwu era.*
ɔrθrθ ɛko.	A shrine established by a man, and occasionally by a woman, to bring general prosperity to the person, especially in a financial sense.
ɔtoto ɛja.	The "bad bush" or burial ground for persons who die from deaths considered unnatural. Twins were sometimes left here to die.
ɔtɔsi.	The shrine associated with the *amadi* patrilineal descent groupings.
ugwu ɛhɔ.	The bush area at Amaizu Village where the shrine of the slave matriclan is located.
uhie ci.	An important Afikpo title.
ukɛ ɛkpɛ.	Age grade.
ukɛ ɛkpɛ ɛzi.	Age grade in a compound.
ulo.	House.
ulote.	Boys' house.

umudi.   The term for (1) a major patrilineage, or (2) a minor patrilineage.

umuNna.   An Igbo term for a (1) major patrilineage, or (2) a minor patrilineage; not as frequently used at Afikpo as *umudi.*

BIBLIOGRAPHY

Adams, R. F. G., with I. C. Ward
    1928   "The Arochuku Dialect of Ibo," *Africa*, 2:57–70.

Allen, J. G. C.
    1935   "Izi Clan Intelligence Report." Unpublished ms.

Anon.
    1957   "Damn the God that Fears Twins! Twins Exiled by Afikpo Tin-Hut God Find Refuge in Church!" *Drum* (Nigeria edition), 74:20–22.

    n.d.   "Intelligence Report on the Aro Clan, Arochuku District, Calabar Province." Unpublished ms.

Ardener, E. W.
    1954   *Double Descent Among the Fanti.* New Haven, Conn.: *Africa*, 24:85–99.

    1959   "Lineage and Locality among the Mba-Ise Ibo," *Africa*, 29:113–33.

Beecroft [Becroft], J., and J. B. King
    1844   "Details of Explorations of the Old Calabar River in 1841 and 1842 . . .," *Journal of the Royal Geographical Society*, 14:260–83.

Charles, E., and D. Forde
    1938   "Notes on Some Population Data from a Southern Nigerian Village," *Sociological Review*, 30:145–60.

271

Christensen, J. B.
  1954   *Double Descent Among the Fanti.* New Haven, Conn.:
          Human Relations Area Files.
Chubb, L. T.
  1948   *Notes on Ibo Land Tenure.* Zaria, Nigeria: Gaskiya Cor-
          poration.
Colson, E., and M. Gluckman (eds.)
  1951   *Seven Tribes of British Central Africa.* London: Oxford
          University Press for the Rhodes-Livingstone Institute.
Dike, K. O.
  1956   *Trade and Politics in the Niger Delta.* London: Oxford
          University Press.
Durkheim, E.
  1933   *The Division of Labor in Society,* trans. G. Simpson.
          New York: Macmillan.
Easterfield, M., and E. K. Uku
  n.d.   "Seeds in the Palm of Your Hand: An African Tribe in
          Transition." Unpublished ms.
Evans-Pritchard, E. E.
  1940   *The Nuer.* Oxford: Clarendon Press.
Forde, C. D. See Forde, D.
Forde, D.
  1937   "Land and Labour in a Cross River Village, Southern
          Nigeria," *Geographical Journal,* 90:24–51.
  1938   "Fission and Accretion in the Patrilinear Clans of a
          Semi-Bantu Community in S. Nigeria," *Journal of the
          Royal Anthropological Institute,* 68:311–38.
  1939a   "Government in Umor," *Africa,* 12:129–61.
  1939b   "Kinship in Umor," *American Anthropologist,* 41:523–
          53.
  1940   "Yakö Marriage," *Man,* 40, art. 66, 57–58.
  1941   *Marriage and the Family among the Yakö of South-
          Eastern Nigeria.* (London School of Economics, Mono-
          graphs on Social Anthropology, No. 5.) London: Lund,
          Humphries.
  1949   "Integrative Aspects of the Yakö First Fruits Rituals,"
          Journal of the Royal Anthropological Institute, 79:1–10.
  1950a   "Double Descent among the Yakö," pp. 285–332 in A. R.
          Radcliffe-Brown and D. Forde (eds.), *African Systems*

of Kinship and Marriage. London: Oxford University Press for the International African Institute.

1950b   "Ward Organization among the Yakö," *Africa,* 20:267–89.

1957   *The Context of Belief: A Consideration of Fetishism Among the Yakö.* Liverpool: Liverpool University Press.

1958   "Spirits, Witches and Sorcerers in the Supernatural Economy of the Yakö," *Journal of the Royal Anthropological Institute,* 88:165–78.

1961   "The Governmental Roles of Associations among the Yakö," *Africa,* 31:309–23.

1962   "Death and Succession: An Analysis of Yakö Mortuary Ritual," pp. 89–123 in M. Gluckman (ed.), *Essays on the Ritual of Social Relations.* Manchester: Manchester University Press.

1964   *Yakö Studies.* London: Oxford University Press for the International African Institute.

1965   "Unilineal Fact or Fiction: An Analysis of the Composition of Kin-Groups among the Yakö," pp. 38–57 in I. Schapera (ed.), *Studies in Kinship and Marriage.* London: Royal Anthropological Institute.

Forde, D., and G. I. Jones

1950   *The Ibo and Ibibio-Speaking Peoples of South-Eastern Nigeria.* (International African Institute, Ethnographic Survey of Africa, Western Africa, Part III.) London: International African Institute.

Forde, D., and R. Scott

1946   *The Native Economies of Nigeria.* London: Faber and Faber.

Fortes, M.

1950   "Kinship and Marriage among the Ashanti," pp. 252–84 in A. R. Radcliffe-Brown and D. Forde (eds.), *African Systems of Kinship and Marriage.* London: Oxford University Press for the International African Institute.

1953   "The Structure of Unilineal Descent Groups," *American Anthropologist,* 55:17–41.

Goldie, H.

1885   "Notes of a Voyage up the Calabar or Cross River in

November, 1884," *Scottish Geographical Magazine,* 1:273–83.

1901 *Calabar and its Mission.* (New ed.) Edinburgh: Oliphant, Anderson and Ferrier.

Goody, J.

1956 *The Social Organization of the LoWiili.* (Great Britain, Colonial Office, Colonial Research Studies, No. 9.) London: Her Majesty's Stationery Office.

1957 "Fields of Social Controls among the LoDagaba," *Journal of the Royal Anthropological Institute,* 87:75–104.

1959 "The Mother's Brother and Sister's Son in West Africa," *Journal of the Royal Anthropological Institute,* 89:61–86.

1961 "The Classification of Double Descent Systems," *Current Anthropology,* 2:3–25.

Gourou, P.

1947 "Géographie du peuplement en Nigéria meridionale," *Bulletin de la société belge d'études géographiques,* 16:58–64.

Green, M. M.

1947 *Ibo Village Affairs.* London: Sidgwick and Jackson.

Gwam, L. C.

1961 *A Preliminary Index to the Intelligence Reports in the Nigerian Secretariat Record Group.* Ibadan, Nigeria: National Archives Headquarters.

Harris, J.

1942 "Some Aspects of Slavery in South-Eeastern Nigeria," *Journal of Negro History,* 27:37–54.

Harris, R.

1962a "The Influence of Ecological Factors and External Relations on the Mbembe Tribes of South-East Nigeria," *Africa,* 32:38–52.

1962b "The Political Significance of Double Unilineal Descent," *Journal of the Royal Anthropological Institute,* 92:86–101.

1965a *The Political Organization of the Mbembe, Nigeria* (Great Britain, Ministry of Overseas Development, Overseas Research Publication, No. 10.) London: Her

Majesty's Stationery Office.

1965b "Intestate Succession among the Mbembe of South-Eastern Nigeria," pp. 91–138 in J. D. M. Derrett (ed.), *Studies in the Law of Succession in Nigeria.* London: Oxford University Press for the Nigerian Institute of Social and Economic Research.

Henderson, R. N.

1963 "A Case Study in the Analysis of Kinship, Age-grades and Segmentary Lineage Systems." Unpublished Ph.D. dissertation, University of California, Berkeley.

1967 "Onitsha Ibo Kinship Terminology: A Formal Analysis and Its Functional Applications," *Southwestern Journal of Anthropology,* 23:15–51.

Heneker, W. C. G.

1907 *Bush Warfare.* London: Hugh Rees.

Jones, G. I.

1961 "Ecology and Social Structure among the North Eastern Ibo," *Africa,* 31:117–34.

Kroeber, A. L.

1938 "Basic and Secondary Patterns of Social Structure," *Journal of the Royal Anthropological Institute,* 68:299–309.

Leach, E.

1962 "On Certain Unconsidered Aspects of Double Descent Systems," *Man,* LXII, art. 214, pp. 130–34.

Leith-Ross, S.

1937 "Notes on the Osu System among the Ibo of Owerri Province, Nigeria," *Africa,* 10:206–20.

LeVine, R. A.

1966 *Dreams and Deeds: Achievement Motivation in Nigeria.* Chicago: University of Chicago Press.

Livingston Booth, J. D.

1955 "Oiling the Wheels of Local Government in Eastern Nigeria," *Journal of African Administration,* 7:55–64.

Lowie, R. H.

1927 *The Origin of the State.* New York: Harcourt Brace.

McFarlan, D. M.

1946 *Calabar: The Church of Scotland Mission, 1846–1946.* London: Thomas Nelson.

Meek, C. K.
 1937 *Law and Authority in a Nigerian Tribe.* London. Oxford University Press.
Murdock, G. P.
 1940 "Double Descent," *American Anthropologist,* 42:555–61.
 1949 *Social Structure.* New York: Macmillan.
Nigeria
 1933 *Report on Social and Political Organization in the Owerri Division* [by C. K. Meek]. Lagos: Government Printer.
 1954 *The Nigeria Handbook.* (2nd ed.) London: Crown Agents for Overseas Governments and Administrations.
Nigeria, Census Superintendent
 1953–54 *Population Census of the Eastern Region of Nigeria, 1953* (8 parts). Port Harcourt: C. M. S. Niger Press; Zaria: Gaskiya Corporation.
Obi, S. N. C.
 1963 *On the Ibo Law of Property.* London: Butterworths.
Offonry, H. K.
 1951 "Ibo Untouchables," *West African Review,* 22:807.
Ottenberg, P.
 1958 "Marriage Relationships in the Double Descent System of the Afikpo Ibo of Southeastern Nigeria." Unpublished Ph.D. dissertation, Northwestern University.
 1959 "The Changing Economic Position of Women among the Afikpo Ibo," pp. 205–23 in W. R. Bascom and M. J. Herskovits (eds.), *Continuity and Change in African Cultures.* Chicago: University of Chicago Press.
 1965 "The Afikpo Ibo of Eastern Nigeria," pp. 3–39 in J. L. Gibbs, Jr. (ed.), *Tribes of Sub-Saharan Africa.* New York: Holt, Rinehart and Winston.
Ottenberg, S.
 1955a "Supplementary Bibliography on the Ibo-Speaking People of South-Eastern Nigeria," *African Studies,* 14:63–85.
 1955b "Improvement Associations among the Afikpo Ibo," *Africa,* 24:1–25.
 1956 "Comments on Local Government in Afikpo Division,

Southeastern Nigeria," *Journal of African Administration*, 8:3–10.

1957 "The System of Authority of the Afikpo Ibo of Southeastern Nigeria." Unpublished Ph.D. dissertation, Northwestern University.

1958 "Ibo Oracles and Intergroup Relations," *Southwestern Journal of Anthropology*, 14:295–317.

1959 "Ibo Receptivity to Change," pp. 130–43 in W. R. Bascom and M. J. Herskovits (eds.), *Continuity and Change in African Cultures*. Chicago: University of Chicago Press.

1961 "The Present State of Ibo Studies," *Journal of the Historical Society of Nigeria*, 2:211–30.

1965 "Inheritance and Succession in Afikpo," pp. 33–90 in J. D. M. Derrett (ed.), *Studies in the Law of Succession in Nigeria*. London: Oxford University Press for the Nigerian Institute of Social and Economic Research.

1968a "The Development of Credit Associations in the Changing Economy of an African Society," *Africa*, forthcoming.

1968b "Statement and Reality: The Renewal of an Igbo Protective Shrine," *International Archives of Ethnography*, forthcoming.

1969 "Personal Shrines at Afikpo," *Ethnology*, forthcoming.

n.d. "Elders and Youths: The Government of an African People." Unpublished ms.

Ottenberg, S. and P.

1962 "Afikpo Markets: 1900–1960," pp 117–69 in P. Bohannan and G. Dalton (eds.), *Markets in Africa*. Evanston, Ill.: Northwestern University Press.

Perham, M.

1937 *Native Administration in Nigeria*. London: Oxford University Press.

Richards, A. L.

1934 "Mother-Right among the Central Bantu," pp. 267–80 in E. E. Evans-Pritchard *et al.*, *Essays Presented to C. G. Seligman*. London. Kegan Paul, Trench, Trubner.

1950 "Some Types of Family Structure amongst the Central Bantu," pp. 207–51 in A. R. Radcliffe-Brown and D.

Forde (eds.), *African Systems of Kinship and Marriage.* London: Oxford University Press for the International African Institute.

Schneider, D. M.
  1961   "The Distinctive Features of Matrilineal Descent Groups," pp. 1–29 in D. M. Schneider and K. Gough (eds.), *Matrilineal Kinship.* Berkeley: University of California Press.
  1962   "Double Descent on Yap," *Journal of the Polynesian Society,* 71:1–24.

Stevenson, R. F.
  1968   *Population and Political Systems in Tropical Africa.* New York: Columbia University Press.

Talbot, P. A.
  1926   *The Peoples of Southern Nigeria* (4 vols.). London: Oxford University Press.

Trewartha, G. T., and W. Zelinski
  1954   "Population Patterns in Tropical Africa," *Annals of the Association of American Geographers,* 44:135–62.

Uchendu, V. C.
  1965   *The Igbo of Southeast Nigeria.* (Case Studies in Cultural Anthropology.) New York: Holt, Rinehart and Winston.

Umo, R. K.
  n.d.   *History of Aro Settlements.* Yaba, Nigeria: Mbonu Ojike.

Waddington, H.
  1931   "Intelligence Report on Afikpo Clan of Ogoja Province." Unpublished ms.

Wallace, J. W.
  1941   "Agriculture in Abakaliki and Afikpo," *Farm and Forest,* 2:89–93.

INDEX